RULER VISIBILITY AND POPULAR BELONGING IN THE OTTOMAN EMPIRE, 1808–1908

Edinburgh Studies on the Ottoman Empire
Series Editor: Kent F. Schull

Published and forthcoming titles

Migrating Texts: Circulating Translations around the Eastern Mediterranean
Edited by Marilyn Booth

Ottoman Sunnism: New Perspectives
Edited by Vefa Erginbas

Armenians in the Late Ottoman Empire: Migration, Mobility Control and Sovereignty, 1885–1915
David Gutman

The Kizilbash-Alevis in Ottoman Anatolia: Sufism, Politics and Community
Ayfer Karakaya-Stump

Çemberlitaş Hamami in Istanbul: The Biographical Memoir of a Turkish Bath
Nina Macaraig

Nineteenth Century Local Governance in Ottoman Bulgaria: Politics in Provincial Councils
Safa Saracoglu

Prisons in the Late Ottoman Empire: Microcosms of Modernity
Kent F. Schull

Ruler Visibility and Popular Belonging in the Ottoman Empire, 1808–1908
Darin N. Stephanov

edinburghuniversitypress.com/series/esoe

RULER VISIBILITY AND POPULAR BELONGING IN THE OTTOMAN EMPIRE, 1808–1908

Darin N. Stephanov

EDINBURGH
University Press

This book is dedicated to my parents, Neli Popova and Nikolai Stephanov, my brother, Julian Stephanov, and my wife, Bistra Strechkova. Without them and the unflinching support of Kent F. Schull, this work would not have been accomplished.

Edinburgh University Press is one of the leading university presses in the UK. We publish academic books and journals in our selected subject areas across the humanities and social sciences, combining cutting-edge scholarship with high editorial and production values to produce academic works of lasting importance. For more information visit our website: edinburghuniversitypress.com

© Darin N. Stephanov, 2019, 2020

First published in hardback by Edinburgh University Press 2019

Edinburgh University Press Ltd
The Tun – Holyrood Road
12 (2f) Jackson's Entry
Edinburgh EH8 8PJ

Typeset in Jaghbuni by
Servis Filmsetting Ltd, Stockport, Cheshire

A CIP record for this book is available from the British Library

ISBN 978 1 4744 4141 4 (hardback)
ISBN 978 1 4744 4142 1 (paperback)
ISBN 978 1 4744 4143 8 (webready PDF)
ISBN 978 1 4744 4144 5 (epub)

The right of Darin N. Stephanov to be identified as author of this work has been asserted in accordance with the Copyright, Designs and Patents Act 1988 and the Copyright and Related Rights Regulations 2003 (SI No. 2498).

Contents

List of Figures	vi
List of Abbreviations	viii
Introduction	1
1. The First Shift in (Modern) Ruler Visibility: the Reign of Mahmud II (1808–39)	6
2. The Trope of Love, its Variations and Manifestations: the Reign of Abdülmecid (1839–61)	37
3. Further Stimuli for and Patterns of *Millet* Accentuation and Differentiation: the Reign of Abdülaziz (1861–76)	95
4. The Second Shift in (Modern) Ruler Visibility: the Reign of Abdülhamid II (1876–1909)	127
Conclusion	199
Epilogue	207
Bibliography	214
Index	233

Figures

1.1	Portrait of Sultan Mahmud II (1815)	7
1.2	Portrait of Sultan Mahmud II (1839)	8
2.1	Portrait of Sultan Abdülmecid (1850)	39
2.2	Badge of the Order of Glory (Nişan-ı Iftihar)	45
2.3	Badge of the Mecidi Order	46
2.4	Sultan Abdülmecid wearing his Imperial Decoration, c. 1851	48
3.1	Photograph of Sultan Abdülaziz	96
3.2	Photograph of Şahzade (Prince) Abdülhamid	113
4.1	Portrait of Sultan Murad V	132
4.2	Hamidiye Mosque during *Selamlık* (Friday prayer)	147
4.3	Students of the Hamidiye School for the Deaf and Mute	154
4.4	Students of the Muslim school in Vidin	155
4.5	Tribal School students from Batavya (Jakarta)	156
4.6	The Kağıthane Fountain in Istanbul	157
4.7	Abdülhamid II's Tophane Fountain in Istanbul	158
4.8	Fountain of Mahmud I at Tophane in Istanbul	159
4.9	The Taksim Fountain in Istanbul	159
4.10	The Nişantaşı Fountain in Istanbul	160
4.11	The Hamidiye Fountain in Selanik	161
4.12	The Kastamonu Fountain	162
4.13	The 1893 Chicago Fair Obelisk	162
4.14	Telegraph monument in Damascus	163
4.15	A gift to Abdülhamid II from Bulgarian Muslims	164
4.16	The Lysicrates Monument from the north-west, c. 1853–4	165
4.17	The Beirut Fountain	166
4.18	The Sakız Fountain	166
4.19	The Kuds (Jerusalem) Fountain	167
4.20	The Adana Fountain	168
4.21	The Diyarbakır Fountain I	169
4.22	The Diyarbakır Fountain II	170

Figures

4.23	The Giresun Fountain	170
4.24	The Kaiser's Fountain	171
4.25	Soul-Nourishing Fountain	172
4.26	Soul-Nourishing Fountain II	173
4.27	The Mosul Fountain	174
4.28	The Namazgah Fountain	175
E.1	Portrait of Emperor Nicholas I	208

Abbreviations

A.DVN.	Sadaret Divan Kalemi Evrakı
A.MKT.	Sadaret Mektubî Kalemi Belgeleri
A.MKT.MHM.	Sadaret Mühimme Kalemi Evrakı
A.MKT.UM.	Sadaret Umum Vilayat Evrakı
BOA	Başbakanlık Osmanlı Arşivi
CH	*Ceride-i Havadis*
C.SM.	Cevdet Saray
DH.MKT.	Dahiliye Mektubi Kalemi
HAT	Hatt-ı Hümayûn Tasnifi
HR.SFR.3.	Hariciye Nezareti Londra Sefareti
I.DH	*Iradeler Dahiliye*
I.HR	*Iradeler Hariciye*
IJMES	*The International Journal of Middle East Studies*
LH	*Levant Herald*
M	*Malumat*
SF	*Servet-i Fünun*
TV	*Takvim-i Vekayi*
Y.A.HUS.	*Yıldız Hususi Maruzat*
YEE	*Yıldız Esas Evrakı*
Y.EE.KP.	*Yıldız Esas ve Sadrazam Kamil Paşa Evrakı*
Y.MTV.	*Yıldız Mütenevvi Maruzat*
Y.PRK.ASK.	*Yıldız Askeri Maruzat*
Y.PRK.BŞK.	*Yıldız Başkitabet Dairesi Maruzatı*
Y.PRK.DH.	*Yıldız Dahiliye Nezareti Maruzatı*
Y.PRK.MF.	*Yıldız Maarif Nezareti Maruzatı*
Y.PRK.MK.	*Yıldız Müfettişlikler ve Komiserlikler Tahriratı*
Y.PRK.UM.	*Yıldız Umum Vilayetler Tahriratı*

Introduction

I began my studies of nation-related phenomena in 1999 at the Central European University in Budapest, Hungary and quickly developed two profound dissatisfactions. The first had to do with the lack of clear definitions of basic terms and strict adherence to them, even in seminal works in the field, which I thought was a fundamental impediment to the scientific method. The second concerned the persistent overemphasis on elite strands of thought and narratives at the expense of studying the unfolding of the modern worldview as a mass mentality early on, starting from a simple question: 'Where did the average person first get what eventually became ethnonationalism from?', to which one might add 'and when and how?'. In short, I could pose the following key question, which still remains largely unanswered: 'What do we really speak of when we speak of the modern ethnonational mindset and where shall we search for its roots?'. Unfortunately, both of these systemic problems persist to this day despite occasional (individual) attempts at (partial or situational) amelioration.

In truth, the past two decades have witnessed a veritable explosion of studies employing a profusion of secondary qualifiers[1] – hybrid,[2] nested,[3] compartmentalised,[4] fragmented,[5] fractured,[6] bounded[7] (identities); porous, permeable[8] (communal boundaries), and so on. Undoubtedly, these have helped push the field much further. Yet, for all the rising complexity and subtlety of more recent scholarship on missing or misrepresented aspects of belonging, basic terms such as 'ethnicity' and 'nationality' (with the added twist of '*millet*' and an alleged '*millet* system' in the Ottoman context), 'patriotism', 'nationalism' and 'identity', more broadly, are still predominantly employed in a static, unqualified (aggregating), interchangeable and largely anachronistic manner. In other words, they are deployed in past settings as all too convenient shortcuts or umbrella terms lumping together and labelling people on the ground who most likely saw themselves and the world around them in alternative, much more complex ways.

This book proposes a more systematic and comprehensive approach to these challenges in the context of the late Ottoman Empire. It proceeds from a firm conviction that the present terminological apparatus is inadequate and counter-productive when it comes to the study of a fitful, meandering, yet compellingly real process of becoming modern and ethnonational in outlook at the popular level. Therefore, as a first step, it experiments with terms such as 'religio-cultural community', 'micro-regional' vs 'supra-regional identification(s)', 'macro-communal/macro-group consciousness', 'macro-territorial attachment' and others, more specialised – such as Bulgar- and Hellene-minded *Rum* – in an attempt to capture forms of belonging in the act of shaping from the micro to the macro level, outside the temporal and spatial frames of the nation-state. Regarding the point of origin, this book theorises average personal attachments in the following three-tiered way, borne out by a careful examination of the existing evidence. First, ordinary people saw themselves in loose confessional (Muslim, Christian, Jewish, and so on) and strict professional (artisan, peasant, merchant and so on) terms. Third, they were (micro) regionally defined – in the case of sedentary populations[9] with which this book is chiefly concerned – as a village and its surroundings up to but rarely farther than the nearest town. After all, this was the zone of habitation and movement for most people. In this, the natural terrain – a mountain, a valley, a river – often played a key role. The terrain set the pace of everyday life in a number of ways – climate, types of livelihood available and types of clothing, tools, customs, regional dialects and other specificities. In short, the majority of people did not identify from the outset with *millets*[10] or ethnonational groups. Moreover, being born and raised in a town or village and its vicinity created horizontal bonds, which frequently cut across religious[11] or professional ties. This was one's 'fatherland' in physical, linguistic, cultural and emotional terms.

Second, in order to connect the ruler to the ruled and map the gamut of literal and figurative, direct and indirect, intended and unintended influences of the former on the latter (and vice versa), this book adopts the meta concept of *ruler (in)visibility* and its cycles as foundational for the cultural-historical analysis it offers. Today, despite the ongoing 'imperial turn',[12] we still tend to underappreciate the powerful connection and dynamics between the ruler and the average subject when in fact for most of the nineteenth century the Ottoman monarch had no viable competitor (be it a constitutionalist, nationalist or other movement) in terms of popular appeal, among Muslims and non-Muslims alike.

Third, this book identifies the annual all-imperial ruler celebrations, a global mass-scale nineteenth-century phenomenon, as an under-researched and extremely promising area of focus in the study of the moorings of contemporary popular belonging. Within the Ottoman realm, these festivi-

Introduction

ties commenced by order of Mahmud II in the capital, the provinces and abroad in 1836, a fact that remains almost completely unknown and has until today received hardly any scholarly attention. Unlike a score of influential works in Ottoman studies and beyond, which have embraced the concept of *difference*[13] as central to their analysis of empire, this book emphasises *sameness*, that is, the credible common denominator these sultanic ceremonies drew between imperial subjects, irrespective of location, language, creed or class, leading to a largely level playing field of loyalties. Thus, it makes the case for ceremonial studies as a worthy subfield in Ottoman studies, well equipped and capable of generating insights into monarchy and modern belonging. The next step will be to take ceremonial studies from the local and the imperial to the comparative, the inter- and trans-imperial, and the global levels, lines of analysis a subsequent monograph will explore (see Epilogue). Since this book covers an entire century, devoting a mere chapter to each sultan, it touches by necessity rather lightly on a high number of highly voluminous bodies of scholarship, such as Ottoman imperial power and ideology, *millet*, modernity, nationalism studies, public space/sphere, governmentality and the modern state, to name but a few. Thus, in a sense, it prioritises breadth over depth, in an attempt to open rather than close the research topic in question. At the same time, one of its aims is to offer the reader an in-depth look at the various aspects and metamorphoses of belonging, examined under a magnifying glass, in a thorough and rigorous manner even at the expense of occasionally dry, rather technical analysis.

Methodologically, the book interweaves elements of *micro* and *macro* history. The argument relies on techniques of close textual analysis, inspired by the work[14] and teachings of Carlo Ginzburg, but adapted to the service of macrohistorical themes. The source base includes a wide range of Ottoman archival documents (reports, directives and internal communications), artistic production (monuments, public projects and charity works dedicated to and/or named after the ruler, architectural designs and decorative sets, photographs/lithographs, poems, songs, prayers, speeches, addresses of gratitude, gifts), as well as newspaper articles, memoirs and personal correspondence in Ottoman and modern Turkish, Bulgarian, Hebrew, Russian, English, French and German.

Chapter 1 introduces and briefly traces the concept of *ruler visibility*, the focal point of the entire book, from the inception of the Ottoman imperial project to the nineteenth century. This umbrella term facilitates two lines of subsequent analysis of the sultan's public image – visibility at home vs abroad, and visibility to Muslim vs Christian target audiences. The chapter then focuses on the reign of Mahmud II (1808–39), who engineered the

3

first shift in modern ruler visibility in the Ottoman Empire. On the basis of hitherto untapped Ottoman archival evidence, this chapter makes the claim that the reform process began much earlier than the standard narrative (the Rose Chamber Rescript (*Gülhane Hatt-ı Şerif*) of 1839) still claims. It also introduces some principles of aggrandisement of the ruler in the eyes of the people, such as piety, devotion to duty and fatherly status (in a 'father-children' metaphor of society), which pertain to the entire book.

Chapters 2 and 3 focus on the reigns of Mahmud II's sons, Abdülmecid (1839–61) and Abdülaziz (1861–76), respectively. They brought Mahmud II's policies of increased visibility regarding the royal image to an apex. The trope of love for the ruler, which flourished under Abdülmecid, broadened and intensified the terms of direct engagement between sultan and subject. It also provided early indications for a trajectory of abstraction in terms of glorification of the sultan, which would gradually lead to a personality cult by the end of the nineteenth century, under Abdülhamid II. Abdülaziz maintained a remarkable continuity with his brother's policies. This sultan standardised and expanded the annual all-imperial royal accession anniversary and birthday celebrations, which grew until 1908. Chapters 2 and 3 gradually shift the focus of the inquiry away from elitist theoretical conceptions of power towards the popular practical celebrations thereof. They look at some channels for the localisation of central policies regarding monarchic celebration and the transformative effects on the Ottoman (especially non-Muslim) populace in the period from 1839 to 1876.

Chapter 4 analyses the second shift in modern ruler visibility, along faith-based lines, during the reign of Abdülmecid's son, Abdülhamid II (1876–1909). It demonstrates that the sultan strove to present himself as a pious Muslim to Muslims at home and abroad, and as a Western ruler to non-Muslims at home and abroad. Therefore, the sultan tended to deprive the former of his direct visibility (public appearances and public display or dissemination of royal portraits), while at the same time channelling and staging it selectively towards the latter. Split chronologically into early-, middle- and late-reign sections, this chapter places a special emphasis on the overall shift from direct to indirect sultanic visibility over time by way of resorting to material objects and abstract metaphors as ruler proxies. Chapter 4 traces the escalation of celebration in the second half of Abdülhamid II's reign in an attempt to capture the deliberate personality cult, centred on the sultan. At the same time, it also analyses a range of alleged provocations and attempts at subversion (ceremonial or otherwise) of symbolic central power in order to shed new light on the later channels for group activation and increasingly ethnic group realisation.

The conclusion brings together various threads of the complex feedback

Introduction

loop between ruler visibility and group consciousness at the popular level. It compiles a thirteen-point list of the key constituent elements and open-ended processes of the modern worldview, derived from the case of the Bulgars of Rumelia and open to testing in other (Ottoman or not) contemporary communal cases. The conclusion emphasises the integral connection between imperial policies, their fostering of 'minority' and 'majority' mindsets, and the eventual modern ethnonational political outcomes. This connection is, in my view, inalienable from a comprehensive and historically accurate understanding of the transition from imperial to national mind-frames, and, ultimately, of modernity itself.

The Epilogue discusses the wider usability of the above-mentioned model of modern belonging. It briefly sketches avenues for comparative, inter- and trans-imperial studies across the nineteenth-century globe, starting with the Russian Empire and the case of the Finns.

Notes

1. Most of these enjoy a substantial following. The examples given here are therefore illustrative rather than exhaustive.
2. Bhabha, *The Location of Culture*; Al-Sayyad, *Hybrid Urbanism*; Tziovas, *Greece and the Balkans*, among others.
3. Herb and Kaplan, *Nested Identities*.
4. Ehala, *Signs of Identity*.
5. Wodak, 'Fragmented Identities', in *Politics as Text and Talk*, pp. 143–69.
6. Geisler, *National Symbols*.
7. Barkey, *Empire of Difference*, p. 277.
8. Stein, 'The Permeable Boundaries', in *Boundaries and Belonging*.
9. For an account of Ottoman history with a view to nomadic populations, see Kasaba, *A Moveable Empire*.
10. For the opposite view, see Barkey and Gavrilis, 'The Ottoman Millet System', *Ethnopolitics*, 24–42.
11. For a similar concept and argument, see Lessersohn, 'Provincial Cosmopolitanism', *Comparative Studies in Society and History*, 528–56.
12. See Mikhail and Philliou, 'The Ottoman Empire', *Comparative Studies in Society and History*, 721–45; Aksan, 'What's Up in Ottoman Studies?', *Journal of the Ottoman and Turkish Studies Association*, 3–21. See also David-Fox et al., 'The Imperial Turn', *Kritika*, 705–12.
13. Rodrigue and Reynolds, 'Difference and Tolerance', *Stanford Humanities Review*; Barkey, *Empire of Difference*; Burbank and Cooper, *Empires in World History*; Kuehn, *Empire, Islam, and Politics of Difference*; Hanscom and Washburn, *The Affect of Difference*, among others.
14. See Ginzburg, *The Cheese and the Worms* and his *Clues, Myths, and the Historical Method*.

1

The First Shift in (Modern) Ruler Visibility: the Reign of Mahmud II (1808–39)

Introduction

In 1810, according to John Hobhouse, a British traveller present, along with Lord Byron, at the British ambassador's farewell audience with Mahmud II, the sultan was an aloof figure, who did not engage in any eye contact with his foreign guests. The whole ceremonial setting in which the two sides met (the Reception Room in the Topkapı Palace's Third Court (*Arz Odası*)) was entirely non-Western, including the sultan's attire, made of yellow satin. The sultan's hands were 'glittering with diamond rings' and he had an 'air of indescribable majesty'. Foreigners were incorporated into this setting by having to don Ottoman clothes ('pelisses') over their own. The audience was difficult to arrange and brief, subject to the will of the Janissaries. Not surprisingly, the treatment of the visitors was anything but deferential. They were whisked in and out of the room in short order.[1]

In 1829, according to Adolphus Slade, a British military officer, present at the British ambassador's audience with Mahmud II, the sultan received the visitors with 'great simplicity'. Personally, he was 'divested of sultanic pomp'. Slade went on to describe the sultan's appearance in the following terms: 'Instead of robes of golden tissue, and a cashmere turban concealed by precious stones, he wore a plain blue military cloak and trousers, with no other ornament than a diamond chelengk [aigrette] in his fez, and steel spurs on his Wellington boots'. This encounter took place in an audience tent, in Büyükdere, on the outskirts of Istanbul, prior to a Western-style military review. Büyükdere, in addition to having an open field conducive to military exercises, was also a favoured locale for ambassadorial summer retreats throughout the nineteenth century. The ambassador's arrival on this occasion, in Slade's estimation, was 'the most respectable Frank show ever exhibited to the Osmanleys'.[2]

Though barely two decades apart, these two audiences seem vastly different.[3] The purpose of this chapter is to inquire into the causes and consequences, single events and long-term processes of change in the

The Reign of Mahmud II

Figure 1.1 Portrait of Sultan Mahmud II (1815) by John Young (1755–1825) (Wikimedia Commons).

notion and practice of Ottoman sultanic power representation during the reign of Mahmud II. The main organising principle, both in this chapter and in the rest of the book, is the concept of ruler visibility.

For the purposes of the forthcoming analysis, ruler visibility is a combination of direct and indirect components. The former include the sultan's physical presence at public ceremonies and the degree of his personal exposure to the public gaze. The latter consist of a set of symbolic markers of the ruler, such as his monogram (*tuğra*) on the one hand and the architectural monuments, such as fountains, mosques and tombs, constructed or restored by him, on the other. In the absence of a consistent, genuine and credible effort on the part of the ruler in the pre-modern period to reach out past elite circles and the confines of the capital and due to the lack of a periodical press and mass culture to popularise his 'good works', both types of visibility were quite limited.[4]

Modern ruler visibility is a composite concept, combining projected traits of personal character with short-term and long-term imperatives of policy, both domestically and abroad. It incorporates not only

Figure 1.2 Portrait of Sultan Mahmud II (1839) by Henry G. Schlesinger (1814–93). Ayşe Orbay, *The Sultan's Portrait: Picturing the House of Osman* (Istanbul: Iş Bank, 2000), p. 451.

physical and symbolic aspects – a monarch's more active participation in public events and ceremonies, and the proliferation of his or her markers throughout the imperial domains – but also the more frequent occurrence of references to and discussions about his or her persona in the press.[5]

On the basis of a study of the marked shift in ruler visibility during Mahmud II's late reign, this chapter disputes prevailing notions of the famous nineteenth-century Tanzimat ('Reordering') reforms in terms of both their timing and nature. It does so through the medium of cyclical all-imperial royal ceremony, with a heightened sensitivity to its target audiences, both at home and abroad, while drawing on untapped Ottoman archival evidence, in combination with other, underutilised sources, such as memoirs and newspapers. In the process, this chapter breaks new ground regarding the relations between the Ottoman non-Muslim subjects and the Ottoman ruler in the 1830s, and, by extension, the avenues of formation of macro group awareness in the Ottoman Empire leading over time to ethnonational consciousness.[6]

Ottoman Ruler Visibility before Mahmud II

One of the main premises of this book is that the evolution of royal ceremonies is a barometer for important sociocultural and sociopolitical changes. As the Ottoman state grew from a frontier principality in northwest Anatolia in the early fourteenth century, its bureaucratic structures became more complex and so did its ceremonial projections of power.[7] At first, the Ottoman *bey* (chieftain) had a *primus-inter-pares* (first-among-equals) status, fought side by side with his allies, and was generally highly visible and accessible.

Over time, the gradual territorial expansion and administrative consolidation of the Ottoman domains brought about conflicting visions of power distribution and the future of the state. As the status of the Ottoman ruler grew so did his attempts at centralisation of power at the expense of the alliance of frontier *ghazi* warriors (*uc beğleri*), who had made Osman and his descendants' conquests possible in the first place.[8] These tensions surfaced for the first time in a major way during the reign of sultan Bayezid I when at the 1402 Battle of Ankara, the allied but disgruntled beys of Aydın, Menteşe, Saruhan and Germiyan, withdrew from his side, costing him the battle, his throne and, ultimately, his life.[9] The act initiated a ten-year interregnum, which almost destroyed the entire Ottoman project.

The conquest of Constantinople on 29 May 1453 brought back another wave of centralising-centrifugal tensions. That same day, Sultan Mehmed II, considering himself, by virtue of his achievement of this long-attempted conquest, superior to his ancestors, did not stand upon the call of *ghazi* music, as was dictated by ancient custom.[10]

Over the next two years, the sultan arrested and executed many frontier warriors who had fought under his command but resented the imperial project, correctly perceiving its implications for them.[11] In the words of Cemal Kafadar, the Ottoman sultans had over the course of two centuries 'transformed themselves, at least in their historical consciousness, from recipients to granters of insignia of vassalage'.[12] Not surprisingly, the timing of the Ottoman acquisition of imperial status, with the conquest of Constantinople, coincided with the drafting of an imperial order by Mehmed II, which was codified into a book of ceremonies by the late 1470s.[13] According to Gülru Necipoğlu-Kafadar:

> This rule book stipulated that the monarch remain aloof; he would no longer sit at banquets or appear regularly at public audiences as he used to do. Except for the two religious holidays in which he agreed to give public audiences, he would remain in seclusion, only receiving privileged dignitaries and ambassadors in his private audience hall four times a week.[14]

Thereafter, as the Empire gained power and international prestige, the sultan's title became longer and more magnanimous whereas his visibility and accessibility, from the standpoint of the general populace, gradually decreased. Descriptions of audiences and processions of Suleyman I and Selim II in the second half of the sixteenth century provide a window into 'classic imperial' Ottoman conceptions of the ruler and the terms of his interaction with his own and foreign subjects. His face showed little or no emotion. He rarely spoke. When he did, he employed intermediaries.[15] Audience halls and processions were arranged in such a way as to preclude direct contact of any kind.[16] The processions themselves did not target the people, and were therefore not publicised, whereas foreigners were more often than not excluded from them.[17]

The accession of Selim II to the throne in 1566, upon the death of his father, Suleyman I, while on campaign in Szigetvar (Hungary), marked another stage in the reduction of direct Ottoman ruler visibility. Until then, Ottoman sultans had the habit of visiting the tomb of Eyüp prior to embarking on a campaign in order to seek the saint's blessing.[18] Selim II left his personal mark on this practice in two ways. First, the fact that his visit occurred immediately following his accession, on his way to the front in Hungary, set a key precedent for all subsequent sultans. Second, beginning with Selim II, no Ottoman sultan personally led the Ottoman army on campaigns any longer. Therefore, the practical purpose of the sultan's visit gave way to an entirely symbolic act signifying the sultan's military leadership. As Ottoman sultans withdrew further from the public gaze over the course of the seventeenth century, the accentuation of their (increasingly theoretical) military leadership became only more pronounced with the addition of a sword girding to the tomb visit. The earliest such sword girdings which can be reliably dated took place in the mid-seventeenth century. It was at that time that the identity of the sacred sword, employed in the ritual, began to be mentioned and the ceremony took the definitive shape and unmistakable content of an investiture rite. Whereas in the past such ceremonial visits to Eyüp had occurred as often as campaigns, beginning with Selim II, they took place only once, upon accession. Only in this way, can we explain the reading of *fetih suresi* (the sura of the Qur'an invoking conquest) during the sword-girding ceremony, a practice which was invariably performed on campaigns.[19]

One of the first sword girdings for which there is sufficient evidence was in fact a double sword girding, a rare occurrence in all of Ottoman history.[20] In 1623, upon his accession, Murad IV was girded with the swords of the Prophet (*Peygamber*) and Selim I (*Yavuz Selim*). The reason for such an extraordinary act, in my opinion, is clear – a quick string of sultanic depositions preceding this sword girding produced a dynastic low moment. Between February 1618 and September 1623 (a span of five years and seven months), three sultans were deposed in quick succession – Mustafa I, Osman II and Mustafa I again.[21] It is probably no coincidence that in the aftermath of such a destabilising episode, Murad IV chose to be girded with two swords – one of Islamic and one of dynastic significance.[22] I believe that even the choice of swords can be explained to the benefit of our understanding of the contemporary workings of core Ottoman power. Murad IV picked Selim I's sword, as his choice of a dynastic sword, over Osman Ghazi's sword, one of the most popular swords in all of Ottoman history, probably in order to avoid any association with Osman II (*Genç Osman*). Symbolic confusion and negative association, with a sultan recently deposed and murdered by the Janissaries, could easily cost him his throne and life.

After their heyday as a formidable military force in the fifteenth and sixteenth centuries, the Janissaries, a professional standing infantry and artillery corps, made up of non-Muslim child levies (*devşirme*),[23] began by the beginning of the seventeenth century to play a role in Ottoman politics very similar to those of the Pretorian Guards in the Roman Empire and the Streltsys in the Russian Empire. With the deposition and the subsequent unprecedented murder of an Ottoman sultan (Osman II) in 1622, 'the pattern was set for the rest of the century'.[24] At the outset, in the late fourteenth century, under Murad I, the Janissaries were conceived as a slave (*kul*) corps, created by and loyal solely to the sultan, without rights of marriage, land or property inheritance.[25] Over the course of the following centuries, however, their activities branched far outside warmaking.[26] In 1632, Murad IV provided them land grants with an obligation to campaign.[27] Gradually, the Janissaries became extensively engaged with trade and tax farming (*iltizam*).[28] By the eighteenth century, the Janissaries had infiltrated the imperial domains and more or less dominated provincial household-based politics in areas as far flung from Istanbul as Syria (*Sham*), Egypt, Tunisia and Algeria.[29] They also played a vital role in the life of the guilds (*esnaf*, *taife*).[30] In fact, by the eighteenth century, virtually all Muslim guildsmen had become Janissaries.[31] As the Janissaries thus began to lose their cutting edge in military matters and the Empire's expansion was arrested (due to a number of factors, not least among them over-extension), they became a rising domestic political force, at once providing crucial checks-and-balances on the exercise of sultanic power and serving as the nucleus of opposition to any measure, which threatened the status quo.[32] One area in which the Janissaries avidly performed the role of 'enforcers' in the pre-modern period was the sultan's conservative image and public conduct, on the one hand, and, in a related fashion, his limited, subdued contact with foreign agents.

While the sultan was gradually withdrawing from public view, as a reflection of his enhanced status, restraining factors and for other reasons, including personal security,[33] he began to craft more carefully the symbolic signifiers of his personage. In the period between the mid-fifteenth century and the late sixteenth century, dominated by the reigns of Mehmed II and Suleyman I, the Ottoman sultans attained a position from which they could credibly dispute with Western sovereigns the title to *universal kingdom*. Understandably, some of them attempted to cast their images in the mould of Western rulers, which entailed occasional departures from mainstream Ottoman (Muslim) thinking regarding ruler representations. Thus, Mehmed II invited Western artists to his court and had portraits painted of him as a Renaissance prince, in contravention of Islamic injunctions and previous sultanic practices. He also issued medals commemorating his capture of Constantinople and bearing his august image.[34] Suleyman I, who competed with the Habsburg emperor Charles V for the title of Holy Roman Emperor, even had a ceremonial helmet-crown made for him which displayed motifs clearly borrowed from the papal tiara.[35] This act was further remarkable for the fact that, unlike the Safavids – their Muslim rivals to the East – the Ottomans did not have a crown among their regalia.

The latter two changes met with disapprobation at home and were reversed no later than the next reign. Bayezid II went so far as to accuse his father Mehmed II of apostasy after his death.[36] There was more to this accusation than mere matters of human visual representation or ceremony, however. As Cemal Kafadar points out, Bayezid II also sought to ease the moral pressures of centralisation and appease some of its discontents, even though the process itself was not halted.[37] In addition, Bayezid II's announcement probably had a purely generational dimension as well: it can be seen as a natural filial reaction, the consequence of an incoming ruler's desire to differentiate himself from the outgoing one. Such reasoning in fact characterised most transitions between reigns, and, as we will see later, by way of the rising capacities of the media in the modern period, it would come to play an ever larger role in royal image making.

The first practice, of having royal portraits painted, survived. It did outlive Mehmed II and, in the form of dynastic albums, lasted until the end of the Empire. These were made for the royal household alone. They were never exhibited in public. Suleyman I, on the other hand, employed the helmet-crown very briefly, in the course of just a few processions, modelled after those of his nemesis, the Habsburg emperor Charles V, and targeting an overwhelmingly Western audience.[38] Afterwards, the helmet-crown was blamed on an allegedly superfluous and whimsical Grand Vizier, Ibrahim Paşa, whose death, by execution, brought an end to such visual experimentation regarding the sultan. As a whole, these were exceptions rather than the rule. The general trend was for sultans to partake rarely of public ceremonies. When they did, they engaged in restrained and strongly ritualised behaviour, usually sharing ceremonial space with few outside the capital's elite.

The ruler's direct visibility was so low in the seventeenth and most of the eighteenth centuries that the sultan could leave the palace in disguise (*tebdil-i kıyafet*), without much fear of being recognised. Most people simply had no way of knowing what the sultan looked like. Foreign diplomats, on the other hand, could not move freely throughout the capital – they needed special permits to proceed from one point to the next and were accompanied by a Janissary guard at all times. As late as the turn of the nineteenth century, foreign emissaries had to make special provisions prior to staging any more or less public event or celebration in the Ottoman capital. For example, in preparation for a fete and public promenade (*temaşa*) at the Russian legation in Istanbul on the occasion of the Russian Emperor Paul I's accession in 1796, the legation's chief interpreter, Joseph Fonton, had to request security arrangements from the Ottoman authorities in order to avoid the occurrence of 'quarrels and disputes (*kavga ve niza*)'.[39] Not only the Janissaries, but also the population of the capital as a whole was at that time still largely unaccustomed and hostile to acts of celebration of foreign sovereignty on Ottoman soil. The memoirs of Western travellers, well into the nineteenth century, corroborate this state of affairs.[40]

The seventeenth[41] and eighteenth centuries were, for the most part, quite uniform in terms of the Ottoman ruler's limited direct visibility, despite some periodic peaks. For example, Ahmed III, whose reign (1703–30) became known as the 'Tulip Period (*Lale Devri*)' encouraged a more ostentatious style of elite entertainment, including large open-air parties with poetry, music and frequent royal promenades along the shores of the Bosphorus. This age opened new possibilities in terms of indirect visibility as well. It inaugurated the passion for lavish fountains with poetic inscriptions eulogising the ruler and it made the open format of waterfront palaces highly appealing and fashionable.[42] The emergent Ottoman Rococo architecture captured the exuberance of this age and left a lasting mark on the Ottoman capital, to which we will return later. At this time, the ruler's monogram (*tuğra*) began to appear on the facades of public buildings, a public statement enhancing his indirect visibility.[43] Yet the changes, some more lasting than others, affected significantly neither the ruler's direct visibility in the long run, nor the manner of his connection to public spaces outside the capital.

It was Selim III (1789–1807) who took the ruler's indirect visibility a step further in connection to his reforming measures. Upon conclusion of the Iaşi Treaty, which ended the war with Russia in 1792, the sultan approached twenty-two prominent men and asked them to pen memoranda on the new order to be implemented in the Ottoman Empire. The resulting papers which, Şükrü Hanioğlu likens to the French *Cahiers* of 1789, focused on proposals for military and fiscal reform.[44] The sultan invited foreign officers to serve as advisers to the Ottoman army and established colleges to teach European military sciences in imitation of French academies. Unlike previous such instructors like Baron François de Tott or Comte de Bonneval (*Humbaracı Ahmed Pasha*), the new advisers came as formal emissaries of the French government and retained their French rank and loyalty to France. The sultan insisted that, contrary to their long-standing habits, the Janissaries should drill and train on a regular basis.[45]

Selim III also broke new ground with the establishment of Ottoman legations abroad in the early 1790s.[46] Inspired by Napoleon I's gift in the shape of his little portrait, which was conveyed by the French ambassador in Istanbul, Selim III procured his own version and sent it back as a token of his appreciation of Napoleon's friendship.[47] In terms of ruler visibility, Selim III, who also engaged in the type of elite entertainment introduced by Ahmed III, was both the last representative of the pre-modern age and the harbinger of the modern one.[48] This should hardly come as a surprise given that his reign began in the fateful year of 1789, which left no part of the European continent unchanged. Selim III's attempt to make a lasting mark at home, however, with the establishment of a new military corps, the 'new order (*nizam-i cedid*)' troops, which would be directly associated with and loyal to the ruler, was short-lived. A Janissary rebellion led to the deposition of the sultan in 1807.

Mahmud II's Early Reign and the Janissary Constraint

The period of this book opens with the year 1808 for a number of reasons. First, at this time, the Ottoman Empire endured one of its most unstable episodes. Between May 1807 and July 1808 (a span of one year and two months), two sultans were deposed – Selim III and Mustafa IV. Both were subsequently murdered. As will be demonstrated shortly, the circumstances of Mahmud II's rise to the throne in 1808 played an important role in the timing and nature of his eventual reform efforts. The volatile conditions in the Ottoman capital coincided with provincial disturbances and centrifugal moves by powerful local notables (*ayan*).[49] Centre and periphery were brought together, albeit temporarily, in a 'Deed of Agreement (*sened-i ittifaq*)', concluded in the same year of 1808.[50]

The details of Mahmud II's rise to power – his hiding in the chimney of a bath, thus narrowly escaping the Janissary assassins sent for him – probably brought home the point that any significant reforms could only be implemented after the Janissary Corps had been completely removed from the political scene. The fate of Osman II in 1622 and Selim III in 1807, both of whom had intentions to reform the Janissary corps, in addition to the fate of other deposed Ottoman sultans over the intervening centuries, certainly favoured such a conclusion. Therefore, a durable grip on power necessitated caution and dissimulation on the part of the ruler for as long as the Janissary Corps existed. It makes little difference whether or not Selim III had an actual influence over his younger cousin[51] and impressed upon his receptive mind ideas of reform early on. The mere fact of Mahmud II's rise to power on the strength of the loyalist Bayraktar Mustafa Pasha, a powerful Rumelian[52] notable, and his Albanian troops, who reined in the Istanbul Janissaries, said much about the new ruler's potential personal disposition regarding the latter. Moreover, it was the provincial Albanians, and not the Janissaries of the capital, who marched beside the new sultan along Divan Yolu following his sword-girding procession.[53] In return for his vital support, Bayraktar Mustafa became Grand Vizier. In other words, from the outset of his reign, Mahmud II drew his legitimacy from sources other than the Janissaries.

On the surface, little had changed in the way the sultan acted in public. The 1810 account by Hobhouse, discussed above, cast Mahmud II's image in light similar to his predecessors going at least as far back as the early seventeenth century. There is evidence to suggest, however, that even with the Janissary constraint on what he could and could not do, Mahmud II had some exposure to Western practices of ruler celebration. An imperial decree (*HAT*) dating roughly from the time of Hobhouse's visit to Istanbul contains a brief summary of the story of English royal accession celebrations: 'In the English state some time around 180 years ago, the things handed down by tradition changed, and it became customary for the English House at that time to celebrate the day on which the kings sat on the royal throne . . .'[54] Apparently, the occasion for this explanation was the annual practice of the two British Navy squadrons in the Golden Horn to fire twenty [sic] ceremonial cannon salvos on the King's accession day. This act always remained unreciprocated (*mukabelesiz*). In fact, as a way of protesting the lack of any Ottoman reciprocity whatsoever, the

Ruler Visibility and Popular Belonging

British ambassador announced his intention to send a notice to the staff of the Ottoman Chief Artilleryman (*Topçubaşı Ağa*) to the effect that they 'did not inadvertently reciprocate (*sehven mukabele etmemek için*)'.[55] It remains unclear whether the Ottomans caught the intended irony in the ambassador's protestations. More importantly, this act of diplomatic exasperation clearly demonstrates that the long-standing Ottoman policy of ceremonial non-engagement with the West on its terms was still in force in 1810.

The growing Greek revolt of 1821 made it plain to see that by the mid-1820s this policy was no longer tenable. It demonstrated convincingly the urgent need for active positive Ottoman image making abroad, in light of the West's vital support for the insurgents. The revolt also contributed in large part to the closing of Selim III's experiment – the Ottoman legations abroad – as their largely Phanariot staff's loyalty to the Ottoman state came under question.[56] This closure reduced the indirect sultanic visibility abroad for more than a decade.

Wars, Political Crises and the Changing Image of the Ruler

Drastic change came on the heels of a protracted period of foreign wars and internal instability. Between 1768 and 1829, the Ottomans were on the losing end of a series of wars with Russia, which did not conceal its grand designs on core Ottoman territories, including Istanbul and the Dardanelles. These wars initiated the so-called 'Eastern Question' and led to the Ottoman loss of the Crimea (1783), weakened control of the Danubian Principalities of Wallachia and Moldavia, and the formation of autonomous Serbia (1829) and independent Greece (1832).[57] At this time, the Ottoman centre also fought powerful warlords at home, such as Osman Pazvantoğlu of Vidin, Tepedelenli Ali of Yanya, and, above all, Mehmed Ali of Egypt, who had grown to be more powerful and independent than any provincial governor in Ottoman history.[58] What all of these external and internal crises called for was a profound reorientation in Ottoman foreign policy and the establishment of a plane of diplomatic reciprocity with and acceptance by the increasingly powerful West. Until recently, this process was uniformly and rather indiscriminately referred to as 'Westernisation', with its inevitable corollary of 'secularisation' in most standard narratives of the period.[59] Despite the universal acknowledgement of the role of Mahmud II as the first successful initiator of this reform process after the abolition of the Janissaries – known as the 'Auspicious Event (*Vaka-yı Hayriye*)' – in 1826, the majority of established historical accounts today still point to the Gülhane Rescript of 1839 at the outset of

Abdülmecid's reign as the starting date of Ottoman modernity. Clearly, the yardstick of modernity in this context is the central Ottoman attempt to establish and safeguard the equality of Christian and Muslim Ottoman subjects before the law, announced with the above-mentioned decree.

While adopting this as its central premise, this chapter shows that the Tanzimat process was in fact well under way by 1839. Moreover, its central engine was not a Western agent, but the sultan himself, who, with the help of his advisers, Mustafa Reshid Pasha featuring prominently among them, designed new celebrations with a view yet again of centralisation, only this time of subject loyalties. Finally, regardless of long-term implications, the immediate contemporary context of the ruler's reformed image was secular only if viewed from abroad. At home, Mahmud II strove to present himself in strictly Muslim terms to Muslims, and universal kingly terms to non-Muslims. In doing so, he initiated two momentous long-term trends, which have been underappreciated by period Ottoman scholars, but which are indispensable to a realistic understanding of the history of communal ethos in the late Ottoman Empire. The first is the direct active engagement with non-Muslims and the monarch-initiated split in the manner of relation of the ruler to his Muslim and non-Muslim subjects, which accordingly conditioned reverse attitudes and modes of attachment. The second is the creation and fostering of an integrative, universalist conception of faith as a binding factor between the Muslim ruler and his non-Muslim subjects, which in more or less credible format lasted for almost a century thereafter and gave Ottomanism its most viable form in the mid-nineteenth century.

The Explosion in Direct Ruler Visibility after the Abolition of the Janissaries

Barely a few weeks after the abolition of the Janissaries on 16 June 1826, Mahmud II had 2,000 soldiers 'arranged in European order and going through the new form of exercise' in the outer court of the Topkapı Palace. Even more striking was Mahmud II's openness to the public gaze: 'the sultan, who was at first stationed at the window within sight, descended after a time and passed the men in review'. It is no coincidence that the British ambassador, Sir Stratford Canning, who meticulously related the scene, felt obliged to make a point of saying 'within sight'. The remark reflects the unusual nature of the sultan's act. Just as striking was the sultan's outer appearance – 'dressed in the Egyptian fashion [that is, in a modern military uniform] armed with pistols and sabre and on his head, in place of the imperial turban, was a sort of Egyptian bonnet'.[60] Equally unusual was the fact that non-Muslims could watch the new troop parade through the city with equanimity, whereas at the beginning of previous campaigns they were often attacked by the Janissaries for desecrating the sacred banner, among other supposed offences.[61]

The sultan's 'Egyptian' transformation in the immediate aftermath of the 'Auspicious Event' deserves a closer look, especially if we keep in mind that he had already invited an Egyptian military instructor to teach the newly founded *Eşkinciyan* (Mounted Yeomen).[62] As a matter of fact, it was precisely the drilling exercise of these new troops wearing modern uniforms, in the European fashion, conducted by the Egyptian instructor and three of Selim III's veterans on the large drilling ground near the Janissary barracks at Etmeydanı on 11 June 1826, that precipitated the 'Auspicious Event' in the first place.[63] That Mehmed Ali, the reformer of Egypt, was after all a Muslim probably made his blueprint of innovation much more palatable to Mahmud II's own Muslim public than any outright acknowledgement of a direct Western importation. After all, prior to 1831, Mehmed Ali was acting as a perfectly obliging, if powerful provincial governor. For example, his defeat of the Wahhabis and the retaking of Mecca in 1813, upon Mahmud II's request, led to the renewed trumpeting of the sultan's *ghazi* title.[64]

As the ruler's direct visibility increased, so did the militarisation of his image. In fact, the two trends were mutually reinforcing. This occurred in a context of profound Ottoman weakness, both at home and abroad, in the aftermath of the disbanding of the Janissary corps, followed by the 1827 debacle at the Battle of Navarino, where the Ottoman fleet was annihilated, and the disastrous Russo-Turkish War of 1828–9. The process of change had multiple dimensions and implications. First, it was a matter of clothing. The bright colours and luxurious materials of former centuries were quickly phased out in favour of dull colours (blue, brown and grey) and coarse materials (wool and cotton).

In 1829, a British military officer still noted a few vestiges of the past in Mahmud II's procession to a military camp and audience given to the British ambassador. For example, the sultan was accompanied by 'pages walking on either side with huge peacock plumes to conceal his resplendent visage from profane eyes'. In addition, foreigners still had to 'be conducted to another tent to be clothed', although – in contrast to the 1810 account by Hobhouse – with 'Spanish mantles, made of inferior cloth'.[65]

By the early 1830s, Mahmud II could only be distinguished from a regular military officer by a collar of diamonds, emeralds and rubies and a diamond clasp on his cloak.[66] Simplicity and accessibility became key motifs in Mahmud II's reformed image of the 1830s in his bid for much needed direct vertical ties of subject allegiance. Thus, Mahmud II became

The Reign of Mahmud II

the first sultan in recorded Ottoman history to walk to Friday prayers through crowded bazaars.[67] The sultan even spent a night on a ship, preferring to have a simple dinner with sailors instead of the splendid banquet given in his honour by Salih Paşa, the commander of the town of Kal'a-yı Sultaniye (Çanakkale).[68]

From 1826 to his death in 1839, Mahmud II clearly chose a course of high (in some cases, extreme) visibility in order to impose a drastic departure from Ottoman norms in most spheres of life under the duress of a prolonged imperial crisis. In a manner reminiscent of Nicholas I of Russia (1825–55), the parade ground allowed him to express a convincing autocratic vision for the Empire. Mahmud II learned to ride a horse in the European fashion and initiated joint military reviews (with, notably, the Russians) for the first time in Ottoman history.[69] In a manner reminiscent of Peter I of Russia (1682–1725), to whom some contemporary observers compared him, Mahmud II founded new elite regiments, such as the Lancers (*Mızraklı*). This novel practice continued under the next three sultans. His Friday prayer processions became much more accessible to foreigners than ever before. They signalled the type of spectacle and source of publicity that would only grow in size in the future.

An 1833 account by John Auldjo, a British traveller, relating one of Mahmud II's Friday prayer processions, already reveals the lack of any visual barriers between the sultan and the common people on the street. Moreover, during this procession, an Ottoman officer politely addressed foreign ladies in fluent French and provided refreshments for them. Most strikingly, when the foreigners took off their hats, the sultan looked 'earnestly' *at* them, 'without turning his head', and went so far as to acknowledge the salute 'by a slight inclination of his body'.[70] The act of the sultan's initiation of eye contact with foreigners, and his response to their greeting, are indicative of the speed of Ottoman integration into the Western system of signs and symbols after the 'Auspicious Event'. What makes this case even more remarkable is the fact that the visual exchange occurred in the context of a public procession, which by its nature carries lower eye-contact expectations than a personal audience of the type described at the beginning of this chapter.

After a lapse of about two decades, following Selim III's deposition, Mahmud II returned to the theme of the ruler's visage as a diplomatic tool, only this time he much broadened both its purpose and its target audience. After reportedly examining with great care the portraits of the tsar and tsarina hanging in a Russian ship's cabin in 1829, the sultan created a medallion bearing his own portrait – a depiction of the sultan in a Western-style uniform. This became known as the 'Imperial Portrait (*tasvir-i hümayun*)' and it quickly became a most coveted domestic award, demonstrating its holder's rare proximity and high loyalty to the sultan.[71] Internationally, the Ottomans maintained such gift exchange at least until the accession of Abdülaziz in 1861, at which point he bestowed upon the French ambassador, Marquis de Lavalette, a portrait of his recently deceased brother Abdülmecid, 'decorated with rich diamonds (*s bogati brillanti ukrashen*)'.[72]

Even more radical was the public display of royal portraits. In the early 1830s, Mahmud II commissioned portraits of himself wearing the new military uniform. In 1835, the sultan began to distribute his portraits to schools and official buildings.[73] They were hung in army barracks and saluted by the troops as if he were present.[74] Various sheikhs would bless them before they were placed in government offices and other public places. A twenty-one-gun salute greeted them as a guard of honour marched past.[75] In flagrant violation of Ottoman Muslim mores proscribing human depiction of any kind, Mahmud II even gave away his portrait to the şeyhülislam, Yazıncızade Abdülvehab Efendi.[76] This was an act of deliberate provocation on the part of the sultan, followed by an exercise of blunt authoritarian force. The top cleric's staunch opposition to portraits soon led to his dismissal as well as the appointment of a permanent portrait artist in the palace service.[77]

The early 1830s also witnessed the appearance of a modern domestic press in the Ottoman language. Not surprisingly, the first Ottoman newspaper, *Takvim-i Vekayi*, which also appeared in French, as *Le Moniteur ottoman*, aided the cause of the sultan's visibility by describing the sultan's daily activities. Its appearance in 1831 was probably in response to Mehmed Ali's initiation of his own publication, *Vaqa'-i Mısriyye* in 1828.[78] In fact, the earlier cooperation between the sultan and his powerful governor gave way to a vicious rivalry by the early 1830s, which posed a serious threat to Mahmud II's personal power and the Empire's integrity for the rest of the sultan's life. The temporary diffusion of the crisis, with the assistance of the Great Powers in the mid-1830s, afforded Mahmud II the opportunity to press with some of his most sweeping economic, bureaucratic-administrative, legal and, as the following pages will show, ceremonial reforms.

The Rising Importance of Ottoman Non-Muslims from the Sultan's Perspective. Further Gains in Sultanic Visibility

The Treaty of Küçük Kaynarca, which concluded the Russo-Ottoman war of 1768–74, humiliated the Ottomans by forcing them to accept, among other indignities, Russian protectorship over Ottoman Christians and the effective ceding of the Muslim-populated Crimea to Russia.[79] In return, the Ottomans received the symbolic compensation of claiming protectorship over non-Ottoman Muslims. This amounted to a claim to caliphal authority, which the Ottoman sultans had not asserted, consistently and prominently, since the mid-sixteenth century, the time of Kanuni Süleyman (Süleyman the Magnificent) and his chief jurist, Ebu'suud. The Treaty of Küçük Kaynarca altered the symbolic power equation between the two sides permanently at a time when Catherine II's designs on Istanbul and the Straits presented a very credible threat to the Ottomans. One of its clauses – article 16 – explicitly afforded Russia the right to make representations on behalf of the Danubian Principalities of Wallachia and Moldavia before the Sublime Porte.[80] As Russia thus encroached more than ever before on long-held Ottoman territories, it became increasingly clear that Ottoman Christians, densely populating some of the new borderlands with Russia, could be used as a 'fifth column', a powerful tool in diplomacy as well as war making. For example, the 1804 Serbian revolt led to the 1806–12 Russo-Ottoman War. Similarly, the 1821 Greek revolt concluded with the 1828–9 Russo-Ottoman War. As Stanford Shaw and others have shown, the relations between Ottoman Christians and the sultan formed a credible link between most, if not all, Russo-Ottoman Wars after 1774.[81]

In 1791, in a memorandum (*layiha*) to Selim III, Rumelia's Chief Military Judge (*kadıasker*) Tatarcık Abdullah Efendi first expressed the need to better address the Ottoman Christians' needs in order to avoid the occurrence of revolts.[82] An early indication of the Ottoman integrative efforts with respect to Ottoman Christians comes from an unlikely source: *Vestnik Evropyi*, a St Petersburg newspaper. In 1809, it claimed that the late Ottoman reformer, Bayraktar Mustafa Paşa, had 'ordered that Muslims should stop using the word *giaour* (infidel), as any Christian of any confession serves the same God that Muslims believe in'.[83] The Greek Revolution of the 1820s, which began precisely in the increasingly contested borderlands of Wallachia and Moldavia, before it spread to the southern Balkan Peninsula, only accentuated the Ottoman centre's concerns. Thus, in 1827, with a special decree (*ferman*) addressed to the local administration of Rumelia, the Sublime Porte set the task of providing the Christians with security and the inviolability of their property.[84] The Russo-Ottoman War of 1828–9, followed by a wave of immigration of Ottoman Christians to Russian-held borderlands (Bessarabia), further helped place the issue in stark perspective. In 1828, the well-known poet and custodian of the holy cities of Mecca and Medina, Keçecizade Izzet Molla, and the *defterdar katibi* (clerk to the financial section of the Ottoman government) Vecih Efendi presented another memorandum (*layiha*) to Mahmud II. In it, they advised that certain concessions be made to the insurgent Christians, pointing out that the state could not afford to be at war with Russia. They went so far as to pose a rhetorical question: 'Is it not better for us to try and preserve even a part of what we might completely lose at war?'[85]

In July 1829, towards the end of the Greek Revolution, Mahmud II addressed the Greek-speaking Orthodox Christians (*Rum*) of Morea in a *ferman* in the following terms: 'There will be in the future no distinctions made between Muslims and re'aya and everybody will be ensured the inviolability of his property, life and honour by a sacred law (*Şeriat*) and my sublime patronage'.[86] The recurring motif of Ottoman non-Muslims' inviolability of property shows more than a passing concern of the sultan's. The clothing law of that same year eliminated headgear as the chief marker of class and confession. According to Donald Quataert, Mahmud II thus legally 'offered non-Muslims and Muslims a common subjecthood/ citizenry'.[87]

The sultan's closer interaction with his own subjects went much further than the flowery language of the *ferman*. Over a period of seven years (1830–7), he made no fewer than five country trips (*memleket gezileri*) to the provinces.[88] The first trip was to Tekfurdağ, not far from Istanbul, and it lasted a day. The sultan went there by steamship on 28 January 1830 and personally supervised the transportation of a shipload of cargo waiting in the port to be dispatched to Şumnu (Shumen in present-day Bulgaria). The sultan's next trip, starting on 3 June 1831 and lasting for thirty-three days, had as its destination Edirne and the provinces around the Dardanelles. As Cengiz Kırlı insightfully points out, each trip went further away from the capital, and the majority of them were clearly designed with the Empire's non-Muslim population in mind.[89] Despite the official purpose of the trips – to examine the living conditions of his subjects and provide charity to the poor – Kırlı convincingly argues that Mahmud II's real purpose was 'to be seen rather than to see his subjects'.[90] During these trips, the sultan indeed consistently provided funding for churches, synagogues and other historic sacred sites. His attitude set an example for high-ranking Ottoman officials to follow.[91] The sultan also distributed monetary payments along the way (fifty-one guruş to each Muslim and thirty-one guruş to each non-Muslim). He even went to small villages and distributed gifts to their inhabitants. While not unprecedented, such benevolent treatment of Ottoman non-Muslims was certainly rare, especially over a period of just a few years. It was clearly outside the norm of previous Ottoman practices.[92] According to Kırlı, 'in an attempt to captivate the sentiments of his subjects

Mahmud II constantly downplayed his godlike figure and presented the image of an invincible yet human and earthly ruler'.[93] True to the clothing regulation he had issued only two years earlier, the sultan wore the new style of headgear and trousers as he was walking among his subjects. Mahmud II continued to reproduce the new image of the Ottoman ruler on his third and fourth trips to Istanbul's neighbouring town of Izmit, in 1833 and 1836 respectively. The former lasted a week and the latter two weeks.[94]

The last trip was the longest and is the best documented. It commenced on 29 April 1837 at Varna (in present-day Bulgaria) on the Black Sea coast of Ottoman Rumelia. Over the course of thirty-nine days, Mahmud II visited more than a dozen towns on or near the Danube. Helmuth von Moltke, a Prussian officer who accompanied him on this trip, noted how the people who did not believe that the sultan was visiting their towns crowded town squares to see him.[95] In a speech Mahmud II had Vassaf Efendi read[96] at Şumnu, the sultan declared:

> I distinguish the Muslims among my subjects only in the mosque, the Christians – in the church, the Jews – in the synagogue; there is no other difference among them. My love and justice are strong for all, and all are my true sons.[97]

Clearly, this statement continued the theme of equality between religious groups in the Empire, first touched upon in the 1829 statement, discussed above. It also presented the relations between the ruler and the ruled through a universalising *father-children* metaphor of society, common to many contemporary empires. Such a metaphor had been employed by Ottoman rulers in the past, but in Mahmud II's time, it gained a new meaning and urgency to it. Its use reflected a central elitist attempt to pre-empt the rise of ethnoreligious claims, inspired by novel notions of popular sovereignty, maintain unity irrespective of cultural affinities and reorient weakened subject loyalties back to the centre in the aftermath of the disastrous 1828–9 Russo-Ottoman War. In fact, the whole 1837 trip was timed around the Russian withdrawal from the fortress of Silistre (Silistra in present-day Bulgaria) in late 1836. The familial metaphor and its mutations would play a key role later under a number of Mahmud II's successors as a symbolic buffer against all attempts to invoke principles of constitutionalism and self-determination. The trope of love towards a ruler's subjects, regardless of their faith, seems to predate by about two decades a similar development in the Russian Empire.[98] The speech further announced: 'You Greeks, Armenians, Jews, you are all servants of God, and you are all my subjects – just as good as the Muslims. Your beliefs are different, but you all obey the laws and my imperial orders'. Apparently, at the end of the speech the sultan inquired whether anybody among the non-Muslims had any complaints or whether their churches needed repairs. In another village, he actually donated money for church repairs.⁹⁹ In another speech during the same trip, the sultan addressed the leaders of non-Muslim communities directly:

> It is our wish to ensure the peace and security of all inhabitants of our God-protected great state, both Muslim and reaya. In spite of all difficulties, we are determined to secure the flourishing of the state and the population under our protection. You [the leaders of non-Muslim communities] bearing in mind our wish, ought to believe us in this deed.¹⁰⁰

The repeated invocation of God and faith in all of the above passages, with the stress falling on their universal and authority-upholding, rather than particularist and potentially divisive functions, constituted the single most important thread in the sultan's legitimating strategies throughout his late reign. It was religion, in the form of a carefully composed set of integrative messages and practices, that underwrote Mahmud II's attempts at ceremonial penetration, consolidation and centralisation of his domains, already under way by the time of this trip. The symbolic integrative process of the annual sultanic birthday and accession day celebrations had already commenced and some of the very same leaders of non-Muslim communities Mahmud II met with in early 1837 were already directly involved in the popularisation of his image.

Ruler Celebrations at Home and Abroad

A report, dated 8 May 1836, by Mustafa Reşid Paşa, the Ottoman ambassador to Paris, announced a decision made shortly before (*hususi karargir olarak*) to initiate annual celebrations of the sultan's birthday (*veladet*) and accession day (*cülus*). In this context, worthy of note are both the Ottoman centre's intention to universally enforce this decision and the profoundly religious terms framing it. Thus, the report declared that 'the eternal performance of this comprehensive auspicious procedure is most beautiful and desirable' and added that 'as it went into effect in Istanbul and the other imperial domains so it should in the Embassies of the Sublime State, located in Europe'.¹⁰¹ There was no mention whatsoever of the foreign origins of these annual ritual practices. On the contrary, this innovation was carefully enveloped in Muslim rhetoric. The sultan's birthday and accession day were 'bestowed solely by the grace of God to the entire Islamic community and Muslim people (*bilcümle millet-i islamiye ve ümmet-i muhammediye hakkında mehza lutuf-u ilah olan*)'. In addition, 'God's sublime will (*maşaallah-ı teali*)' and 'acts of divine favour (*inayat-ı samadaniye*)' were also invoked with reference to the planned sultanic celebrations.

That the sultan should order these celebrations as soon as he set up the Ottoman Foreign Ministry (*Hariciye Nezareti*) which re-established the Ottoman foreign legations (first in Paris and London, followed by Vienna and Berlin), is a testament to their perceived importance. The immediate issue of the calendar for these new official holidays – lunar (Muslim) or solar (Christian) – raises questions regarding the target audience Mahmud II had in mind and the frame he envisaged for the entire endeavour.

A document most likely dating from early 1836 provides a glimpse of the tortuous path of these reforms in terms of the sultan's domestic legitimating strategies. It contains a lengthy description of the elaborate ceremonies performed in the Ottoman capital on the birthday of the Prophet (*mevlid*) each year. Decorations and illuminations, public recitations of the life of the Prophet and cannon salvos from specially placed land batteries and the fleet in the Bosphorus at the five prayer times during the day completed the list of 'necessities of veneration (*levazım-ı ihtiramiye*)'. The Prophet's birthday (Rebiülevvel 12) was always celebrated according to the Arab lunar calendar (*şühur-u kameriye-yi arabiye*). Therefore, 'as an act of piety and gratitude (*teyemmünen ve teşekküren*)', it was firmly decided (*tasmim*) to celebrate the sultan's own birthday and accession day, according to the solar calendar (*şühur-u şemsiye*). On this matter, a special sultanic decree was forthcoming.[102]

The choice of the solar calendar was clearly dictated by the sultan's need to gain a following with non-Muslims at home and abroad. Indeed, the first reports of sultanic celebrations come from the volatile Danubian Principalities of Wallachia (*Eflak*) and Moldavia (*Boğdan*) the following year.[103] The documents are quite succinct, but they shed some light on the initial terms of interaction between centre and periphery in the organisation and execution of these newly minted official holidays. For example, the hospodar (*voyvoda*) of Wallachia duly reported to the centre that preparations were under way for the celebration of the sultan's accession day.[104] This act was apparently brought to the sultan's attention and 'a response with appropriate kindness (*iltifatlıca münasibi vechle cevabname*)' was being prepared in return.[105] Based on the evidence, the royal birthday seems to have been much more important at this early stage. This probably stemmed from the fact that, unlike the royal accession, there was a local Muslim precedent in the birthday of the Prophet. Therefore, the sultan's birthday had more resonance at home.

It was on the 'auspicious eve (*leyle-yi mübarekesinde*)' of the royal birthday that the hospodar of Wallachia sent to Istanbul two circulars 'regarding what was done in preparation of the necessary acts of illumination and rejoicing in Bucharest with a view to expressing the requisites of devotion (*ubudiyet*) and submission (*rıkkiyet*) [lit. "servitude"]'.[106] Despite this statement's undeniable rhetorical qualities, it did also touch on several important aspects of these celebrations, as the centre intended them.

First, this passage clearly conveyed the importance of the undertaking. In two lines of text, words denoting 'necessity' appeared twice – 'necessary acts (*icra-yı levazım*)' and 'requisites (*muktaza*)'. Interestingly, these Ottoman synonyms referred to both the outer (illumination and rejoicing) and inner (devotion and submission) manifestations of attachment to the sultan. In other words, from the outset, there were clear indications of the centralising purposes of these events. What is just as impressive is the subtle innovative use of *faith* in this process of loyalty creation and cultivation. The full primary meaning of the Ottoman word *ubudiyet*, rendered as 'devotion' here, was purely religious – 'devotion to God with faith and obedience'.[107] That the majority of subjects in question were Christian mattered little. Instead the emphasis fell on the integrative function of *faith*, its marriage to the concept of central authority (that is, purposes of state) and the immediate implication of loyalty by way of submission. This seems to be the next step in the sultan's changing attitude towards Ottoman Christians, discussed above.

The importance of this undertaking can be also gleaned from the explicit recognition of the preparations for it. In fact, another decree reveals the actual scale of activity and direct involvement of the centre in the provincial celebrations. Apparently, the admiral of the Ottoman Fleet (*Kapudan Paşa*) personally appointed an agent with the task of transporting a portion of previously purchased wooden material from the Imperial Dockyards (*tersane-yi amire*) in Istanbul to the Danubian port of Braila (*Ibrail*). A trusted aide of the Wallachian hospodar (*eflak kapukahyası*)[108] acknowledged their receipt by way of two circulars.

The longest, by far most florescent but also most telling account of the way these new celebrations reconfigured the centre–periphery and sultan–subject relations was written by the hospodar of Wallachia, Alexander Ghika.[109] It was dated 12 November 1837, that is, about six months after his personal audience with Mahmud II in Silistre during the sultan's tour of Rumelia.

The letter contains the attempt of a high Christian dignitary with vested interests to accommodate the anxieties of the centre regarding subject loyalty.[110] It shows a different perspective on the nature and purposes of the new celebrations. The theme of a people, bound by faith and duty to the sultan, captures the essence of the entire project. According to Ghika, 'the public perseverance in congratulating and felicitating [the sovereign] is a public duty for all men (*tehniyet ve tebrikete müsaberet-i amme ibad uzere resm-i vücubiyet olmayi*)'.[111] Once again, 'the duty of devotion (*vacibe-yi ubudiyetleri*)'[112] resurfaces, only this time from the multiplied perspective of the populace. Interestingly, *vücub* is a term from canon law, which indicates 'incumbency as a religious duty not directly ordained of God'.[113] The word for 'men' – *ibad* – also means 'servants of God'. It may well have been the word the sultan used in the tour speech analysed above. Not surprisingly, the motif of popular prayer for the ruler figures prominently in the letter. What is most surprising, however, is that the supplicants in question are Christian. This is the earliest such instance so far identified. An element of totality and unity invariably accompanied these prayers. For example, 'all joined together in prayer and supplication by all for the long life of His Majesty',[114] and again 'all (*cümle*)' took part in 'benediction prayers (*da'vat-ı hayriye*)'.

Finally, Ghika took the liberty of improvising on the trope of love and even employed a Muslim metaphor in his narrative. According to him, 'in this way, with hope and excitement, [Wallachians] shared in the public rejoicing (*bu güne umumi sürurdan behredar olmak ümid ile iqa'*)'. Their 'gratitude and praise fell like tulip flowers (*laleendaz şükr ve sena oldukları*)'. The mention of this flower (*lale*), which could be rendered calligraphically the same way as 'Allah', would surely resonate with any Muslim reader, and all the more so the Ottoman sultans who had held it close to their heart for centuries.

It seems that at the time of Alexander Ghika's letter to Istanbul, royal birthday celebrations were already commencing throughout the neighbouring Ottoman province of Rumelia. A report from Rumelia's governor (*vali*) indicates the mechanics of centralisation and coordination of these efforts. According to this report,

> with the purpose of performing [these celebrations] in most places, elders (*muhtarlar*) were elected and appointed in all townships (*nahiye*) of Rumelia's districts (*kaza*), and from now on this comprehensive meritorious procedure was extended to the district of Premed, as a forerunner for Albania . . .[115]

The governor's report indicated further that a letter from his own trusted aide, stationed in Istanbul to represent his interests (*kapukahyası efendi*), requested from the centre individual seals to back up the authority of each elder. As a result, an imperial order was duly forwarded to the Imperial Mint (*darbhane-yi amire*) to produce the seals in question.[116]

In the capital, the celebrations in late 1837 occasioned the first signs of recognition by the West. According to a report from the centre, even before the edict announcing the royal birthday celebrations had been distributed, official greetings (*tebrikname*) on behalf of the English and other ambassadors began to arrive in large numbers. The list included the ambassador of Iran, Hudadad Khan, and his Chief Scribe (*serkatibi*), Mirza Ja'fer, a fact that stood out and called for 'a special display of gratitude and manifest satisfaction (*mahsusca ibraz-ı teşekkur ve izhar-ı memnuniyet eylemesi*)'.[117]

Since in late 1837 the Ottoman Ambassador to France, Nuri Efendi, was also the acting Minister of Foreign Affairs (*umur-u hariciye nazırı*), it was only fitting that the first celebrations abroad should be held in Paris. A report confirmed the decoration of the embassy on the occasion of the accession anniversary that year.[118] Curiously, the novel sultanic celebrations were felt even in faraway Erzurum where a zealous governor by the name of Esad Paşa had a special poem recited and a chronogram composed in honour of the sultan's birthday.[119] Both were sent to the centre, as proof of the locals' 'show of gratitude and joy (*izhar-ı teşekkür ve meserreti*)'.[120]

By 1838, the sultanic celebrations abroad really gained momentum. Two of the reports, from the Ottoman legations in Vienna and Berlin, and a clipping from a British newspaper regarding the Ottoman festivities in London, deserve particular attention. They synthesise all celebration motifs, discussed above, and best delineate the experimental nature of modern Ottoman ruler visibility, including the fascinating hybridity between Western form and Ottoman content, and vice versa, all harnessed for the cause of state. The report from Vienna is unique for its length and elaborate detail. What is more, a marker of the sultan's direct visibility served as the deliberate epicentre of both the actual ceremonial event at the embassy and the narrative thereof.[121] The description of the royal birthday celebration began (1) and ended (2) with a reference to the royal portrait:

> (1) . . . the circle of manifest majesty around the virtuous portrait of his imperial majesty was decorated fittingly and at that circle, under the graceful auspices of his majesty the sultan, a ceremonial social gathering in the European style, a soiree (*suvare*) was prepared with serious attention, and the three hundred greatest Austrian ladies and gentlemen as well as all ambassadors of friendly states were invited.[122]

> (2) . . . and the portrait was entered into a place of fitting superiority, with the awe-inspiring virtues of his majesty, the show of sublime praise for the padishah, the remembrance and reminiscence of his glorious exploits, and after an hour or two the invitees took leave, delighted and honoured.[123]

At the embassy in Berlin, the imperial portrait was also placed prominently – in the 'most presentable room (*en mu'teber odasına*)' – but it was clearly not the focal point of the entire banquet. That the royal portrait and the classic sultanic title – 'the shadow of Allah' – should coexist in the same phrase is jarring and ironic, but such indeed was the scope of change and the paradoxes it occasionally entailed.[124] In a vein of religious symbolic continuity, in Vienna the sultan's exploits were referred to by the same word (*menaqıb*) as the Prophet's own. The Berlin account went a step further and described a recitation of the names and titles of the sultan, not unlike the readings of the Prophet's exploits on his birthday every year, to which all Ottomans would have been accustomed since early childhood. In Berlin, these readings were punctured by enthusiastic cries of 'May the Sultan Live a Thousand Years!'. The sultan's name was 'sanctified (*mütekaddis*)'; he was 'a holy personage (*zat-ı kudsiyet*)'. Unlike Vienna, the apex (*zirve*) of the Berlin event was the drawing and ceremonious attachment of the sultan's traditional monogram (*tuğra*).[125] In London, the Ottoman ambassador Sarım Efendi chose to display the *tuğra* at the heart of an elaborate gas illumination set in front of the embassy building, which also featured a crescent and star, with a stylised Ottoman sun on top. Each of the *tuğra*'s sides, however, was graced by the sultan's initials in English – *S.M.*[126] This was very likely the first such instance in Ottoman history.

Conclusion

The fascinating details of these first annual Ottoman ruler celebrations and the dissonance between their flows and accents from locale to locale reveal the creative heterogeneity of an extremely formative, but still little understood epoch of late Ottoman history. What Mahmud II began in the last years of his reign for strategic and geopolitical reasons, grew during the reigns of his children and grandchildren. As the following chapters demonstrate, over time the sultanic ceremonies created increasing and more regularised opportunities for imperial populations, near and far, to experience the centre, and, consciously or not, situate themselves in relation to it, within the fabric of a rapidly changing Ottoman society. As a result, these ceremonies forged a gradual revolution in thinking, creating, for the first time, an imperial public space/sphere in the modern (macro) sense of the term and a playing field for communal alignments, which had never been necessary or possible on a macro scale before.

Notes

1. Hobhouse, *A Journey through Albania*, pp. 367–71.
2. 'The British Ambassador's reception by the Sultan', from Slade, *Records of Travels*, quoted in Kelly, *Istanbul: A Traveller's Companion*, pp. 305–6.

3. For a similar visual juxtaposition *Istanbul: A Traveller's Companion*, see the 'before' and 'after' images in Hanioğlu, *A Brief History*, pp. 64–5. See also Kırlı, 'Surveillance and Constituting the Public', in *Publics, Politics, and Participation*, pp. 295–6.
4. One possible exception to the general rule of low ruler visibility in the pre-modern period may have been the practice of subject petitions to the sultan on his Friday prayer procession to an imperial mosque, with the caveat that it is hard for us today to gauge how visible/accessible the sultan really was to petitioners and bystanders even at this point.
5. In designing this concept for the first time, with Sultan Abdülhamid II in mind, I was much influenced by Selim Deringil's work and what he called 'vibrations of power without being seen'. See Deringil, *The Well-Protected Domains*, p. 18. For the most sophisticated work focusing on the person and reign of Abdülhamid II, see Georgeon, *Abdülhamid II* and Georgeon, 'Le sultan caché', *Turcica*, 93–124. For a very insightful comprehensive essay employing a concept of visibility from Selim III to Mehmed V Reşad, see Eldem, 'Pouvoir, modernité et visibilité', in *Le Corps du leader*, pp. 171–202.
6. The bulk of the existing scholarship on the late Ottoman relations between the Muslim ruler and his non-Muslim subjects still treats them as a self-contained, mostly antagonistic set, taking for granted non-Muslim types of group consciousness, based on theorised 'proto-national' (millet) institutions. In a gesture typical of the ethnonational, temporally continuous mindset prevalent today, an equivalent of our present-day concept of 'nationality' is sought after and, if not found, then sewn into the fabric of societies past.
7. For a complex, masterful study of the transformations of Ottoman power in the pre-modern period, see Murphey, *Exploring Ottoman Sovereignty*. For the global context, see Duindam, *Dynasties*.
8. In Islamic theory, the concept of '*ghaza*' refers to a conquest in the name of the faith. The warriors of the faith (*ghazi*) in the early days of the Ottoman state came from various backgrounds and more often than not had a dual military-spiritual function (*ghazi dervish*). See Kafadar, *Between Two Worlds*.
9. For details of the battle and Bayezid I's subsequent fate, see Finkel, *Osman's Dream*, pp. 28–30. Kafadar refers to Bayezid's policies as 'an earlier centralisation-cum-imperialisation drive'. See Kafadar, *Between Two Worlds*, p. 97.
10. Kafadar, *Between Two Worlds*, p. 146.
11. Ibid., p. 97.
12. Ibid., pp. 146–7.
13. See Necipoğlu, 'Framing the Gaze', *Ars Orientalis*, 303.
14. Ibid., 303. See also Necipoğlu, *Architecture, Ceremonial, and Power*, pp. 3–30.

15. See de Busbecq, *The Life and Letters of Ogier Ghiselin de Busbecq*, vol. I, pp. 152–6, 158–60, 281–5, and 'The Visit of Sultan Selim II', from Fresne-Canaye, *Le Voyage du Levant*, quoted in Kelly, *Istanbul: A Traveller's Companion*, pp. 179–82.
16. See Necipoğlu, *Architecture, Ceremonial, and Power*.
17. For the highly elaborate and restrictive protocol of foreign ambassadorial processions in Istanbul, see Talbot, 'Accessing the Shadow of God', in *The Key to Power?*.
18. Eyüp al-Ansari, a companion of Muhammad who participated in one of the earliest Arab sieges of Constantinople, was allegedly buried outside the city walls. After the fall of Constantinople, the site where his remains had been laid to rest became a major funerary complex and one of the holiest Muslim sites in the whole Ottoman Empire.
19. This entire section is based on Kafadar, 'Eyüp'te Kılıç Kuşanma Törenleri', in *Eyüp: Dün/Bugün: Sempozyum, 11–12 Aralık 1993*, and Karateke, *Padişahım Çok Yaşa!*, pp. 51–2, with reference to Selaniki, *Tarih*, p. 43, and Çelebi, *Seyahatname*, p. 160. See also Finkel, *Osman's Dream*, p. 153. Not surprisingly, she entitled her chapter, which opens with Selim II, 'The Sedentary Sultan'. See Finkel, *Osman's Dream*, pp. 152–96.
20. The other two such occurrences – Mahmud II's sword girding in 1808 and Abdülhamid II's sword girding in 1876 – are also highly significant and will be analysed later.
21. On the traumatic events surrounding the deposition of Osman II (Genç Osman), see Piterberg, *An Ottoman Tragedy*.
22. Karateke makes note of each sword's significance. See Karateke, *Padişahım Çok Yaşa!*, p. 54.
23. See Yılmaz, 'Becoming a Devshirme', in *Children in Slavery*, pp. 119–34.
24. Finkel, *Osman's Dream*, p. 202. Janissary revolts also took place in 1651, 1655, 1687, 1703, 1730, 1733, 1734, 1740, 1742, 1743 and 1783. See Mansel, *Constantinople*, p. 224.
25. On the Janissary foundation, see Kafadar, *Between Two Worlds*, pp. 112–13.
26. At their apex militarily, the Janissaries instilled fear in Ottoman enemies with their superb firearm/artillery expertise.
27. Finkel, *Osman's Dream*, p. 210.
28. Ibid., p. 359.
29. See Hathaway, 'The Military Household in Ottoman Egypt', *International Journal of Middle East Studies*, 46.
30. See Quataert, *The Ottoman Empire*, pp. 135–7.
31. Guilds were artisan associations, which safeguarded the livelihood of their members by restricting production and controlling quality and prices. Quataert, *The Ottoman Empire*, p. 135.
32. This is an over-simplification attuned to the purposes of the present overview. For the most sophisticated, if controversial, analysis of the Janissaries' role in seventeenth-century Ottoman politics, see Tezcan, *The Second*

Ottoman Empire. See also Kafadar, 'Janissaries and Other Riffraff', in *Identity and Identity Formation* and Kafadar, 'On the Purity and Corruption of the Janissaries', *Turkish Studies Association Bulletin*, 273–80.

33. In 1389, during an inspection of the battlefield of Kosovo Polje following his victory over Prince Lazar Hrebeljanovic, Murad I was assassinated. Thereafter, the protocol of royal audiences changed so that on approaching the sultan, each of the ambassador's hands would be held behind his back, a rather humiliating position. See Talbot, 'Accessing the Shadow of God', p. 121.
34. Necipoğlu, 'Dynastic Imprints on the Cityscape', in *Cimetières et traditions funéraires*, vol. II, p. 35.
35. Necipoğlu, 'Suleyman the Magnificent', *The Art Bulletin*, p. 403.
36. Necipoğlu, 'Dynastic Imprints on the Cityscape', p. 27.
37. Kafadar, *Between Two Worlds*, p. 97.
38. Necipoğlu, 'Suleyman the Magnificent', 411–16.
39. See HAT 1412/57520 in the Turkish Prime Minister's Ottoman Archives in Istanbul.
40. See Brewer, *A Residence at Constantinople* and White, *Three Years in Constantinople*, among others.
41. On the implications of the sultan's withdrawal to the Harem for domestic politics in the seventeenth century, see Peirce, *The Imperial Harem*.
42. See Hamadeh, 'Splash and Spectacle', *Muqarnas*, 123–48, and her book *The City's Pleasures*, as well as Artan, 'Architecture as a Theatre of Life'. For more recent work on the architecture of eighteenth-century Istanbul, see Ünver, 'Architecture for a New Age'.
43. Karateke, 'Legitimizing the Ottoman Sultanate', in *Legitimizing the Order*, p. 51.
44. Hanioğlu, *A Brief History*, p. 42.
45. Ibid., p. 44.
46. See Hurewitz, 'The Europeanization of Ottoman Diplomacy', *Belleten* as well as Shaw's *Between Old and New*, p. 248.
47. Eldem, *Pride and Privilege*, p. 58. This is the most comprehensive study of Ottoman orders and decorations.
48. Not surprisingly, Shaw's major study of Selim III was entitled *Between Old and New*.
49. See Yaycıoğlu, *Partners of the Empire*.
50. Hanioğlu, *A Brief History*, p. 57.
51. Eldem finds that he did, at least in matters of sultanic iconography and symbolism. See Eldem, 'Pouvoir, modernité et visibilité', p. 175.
52. Rumelia is the common Ottoman name for the European part of the Empire.
53. See Karateke, *Padişahım Çok Yaşa!*. Divan Yolu, the former Byzantine Mese, was Istanbul's main thoroughfare and the ceremonial route of a new sultan's sword-girding procession.

The Reign of Mahmud II

54. '*Ingiltere devletinde yüz seksen sene mukaddem ba'zen nakliyat vuku' bulup ol esnada sandali-yi kralı'ya ku'ud eden krallarının günü olarak Ingilterelu beytinde şenlik etmek mu'tad olmak . . .*', HAT 1289/50022.
55. Ibid. The fact that the Ottomans got the number of British cannon salvos wrong is yet another indication of their (deliberate) ignorance of Western protocol at the time. The actual number was and still is twenty-one.
56. The Phanariots were members of a loose, but extremely influential trading and diplomatic network of Hellenised Christians, based in the Phanar district of Istanbul. Since some of them were involved in the revolts in Wallachia and Moldavia, which initiated the Greek Revolution, they instantly fell out of favour. In fact, a few of their number fell victim to the backlash in Istanbul. The widespread support for the insurgents in the West, and the fact that most Ottoman diplomatic agents and interpreters at the time were Phanariots further threatened their status within the Ottoman state. See Philliou, *Biography of an Empire*.
57. For the classic text on the 'Eastern Question', see Anderson, *The Eastern Question*. For a collection of documents from the Ottoman perspective, see Kuneralp, *Ottoman Diplomatic Documents*.
58. On Osman Pazvantoğlu of Vidin, see Gradeva, 'Secession and Revolution in the Ottoman Empire', in *Ottoman Rule and the Balkans*, pp. 73–95; on Tepedelenli Ali, see Flemming, *The Muslim Bonaparte*; on Mehmed Ali, see Fahmy, *All the Pasha's Men*.
59. The most influential such works are Lewis, *The Emergence of Modern Turkey* and Berkes, *The Development of Secularism in Turkey*.
60. Lane-Poole, *Life of Sir Stratford Canning*, vol. 1, p. 421; Stratford Canning to George Canning, 20 June 1826, as quoted in Mansel, *Dressed to Rule*, p. 103.
61. Aksan, 'Military Reform and Its Limits', in *The Early Modern Ottomans*, p. 129, with reference to MacFarlane, *Constantinople in 1828*.
62. Hanioğlu, *A Brief History*, p. 58.
63. Ibid., p. 58, and Mansel, *Dressed to Rule*, p. 237.
64. See HAT 1522/32 and C.SM. 89/4472.
65. 'The British Ambassador's reception by the Sultan', from Slade, quoted in Kelly, *Istanbul: A Traveller's Companion*, pp. 305–6.
66. Auldjo, *Journal of a Visit to Constantinople*, pp. 97–8.
67. This occurred on a tour of the Straits in 1831, another novel sultanic practice.
68. Kırlı, *The Struggle over Space*, p. 265 with reference to Özcan, 'II. Mahmud'un Memleket Gezileri', in *Prof. Dr. Bekir*, pp. 364–8. I would like to thank Virginia Aksan for bringing Cengiz Kırlı's very important work to my attention.
69. 'The British Ambassador's reception by the Sultan', from Slade, quoted in Kelly, *Istanbul: A Traveller's Companion*, p. 306; Auldjo, *Journal of a Visit to Constantinople*, pp. 172–4.
70. Auldjo, *Journal of a Visit to Constantinople*, pp. 94–5, 98.

71. Eldem, *Pride and Privilege*, p. 126.
72. *Tsarigradski Vestnik*, 8 July 1861. See also Eldem, 'Pouvoir, modernité et visibilité', p. 189, footnote 38.
73. See Kırlı, *The Struggle over Space*, p. 271, with reference to Lütfi, *Tarih-i Lütfi*, vol. 5, pp. 50–2; Heyd, 'The Ottoman Ulema', in *Scripta Hierosolymitana*, vol. 9, p. 70. For the most detailed exposition, see Eldem, 'Pouvoir, modernité et visibilité', 175–86.
74. Mansel, *Dressed to Rule,* pp. 103–4, with reference to conversations with Erdem and Finkel and quoting Pardoe, *The City of the Sultans*, p. 256.
75. Deringil, *The Well-Protected Domains*, p. 22, referring to Gündüz, *Osmanlılarda Devlet-Tekke Munasebetleri*, pp. 150–1.
76. Kırlı, *The Struggle over Space*, p. 271, with reference to Lütfi, *Tarih-i Lütfi*, vol. 4, p. 65.
77. Ibid., with reference to Baykara, *Osmanlılarda Medeniyet Kavramı*, p. 55.
78. Ibid., p. 269, with reference to Koloğlu, 'Osmanlı Basını', in *Türkiye Ansiklopedisi*, vol. 1, pp. 69–70.
79. Despite Roderic Davison's subsequent eloquent proof that such protectorship was neither contained in nor implied by the actual clauses of the treaty, at the time Russian diplomats made a credible claim to it abroad, which framed the discourse of the 'Eastern Question' and the place of Ottoman Christians in it for at least a century thereafter. Russia's claim to such protectorship and the Ottomans' refusal to accept it in fact led directly to the Crimean War of 1853–6 and the Russo-Ottoman War of 1877–8. On Davison's argument, see his 'Russian Skill and Turkish Imbecility', in *Essays in Ottoman and Turkish History*, pp. 29–50.
80. Ibid., pp. 29–30.
81. Shaw, *History of the Ottoman Empire*, vol. 2, p. 138.
82. Safrastjian, 'Ottomanism in Turkey', *Etudes balkaniques*, 73, with reference to Kaynar, *Mustafa Reşit Paşa ve Tanzimat*, pp. 14–15.
83. Safrastjian, 'Ottomanism in Turkey', pp. 73–4, with reference to *Vestnik Evropyi*, pp. 78–9.
84. Todorova, *Anglia, Rossia i Tanzimat*, p. 45, with reference to *Turski Dokumenti za Makedonskata Istorija*, p. 13. See also Safrastjian, 'Ottomanism in Turkey', p. 74.
85. Safrastjian, 'Ottomanism in Turkey', p. 74, with reference to Sungu, 'II. Mahmud'un, Izzet Molla ve Asakir-i Mansure haqqinda Bir Hattı', *Tarih Vesikaları*, p. 173.
86. Ibid., with reference to von Prokesch-Osten, *Geschichte*, p. 57.
87. See Kırlı, *The Struggle over Space*, pp. 266–7, with reference to Quataert, 'Clothing Laws', *International Journal of Middle East Studies*, 413.
88. This section is based on Kırlı, *The Struggle over Space*, pp. 263–8, who drew on Özcan, 'II. Mahmud'un Memleket Gezileri', pp. 361–79.
89. 'Although he travelled extensively in the Rumelian provinces where Greek-speaking Orthodox Christians and Jews lived predominantly, the only

Anatolian province that he [Mahmud II] visited where Muslims constituted the majority of the population was the imperial seat's neighbouring town of Izmit', Kırlı, *The Struggle over Space*, p. 266.
90. Ibid., pp. 263–4.
91. Lory analysed the case of an 1830 charitable donation by the Grand Vizier for the repairs of a Christian church in Manastir (Bitola). See Lory, 'The Vizier's Dream', *History and Anthropology*, 309–16.
92. For a detailed discussion of the circumstances of church construction and repair in the Ottoman Empire over the previous centuries, see Gradeva, 'Ottoman Policy', *Etudes balkaniques*, 14–36. See also Karateke, 'Opium for the Subjects?', in *Legitimizing the Order*, p. 126.
93. Kırlı, *The Struggle over Space*, p. 265.
94. Ibid., p. 265.
95. Ibid., p. 266, with reference to von Moltke, *Lettres sur l'Orient*, p. 139.
96. This act of delegation seems to have been a deliberate nod to the sultan's past invisibility and inaccessibility, especially vis-à-vis provincial crowds utterly unaccustomed to experiencing the sultan's physical presence in any way whatsoever.
97. Todorova, *Anglia, Rossia i Tanzimat*, p. 46, with reference to Karal, 'Gülhane', *Belleten*, 595.
98. See Wortman, *Scenarios of Power*, especially part 1, 'Alexander II and the Scenario of Love'.
99. Karateke, 'Opium', p. 126, with reference to von Moltke, *Briefe über Zustände*, pp. 131, 142.
100. Safrastjian, 'Ottomanism in Turkey', pp. 74–5, with reference to Inalcık, *Tanzimat ve Bulgar Meselesi*, p. 28.
101. '*bu usul-u meyamen-i şümulun daima icrası pek ahsen ve mergub olup asitane-yi şevketaşiyanede ve sair mamalik-i şahanede cari olduğu misellu Avrupada bulunan saltanat-ı seniye sefaretlerinde dahi icra olunmak lazım*', HAT 676/33014.
102. HAT 492/24119.
103. On Wallachia, see HAT 1328/51815, 1158/45938, 1158/45939; on Moldavia, see HAT 1158/45937.
104. The hospodars of Wallachia and Moldavia were Christian rulers appointed by the sultan and invested with authority through a special ceremony held in Istanbul. They had a rank only slightly below that of a Grand Vizier, and therefore higher than that of a regular provincial governor.
105. HAT 1328/51815.
106. '*Bukreş'te dahi muktaza-yı ubudiyet ve rıkkiyet tasavvuratla icra-yı levazım-ı şehrayin ve meserrete mübaderet eylemesi olduğuna mütedair . . .*', HAT 1158/45938.
107. For this definition, see Redhouse, *Turkish Ottoman-English Dictionary*, p. 1193.
108. See Bayerle, *Pashas, Begs and Effendis*, p. 94.

109. The Ghikas were a prominent Hellenised noble family of Albanian descent. They were among the principal beneficiaries of the Ottoman removal of Greek-minded Phanariots from top positions in the Principalities after the Greek Revolution.
110. HAT 1160/45957C.
111. Ibid.
112. Ibid.
113. See Redhouse, *A Turkish and English Lexicon*, p. 2129.
114. '*bil'umum isal-ı dua ve şevketlü efendimizin tul-u ömrünü istida birla*', HAT 1160/45957C.
115. '*ekser mahallerinde icra kılındığı vechle Rumeli kazalarında kain bilcümle nahiyelerde [sic] muhtarlar nasb ve ta'yin olunup bundan böyle işbu usul-u mahasin-ı şümül'ün Arnavutlukta dahi icrasına mukaddeme üzere Premed kazasına dahi muhtarlar nasb ve ta'yin kılınması olduğundan . . .*', HAT 637/31386.
116. Ibid.
117. HAT 947/40757.
118. HAT 1184/46714.
119. '*inşadkerdesi olan kasidesiyle bir kıta tarihi*', HAT 759/35846.
120. Ibid.
121. HAT 1200/47094.
122. Ibid., '*tasvir-i hümayun-u mahasinnümun-u hazret-i şahane'nin daire-yi şevketbahirenin dahi tezyinat-ı layıkası icra ve avrupa usulünce saye-yi inayetvaye-yi hazret-i mülukanede daire-yi mezkurede resmen ceşn-i cemiyet-i suvare tertibine i'tina olunarak avusturuya devletinin üçyüz kadar ekabir ve ekabiresi ve kaffe-yi duvel-i mütehabe süferası davet olunup*'
123. Ibid., '*badahu tasvir-i hümayun-u hazret-i şahane ca-i valai girilip mahasin ve mahabet-i hazret-i şahane ve sitayiş-i maali nümayişi cenab-ı padişahane menakıb-ı celilesi yad ve tezkar olunması ve bir iki saat sonra med'uviyet memnun ve mukerrim olduğu halde avdet etmesi oldukları*'.
124. Ibid., '*tasvir-i hümayun melaiknümun hazret-i zil-i Allahi . . .*'.
125. HAT 831/37516.
126. HAT 1187/46783.

2

The Trope of Love, its Variations and Manifestations: the Reign of Abdülmecid (1839–61)

Introduction

On 1 July 1839, Sultan Mahmud II died and the throne passed to his eldest son, Abdülmecid. A few months later, on 3 November 1839, the new sultan signed the so-called Gülhane Rescript, ushering in the reforms known as the Tanzimat. The purpose of the next two chapters is to trace and analyse some intended and unintended modernising effects of the discourse of reform, in tandem with the older policy of modern ruler visibility, on the public (especially non-Muslim) mind, observable from the peculiar vantage point of royal public ceremony. These effects include the process of naming (oneself and 'the other'), motifs of sacred and secular time and space, evolving notions of a social pact and social (organic and familial) metaphors, innovative concepts of necessity and duty, as well as the importance of group unity and loyalty. In their totality, these effects contain the essence of a novel, modernising project, especially in the sense of connecting and familiarising the people (ruled) with the centre (ruler), and establishing a legitimate sphere for mutually beneficial symbolic interaction between the two, both on the individual and the group level. Over time, as the following chapters demonstrate, under the guise of commemorating the ruler, the celebrations provided a fertile ground for the expression of communal interests and the advancement of inter-communal rivalries leading to gradual group mobilisation and resultant hardening of previously porous group boundaries. In the end, all of these effects inscribed the fields of modern public space/sphere and modern politics in the Ottoman Empire, which the celebrations had help forge.[1] Ironically, they were then entirely appropriated for a newly realised ethnonational mental universe, which rather than unite, did indeed splinter, first the imperial public, and then, with a certain, irreducible measure of historical contingency, the Empire itself.

The reigns of Abdülmecid (1839–61) and Abdülaziz (1861–76) constitute the most formative period for the above-mentioned transformations.

Following in the footsteps of their father, Mahmud II, both of these rulers enjoyed high levels of visibility and accessibility vis-à-vis their subjects from the 1840s to the 1860s, a time when autocracy still had no viable domestic alternative. Therefore, they share many of the same parameters of the symbolic ruler–ruled interaction. This period is critical for our understanding of the practical, lived dimensions of abstract communal concepts such as '*millet*' (a community of co-religionists) and, by extension, the gradual formation of ethnonational consciousness in the Ottoman Empire.[2]

At the same time, there are also some differences between the two sultans, based on areas of individual preference and accentuation in their policies of image management on the one hand, and adaptive expectations in the escalating give-and-take of popular ceremonial involvement on the other. The differences justify the treatment of these, in many respects similar, reigns in separate chapters. Though primarily focused on the *Bulgar Rum* community, these chapters also shed light on the activities of both Muslim and other non-Muslim (Hellene-minded *Rum*, Armenian (*Ermeni*) and Jewish (*Yehudi*)) celebratory groupings.[3]

This chapter proceeds in the following order. First, it analyses Abdülmecid's visibility upon coming to power, along with the sultan's target audiences and policy objectives, against the background of Mahmud II's precedents. Second, it reviews the new Ottoman practice of cyclical bestowal of medals and orders as tokens of subject loyalty in conjunction with the sultanic celebrations, themselves cloaked in rhetoric of antiquity. Third, it initiates a systematic discussion of the trope of love for the ruler, from its inception in the late 1830s to its elitist formulation in the early 1840s. Fourth, it analyses Abdülmecid's public image on the eve of and during his 1846 tour of Rumelia.[4] Fifth, it reveals the important connection between the discourse of reform and the songs of praise and prayer for the sultan, arguably the tour's most influential legacy. Sixth, it then traces some other lasting effects of this under-researched sultanic event and evaluates the beginnings of a mass Bulgar consciousness. The final section explores new avenues for macro-communal identification and macro-territorial attachment.

Abdülmecid's Visibility and its Target Audiences. Continuities and Discontinuities from Mahmud II's Reign

The rise of Abdülmecid to power reaffirmed and expanded Mahmud II's policy of direct ruler visibility. Whereas Mahmud II could only gain control over the terms of his own public appearance in 1826, that is, eighteen years into his reign, his son could do so immediately upon coming to the

Figure 2.1 Portrait of Sultan Abdülmecid (1850) by Rupen Manas (Wikimedia Commons).

throne. Therefore, the customary sultanic procession through the streets of Istanbul, following the secluded rite of Abdülmecid's sword girding in 1839 looked and felt worlds away from his father's, back in 1808. Not only were the Janissaries replaced by elite military units wearing brightly coloured Western uniforms, but the sultan also took measures to turn the procession into an interactive spectacle for the foreign diplomatic corps in the Ottoman capital.

The leading article on the cover of the first official Ottoman newspaper (*Takvim-i Vekayi*), founded by Mahmud II only eight years earlier, provides a window on the intended terms of engagement between Abdülmecid and the foreign powers only eleven days after he became sultan. As the sword-girding procession filtered through the Eğri Gate, 'the ambassadors of powers on terms of mutual friendship with the Ottoman Empire (*düvel-i mütehabbe süferası*)' were accommodated with specially erected tents nearby. This was not the only departure from precedent. Equally striking was the invention of a special messenger, who, upon the sultan's passage, should greet the privileged spectators on his sovereign's behalf. Both of these innovations survived until the end of the Empire and will be the object of analysis in subsequent chapters.

According to the same article, it was a certain Tevfiq Bey, a scribe in the imperial chancellery, who performed the messenger's role in this case. Tevfiq Bey's greeting was 'with the purpose of commanding [the foreigners'] esteem and zeal with respect to the act of his majesty's courtesy and favour'.[5] The author went to great lengths to justify this innovation and reveal in stages its profound effects on the diplomats. First, it elicited 'a show of perfect joy and just pride'[6] from them. It is worthy of note that these terms are identical to those that usually refer to the sultan's rapport with his own subjects. The logic of this choice becomes clear with the next stage, whereby the writer in no uncertain terms placed the foreign rulers under the sultan's sovereignty (*hak-ı alisinde metbuları olan hükümdaran*). This state of affairs in turn demanded 'good thoughts and desirable intentions (*efkar-ı hasene ve niyat-ı mergubeleri iktizasınca*)' from them, 'a sign of pure affection (*safvetnişan*)'. The article then culminated with an open-ended inquiry into the proper format – written or oral – of the foreign diplomats' homage to the sultan. In the process, it painstakingly spelled out the contents of the foreign ceremonial gestures:

- expressing and displaying well wishes and mutual, sincere friendship (*ibraz ve ifa-yı hayrhahi ve musadakat*);
- carrying out the requisites of respect and mutual, sincere friendship (*icra-yı levazım-ı riayetkari ve muhalasat*);

- manifesting the requisite of pure affection and mutual friendship (*izhar-ı muktaza-yı safvet ve muhadenet*);
- performing the ceremony of loving friendship and mutual peace/reconciliation (*icra-yı merasim-i vidd ve musalemet*);
- expressing the requisites of gratitude and praise (*ifa-yı levazım-ı teşekkür ve mahmedet*).

These highly nuanced behavioural modes were listed in consecutive lines of text and represent a curious intertwining of bonds of vertical attachment normally demanded from the sultan's own subjects, on the one hand, and bonds of horizontal, reciprocal nature reserved for the sultan's interaction with Western powers, on the other. An example of the former is the repeated reference to 'requisites/needs (*levazım/muktaza*)', an indication of asymmetric power, which, as we already saw in the previous chapter, began to be invoked in sultanic celebrations across the Empire, beginning in 1836. In addition, the last of these five expressions was usually employed, verbatim, with reference to the sultan's own subjects. However, this sequence is in the end dominated by an abundance of synonymic terms (*musadakat-muhalasat-muhadenet-musalemet*), which, in addition to revealing the richness of the Ottoman language, strongly emphasise the mutuality of an Ottoman-intended friendship between the sultan and Western rulers.[7] Most remarkably, this friendship is bordering on and at times flowing into love. The terms '*vidd*' ('loving friendship') and '*safvet*' ('pure affection') reflect these two emotional states, respectively.

This passage has multiple dimensions, centred on the overarching domestic political need to create a momentum for the new ruler and anchor the legitimacy of novelty in the (elite) public mind. Yet even if many of these statements remain rhetorical, not backed by hard realities, they provide important clues as to the direction in which this reign is headed from the outset – towards openness and reciprocity with the West in the manner enforced by Mahmud II. This first impression also echoed in the foreign press. Here is how *The Times* described the new sultan's physical appearance at an audience with Prince de Joinville only a few months into his reign: 'He wore the same costume as that adopted by his father. He wore, like the rest of the Turks who were present, a little black coat . . .'[8] Possibly in order to still be able to somehow stand out within his own retinue, the sultan did retain some rather archaic marks of distinction – a diamond clasp, a diamond aigrette (*celenk*) on his fez and a similarly executed decoration around his neck.[9] Exceptions notwithstanding, the overall course towards simplicity in personal outlook, initiated by Mahmud II, would be a lasting feature of sultanic policies until the end of the Empire. The journalist also noted that the sultan had 'a weak appearance' but projected 'an air of great benevolence'.[10] For better or worse, both of these characteristics would soon become firmly embedded into Abdülmecid's public image. As it turned out, the new sultan, still a boy of sixteen upon coming to power, was the antithesis of his strong-willed, authoritarian father. Instead, he made a name for himself as being quite irresolute as a person and inconsistent as a policy maker, with a penchant for delegating power to his ministers rather than ruling directly.

Some of Mahmud II's advisers, with Mustafa Reşid and Sadık Rifat assuming prominent positions among them, largely retained their power and gradually gained the confidence of the new ruler, even as they were shuffled from one position to the next, according to long-standing Ottoman bureaucratic practice. Therefore, as Mahmud II had carried out reforms in ceremony, taxation, administration, the army and other fields simultaneously, so did Abdülmecid. There is evidence to suggest that the tax collectors (*muhassıl*) were serving as agents for not only fiscal but also loyalty centralisation across the Empire. For example, a royal decree, which can be dated with sufficient reliability to the beginning of Abdülmecid's reign, conveys the greetings of a number of high-ranking provincial administrators, including the chief tax collector of Işkodra (Shkoder in present-day Albania), on the occasion of the sultan's accession.[11] Conditioned by Mahmud II's latter-year annual ruler celebrations, they all related what had transpired locally, in the words of the centre, 'with a view to the expression and performance of a ceremony of congratulation and the requisites of devotion'.[12] What matters most is not the act of congratulating a new sultan, which was customary, but the innovative ceremonies, held locally, and the further development of the stock phraseology, inherited from Mahmud II, that framed these events.

Apparently, the provincial tax collectors' involvement with the centrally mandated process of nurturing direct popular loyalties to the sultan was transformed immediately upon Abdülmecid's rise to power as was the tax extraction process itself. What had been heretofore *muhassıl* trial periods in regions, such as Albania, as well as in Hüdavendigar and Gelibolu, grew into an Empire-wide phenomenon in April 1840.[13] Another decree, dating approximately from the same time, explicitly mentioned the fact that these tax collectors were 'designated and appointed in the manner of the founding and executing orders of the Auspicious Tanzimat'.[14] The decree provided a long list of locales, which had already reported, by way of special messengers back to the capital, the arrival of their appointees.[15] The assumption of their duties was allegedly cause for 'prayer with gratitude and praise, joy and just pride'[16] as well as inquiries from the population 'as to the manner of demonstrating perseverance (*ne suretle muvazebet etmekte*)' to the centre thereafter. In response, the centre confirmed the mode established with the accession congratulations a few months earlier – 'circulars containing declarations of the requisites of gratitude and devotion' – as the correct mode of submitting communications and other reports to 'the imperial attention (*manzurat-ı şehriyari*)'. Finally, the decree prescribed that the provincial messengers 'be sent back to their regions with a delivery of words of appreciation'.[17] It is important to note that, contrary to expectation, the groundbreaking use of the term '*millet*' in the Gülhane Rescript to indicate faith-based (including non-Muslim) communities of the Ottoman Empire did not reappear in this decree. Instead, the document simply referred to 'native population and subjects and tribute-paying community (*ahali-yi memleket ve teb'a ve raiyet*)'. The word '*teb'a* ("all subjects without distinction of religion")' was indeed a neologism, making its debut in the Gülhane Rescript.[18] However, it clearly did not have much disruptive potential domestically. Perhaps in this respect, as in others, the sweeping but ambiguous Gülhane Rescript was meant to appease foreign (especially British) demands and the unappealing power implications of *millet* at home were avoided simply by avoiding the term itself.[19] This may be yet another indication that we should not take this decree's stipulations literally, as has been done for a long time by most of its analysts.[20] Within a few years of the Gülhane Rescript's issue, however, the term '*millet*' was indeed taken up locally in financial dealings with the Ottoman state. As Andreas Lyberatos has shown, in 1841 the Orthodox Christian community of Filibe (Plovdiv in present-day Bulgaria) signed a document of fiscal responsibility (in Greek), whose title included an explicit mention of '*ethnos*', a literal translation of '*millet*'.[21] Two years later, the term '*millet vekili*' ('agent of the community of co-religionists') also gained currency, supplanting the older '*memleket vekili*' ('home district agent') in a trusteeship for the management of the community's finances and its economic relations to the state, which had been set up under Mahmud II back in 1833.[22] Thus, the term '*millet*' was beginning to strike root locally; the trajectory of its proliferation and perpetuation was launched.[23]

Abdülmecid's Visibility and its Domestic Objectives

The same article, which narrated Abdülmecid's sword-girding procession through the streets of Istanbul, and mapped his intended mutual friendship (and love) with the foreign powers, also carried clues about the sultan's expectations from his own subjects. The text directly preceding the excerpt, which was analysed above, mentioned 'troops of a pledged fidelity (*asakir-i sadakatrehin*)' who uttered 'prayers for His Majesty's long life, good fortune, and grace of victory through divine guidance, repeatedly graced by the expression of a purity of heart/love and devotion'.[24] Here is the logic, then, of the psychological process of tying a soldier's mind and heart to the ruler. The sultan displayed a 'grace (*hüsn, zib*)', which was 'victorious through divine guidance (*muvafakkıyet*)' and in return obtained a 'pledge (*rehin*)' of 'fidelity/devotion (*sadakat, ubudiyet*)'. This is a symbolic pact between sultan and soldier but, as subsequent analysis will demonstrate, it can be credibly conceived as a much wider type of social pact. Even though most of these abstract terms have multiple, layered meanings, none is more complex than '*ihlas*'. Rendered as 'heart/love' in the above passage, it also carries denotations of 'duty' and 'worship/belief'. In fact, the full translation of its figurative meaning reads as follows: 'a being or becoming sincere, free from guile or afterthought in duty, love, or friendship; pure sincerity of heart; sincere worship or belief'.[25] In sum, '*ihlas*' denotes a strong attachment with both positive and normative, sensual and rational, individual and totalising dimensions. Interestingly, even though both foreigners and Ottomans were symbolically being drawn to the sultan via notions of friendship, love and devotion, the words of bonding for each type of audience are completely different. Whereas the '*musadakat-muhalasat-muhadenet-musalemet*' sequence, along with '*vidd*' and '*safvet*', were exclusively used with reference to foreigners, the same is true of '*ihlas*', '*sadakat*' and '*ubudiyet*' vis-à-vis Ottomans. As a result, each set of references unmistakably tipped the scales of relative weight (in terms of a respective amalgamated attitude to the sultan) in a different direction: the former towards friendship and reciprocity, the latter towards love, fidelity and devotion.

The Growing Use of Medals and Orders as Monarchic Moorings

One of the most effective practical strategies for drawing both foreign and domestic dignitaries more firmly into the sultan's orbit was the royal bestowal of medals and orders. Sultan Selim III initiated the Ottoman use of Western-style decorations in 1798. In gratitude for Admiral Nelson's 1798 naval victory over Napoleon in Egypt, Selim III bestowed upon him a *çelenk* (a bejewelled aigrette, normally worn on a turban).[26] As with Selim III's other reform efforts, this practice remained rather ad hoc, which hindered reciprocation. It was only in Mahmud II's later reign that this aspect of the process of Ottoman integration into the Western system of signs and symbols became more regularised, part of a wider,

The Reign of Abdülmecid

concerted Ottoman quest for reciprocity with the West, as well as visibility at home.[27] The precedent for a standardised royal distribution of medals and orders, however, took place on the eve of Abdülmecid's birthday, less than a year into his reign. A decree of the Interior Ministry explicitly linked forthcoming promotions in rank and 'a lavish bestowal of gems of

Figure 2.2 Badge of the Order of Glory (Nişan-ı Iftihar), founded by Sultan Mahmud II in 1831. Jules Martin and Raymond Richebe, *Armoiries et décorations* (Paris: P. Ollendorff, 1897), p. 486. Courtesy of Sinan Kuneralp.

Figure 2.3 Badge of the Mecidi Order founded by Sultan Abdülmecid in 1852. Jules Martin and Raymond Richebe, *Armoiries et décorations* (Paris: P. Ollendorff, 1897), p. 487. Courtesy of Sinan Kuneralp.

favour and kindness (*isar-ı cevher-i inayet ve atufet*)' with the royal public holiday.[28] Significantly, among the designated recipients were not only government officers from the capital, including War and Finance Ministry officials, but also 'some appointed to provincial tax collecting positions (*bazı taşra muhassıllıklarında müstahdem olub*)'.[29] Such attention confirms yet again the importance of tax collectors in the government's plans for cultural penetration and indoctrination of provincial populations, a fact that has never been recognised, much less studied by Ottoman scholars.[30] Already, at this early stage, the decree noted the high number of 'wishes and requests (*niyaz ve iltimas*)' of government officers for decorations which had to be dealt with in an organised manner. Therefore, the decree announced the creation of a register (*defter*) with the names of outstanding government employees, along with their accomplishments (*şöhretleri*). Before being presented to the sultan, the successful petitions were to be marked in red.

The two most significant aspects of the decoration procedure are, first, the 'eager anticipation (*muntazır olan*)' it was supposed to create among candidates, and, second, the indication that 'from now on (*bundan böyle*)' it was to be repeated at other royal birthdays. As it turned out, unlike the *muhassıls*, this was a lasting measure, which fostered a vigorous competition for visible markings of royal favour cutting across socioeconomic, sociocultural and even state boundaries. In doing so, it redefined and reinforced elite attachments to the monarch, both at home and abroad, and helped perpetuate the imperial order.

The Uneven Expansion and Artificial 'Ageing' of the New Royal Holidays under Abdülmecid

As the royal celebrations grew from a narrow base consisting of the elite's upper echelon, whose members had enjoyed a near monopoly on access to the royal personage for centuries, they engaged much wider strata of the population, both in the capital and well beyond. In the first few years of Abdülmecid's reign, however, the process seemed to lack some of the clear direction and sharp focus of the years leading up to Mahmud II's untimely death. With the new sultan's rise to power, members of the *ulema*, many of whom were directly or indirectly antagonised and marginalised by Mahmud II, gained an enhanced role at the court.[31] Not surprisingly perhaps, the experiment with sultanic celebrations in the solar calendar, a key component of Mahmud II's drive for ceremonial reciprocity with Western rulers, was abandoned in favour of strictly lunar festivities. Moreover, for reasons already reflected upon,

Ruler Visibility and Popular Belonging

Figure 2.4 Sultan Abdülmecid wearing his Imperial Decoration, c. 1851, lithography by Llanta (by permission from Edhem Eldem's collection).

The Reign of Abdülmecid

the royal accession anniversaries (*cülus*) were neglected in favour of the royal birthdays (*veladet*). Nonetheless, the size of the spectacle grew, both at home and abroad.

In the late 1830s, each of Mahmud II's two annual sultanic celebrations in Istanbul entailed one day of cannon salvos (five times a day)[32] from the royal fleet in the Bosphorus and specially placed land batteries, and one night of candle illuminations of mosques, private houses and shops.[33] By contrast, already in 1841, Abdülmecid's birthday in the capital was marked with a three-night illumination of the above kind.[34] By 1844 or so, the royal birthday salvos of the imperial fleet echoed in recently independent Athens, an act that allegedly called for 'a requisite of respect (*lazime-yi riayetkari*)' in return.[35] By 1848, the same five-times-a-day salvos in Istanbul lasted for seven days.[36]

In a clear demonstration of Eric Hobsbawm's notion of 'invented traditions',[37] the language of the annual decrees announcing the festivities abruptly shifted from describing them as novelty to describing them as custom. For example, in 1841, the decree of the Interior Ministry regarding the royal birthday brought up issues that needed further clarification, thus conveying a sense of a holiday still in the making. The very next year, however, the decree of the same ministry already referred to the sultan's audience held on the occasion of his birthday, as 'issuing from a good custom of the sublime state (*ka'ide-yi hasene-yi devlet-i aliyeden olarak*)'. In fact, the first five lines of text contained no fewer than four such references to 'custom' for a ritual that was barely six years old.[38] Nor was such language limited to circulars of the Interior Ministry. In a document dated just five days after the one discussed above, the Ottoman ambassador to London, Sarım Efendi, twice referred to 'custom' in just four lines of text.[39]

The Trope of Love for the Ruler and its Slow Initial Reception

Perhaps the most impressive aspect of the trope of love for the ruler was the connection openly established early on between the visible individual behaviour at the annual sultanic festivities and the invisible (mystic) personal attitude towards the sultan. This connection manifested itself in a language with strong visualising tendencies and intense symbolic capacities, contained in official newspaper articles and decrees, right from the start of the celebrations in 1836. An article in *Takvim-i Vekayi* from 1 October 1836, which related Mahmud II's commencement of accession anniversary celebrations in Istanbul, equated 'the ceremonial manifestation of joy (*izhar-ı merasim-i şadumani*)' with 'the illumination of the eye of the heart and the soul (*tenvir-i basıra-yı dil ve can*)'.⁴⁰ The reign of Abdülmecid then took this relationship to another level both in terms of the theoretical conception of the top-down message, and, as the next section will demonstrate, in terms of the enthusiastic outpouring of popular responses to it.

The same 1841/42 Interior Ministry decree, mentioned above in the context of illuminations, provides a fascinating picture of the symbolic meaning of ceremonial actions and the visualised terms on which they brought sovereign and subject closer together than ever before. This document established quite literally a two-way operating system of (outward behavioural) 'signs' whereby the sultan manifested 'signs of royal mercy/ compassion (*merahimayat-ı hazret-i mülukane*)' on the one hand, and the elite office holders exhibited 'a sign of devotion (*şiar-ı ubudiyet*)' on the other. More striking still is the visual imperative, which constitutes the ultimate criterion for the validity of this exchange. Thus, it was only when the cream of the elite came to the palace to congratulate the sultan on his birthday and prepare a three-day banquet in his honour that 'the sign of devotion was suitably seen (*şiar-ı ubudiyet muvafık görünmüş*)'. Similarly, this banquet, put together by the Admiral of the Navy (*kapudan paşa*), who had exerted himself on behalf of the elite, was 'seen as the eye of our [elite's] devotion (*meşhud basıra-yı ubudiyetimiz olan*)'.⁴¹

Clearly, the exchange of declarations of commitment between the two parties is unequal. Terms relating to group bonding to the ruler were used on nine separate occasions in just four consecutive lines of text. However, there is also a subtle intimation in the text that the ruler may be less than completely aloof, as his image had been conceived and perpetuated for centuries. Towards the end of the decree, there is an explicit indication that 'the performance of the ceremony of gratitude and rejoicing (*icra-yı resm-i teşekkür ve şadumani olunması*)' serves as 'the object of the sublime heart's desire (*madde-yi dilhah–ı ali*)'. This reference to the ruler's emotional engagement with his people and the use of the same term to denote the sultan's and his subjects' private emotions – 'heart (*dil*)' – point to a subtle tendency towards cutting the distance between ruler and ruled, and placing them on the same mental plane, even as the former was being elevated in the eyes of the latter. There is still a prevailing sense, however, of the chasm between the elite and ordinary people, and a lingering unease with the crowd's potential capacity for disorder, probably stemming at least to some degree from centuries of cyclical Ottoman urban unrest. The word '*millet*' does not appear in this document. Instead, the words for a mass of subjects, a faceless malleable group, include the traditional '*bendegan*' (slaves, servants of the ruler, subjects) and the neologisms '*halk*' (the common people, crowd, mob) and '*tebaa*' (subjects).⁴²

The Reign of Abdülmecid

In contrast to the florescence of government documents, the earliest accounts of provincial celebrations of the sultan as seen from below, many fewer of which have survived, come through as much more restrained, almost dry. One such example is an undated report (*mahzar*) from the town of Tırnova[43] in Rumelia, containing the response of the local (town and district) inhabitants to the new sultan's accession (1 July 1839).[44] The report was signed and sealed by an astonishing number (118) of local notables, both Muslim and Christian, a literal 'who's who' of the district. It relates in detail the content of the local ceremonies on the occasion of Abdülmecid's accession. The report deploys standard metaphors of the ruler rather than engage in the abstract, risky business of metaphoric invention. It conveys an austere notion of the new sovereign – 'a holy personage (*takaddüs hazretleri*)', 'a padishah of the Islamic faith (*padişah-ı din-i islam*)'. It also refers to prayers for the crushing defeat of the enemies of the faith. When it comes to the terminology denoting in some sense or other 'the people', this report might as well have been written centuries earlier. It refers to Muslims as 'population (*ahali*)', non-Muslims as 'tax-paying subjects (*reaya*)' and both as 'slaves (*kul*)'. The only exception to the generally subdued tone of the report is the unique expression describing the provincials' potential reaction should they hear back from the Grand Vizier regarding 'the royal joy (*mahzuziyet-i mülukane*)' on account of their actions – 'the requisite of our inner exhilaration [lit. "a heart's being dilated and cheered"] and perfect joy would overwhelm all of us, Muslim and non-Muslim subjects'.[45] Notably, different words mark the joy of the sovereign (*mahzuziyet*) and his subjects (*mesruriyet*). The two sides still remain very far apart.

The Trope of Love, the Social Pact and the Cosmic Order. A Close Look at Two Letters to the Sultan

Two letters, written by the *voyvoda* (prince) of Boğdan (Moldavia), Mihail Sturdza (*Mihal Isturzazade*)[46] to Sultan Abdülmecid in 1840 and 1844 already paint the relationship between the ruler and the ruled in very different colours. This correspondence was occasioned by the births of the sultan's first and third sons – Mehmed Murad Efendi in 1840 and Mehmed Reşad Efendi in 1844, respectively.

According to the first letter, dated 19 December 1840, the birthday of Mehmed Murad Efendi was marked with ceremonious (*resmi*) cannon salvos, firework illuminations and benediction prayers in the town of Yaş (Iaşi in present-day Romania) and the other towns of Moldavia, as was the case in Dersaadet (Istanbul) and the rest of the imperial domains.[47]

Specifically, five-cannon salvos were fired five times a day for seven days. Moreover, the dissemination of an exact copy of the imperial decree (*ferman*), carrying the news of the prince's birth, in the main port of Kalas (Galati in present-day Romania) and other places, was accompanied by 'the ceremonious performance of cannon salvos and fusillades, and artistically fashioned firework illuminations at the necessary sites'.[48] The list of 'necessary sites' included road stations (*menzil*) and business places (*maslahat yerleri*), the houses of boyars and officers (*boyaran ve zabitan kulları haneleri*), market squares (*esvak*) and shops (*dükkan*). Illumination and music were common, both at the level of the individual property owner, who employed 'candle light (*iqad-ı kınadil*)' and 'chords of saz (*aheng-i saz*)',[49] and on the group level, whereby 'town illuminations with saz (*saz ile icra-yı şehrayin*)' were set up. Finally, there was 'the ritual slaughter of sacrificial sheep and the distribution of coins and dinars [gold pieces] to the poor and the needy for the imperial good fortune'.[50]

According to the second letter, dated 22 November 1844, the birthday of Mehmed Reşad Efendi was communicated to the boyars and inhabitants of Moldavia by way of circular (*ta'mim*), setting off similar festivities: 'For several nights, the entire town of Yaş and the houses of boyars, and the market squares, and the shops (?), and the business places had been skilfully and . . . decked and coloured, illuminated with tapers and candles . . .'[51]

At the outset of his first letter, Mihail Sturdza draws the contours of a kind of social pact between sovereign and subjects on which all Ottoman imperial order seems to rest. He does so by creating an elaborate organic and grand spatial metaphor of Ottoman society: 'Under the large tree (with spreading branches) of justice of the sublime eternally lasting state, supported by the spear of god, fixed and high in the sky, as the original saying goes, various communities and peoples (of the same faith) seek shade . . .'[52] This sweeping sentence introduces two related motifs, which permeate the entire letter, defining the image of the ruler and the terms of his veneration by the people. The first is the imperative of piety. 'Supported by the spear of God (*Müeyyid min atr-ı Allah*)' is the opening phrase of the first letter. The incantatory exclamation – 'Praise! And again Praise! And again Praise be to God (*Hamden sümme hamden sümme hamden*)!' – introduces the second one. Religious imagery is an omnipresent, continuously improvised accompaniment of imperial power, in sync with all of its metaphoric reincarnations within the text. For example, the mention of 'the throne of the All-Bounteous (*dergah-i mennan*)' in the context of the popular prayers and emotional build-up to the birth of the prince leads, several lines down, to the natural conclusion that the newborn prince is 'honouring the throne of existence (*teşrifnümud erike-yi vücud*)'. Thus, from a metonymy of celestial power, 'throne' becomes a metonymy of its earthly equivalent.

Closely related to piety is the notion of the ruler's personal sanctity. According to the first letter, the sultan's first-born son hailed 'from his Majesty's holy garden of roses (*gülistan-ı pak-ı şahaneden*)'. The same motif of 'holiness' reappeared in identical circumstances in the text of the second letter where the sultan's third son came 'from the loins of his holy Majesty the shadow of Allah (*sulb-u pak-ı hazret-i zil-i allahiden*)'. As the next section will demonstrate in greater detail, faith-imbued phraseology provides both the frame and the texture of sultanic claims to legitimate authority and, by extension, subject submission, humility and devotion. Yet there are also literal, hard-fact dimensions of religious rhetoric. The choice of the number 'five' for the size and frequency of daily cannon salvos, mentioned above, was clearly dictated by the number of daily prayers in Islam.

The second motif is the imperative of justice, a ubiquitous and rigid demand levied on Muslim and Christian rulers alike, and figuring prominently in Muslim and Christian doctrines of state. If the Ottoman state can be visually represented by a tree of justice, then it follows that its monarch's rise to power is tantamount to 'the accession of current imperial justice (*cülus-u adalet-i me'nus-u hümayun*)'. There is also a reference to 'the justice-commanding padishah (*padişah-ı adaletferma*)' in this letter. Not surprisingly, the second letter contains two more references to 'justice', one of which is tied to the Grand Vizier, the sultan's proxy in terms of secular power.

A third, related motif, not present in the above passage, but otherwise observable throughout the letters and at least as important for the social pact, is 'grace (*inayet*)'. Clearly, this is yet again a case of a divine attribute extended down to the ruler. The second letter explicitly acknowledges this by wishing the newborn prince 'the divine guidance and assistance of the grace of blessed divine companionship (*tevfik-i inayet-i refik-i samadani-yi berekatiye*)'. As with 'justice' in the second letter, 'grace' in the first one is extended further down to the sultan's subjects by way of his 'grace-giving (*inayetbahş*)' decree, carrying 'the contents of deposited exalted grace (*mazamin-i inayetrehin-i münifesi*)'.

Curiously, mercy, another key traditional attribute of the ruler, and, as it would turn out, in the case of Abdülmecid, a central and lasting characteristic of his public image, does not appear at all in a direct link to the sultan in the two letters. Its only appearance is by way of 'the Grand Vizier's clement and benign flagstaff (*mahatalem-i re'fette'vem-i asafaneleri*)' in the second letter. It could well be that the *voyvoda* of

Moldavia was simply not willing to take any risks in this respect, barely a year into Abdülmecid's reign, with the sultan's *scenario of power* not yet fully shaped. Words for the ruler's benevolence and generosity are also notably lacking, save for the standard, formulaic and therefore somewhat dry 'kindness and favour (*lutuf ve ihsan*)' at the end of the first letter.

What the *voyvoda* did not hesitate to do was to place the Ottoman royal house firmly within the fundamental cosmic order by interspersing his letters with an extravagant panoply of natural and grand spatial metaphors. In addition to the above-mentioned 'sky (*sema*)', these include 'wind (*rüzgar*)' and 'the horizon (*ufuk*)'. Along these lines, the Ottoman princes are 'stars (*encüm*)'. More precisely, each of the two newborn princes is 'a resplendent star, a pleasant moon (*kavkab-ı zahire kamer-i ta'lat*)'. In the first letter, the newborn is 'embellishing the world (*cihanara*)'. In both, he is 'honouring the throne of existence, and embellishing the love of the living (*teşrifnümud erike-yi vücud ve arayişresan mihr-i şühud*)'. In what amounts to perhaps the most exuberant symbolic gesture of all, each newborn is placed at 'the cradle of the universe [lit. "all creation"] (*kehvare-yi kainatta*)'.

These outbursts of extreme verbal florescence could hardly fail to ingratiate the sovereign. Moreover, by way of analogy, they pointed to yet another characteristic of the dynasty – its alleged eternity. For this much cherished attribute, the texts contain quite literal expressions as well – 'the perpetual royal household (*dudman-ı huludiktiran-ı husrevane*)' in the first letter and 'the eternal throne of the caliphate (*serir-i ebedkıyam-ı hilafet*)' in the second one, not to mention 'the sublime eternally lasting state (*devlet-i aliye-yi ebedi ed-devam*)' of the metaphor of Ottoman society discussed above. By the 1840s, however, this Ottoman claim had been substantially undermined and there was an increasingly acute need to strengthen the foundations of dynastic sovereignty and legitimacy. Mahmud II had already pointed the way towards a radical solution by seeking to captivate the hearts and minds of the subject population, especially non-Muslims. At the time of the writing of these letters, the challenges ahead could only have been compounded by the ongoing uncertainty of the power consolidation process under the young Abdülmecid. For all of these reasons perhaps Mihail Sturdza felt obliged to (1) confirm and lay out early on his conservative view of the essence of the role of the ruler – 'the procurement and perfection of safety, public order and circumstances in the shining direction of affluence, joy and tranquillity'[53] – and (2) go to great lengths to demonstrate his subordinate population's exemplary conduct in fulfilling their part of the social pact.

The Reign of Abdülmecid

The two relatively short[54] letters contain an unusually large number of terms and phrases characterising the attitudes of the Moldavian people, including the *voyvoda* himself, towards their distant overlord. Among them, by far the strongest emphasis falls on the many shades of joy the population experienced and, above all, on the emotional and devotional attachments to the sultan, channelled through the medium of prayer.[55] The range of these attitudes can be best analysed based on a juxtaposition of the individual and the group levels before and after the royal birth.

According to Mihail Sturdza, since the moment of the sultan's accession, his subjects were 'putting forth their hands (as beggars) in assiduous prayer . . . [for the birth of a son]'. They did so 'with all their heart and soul, expectant and awaiting the realisation of the hope for benediction'.[56] Apparently, when the imperial decree announcing the royal birth finally arrived, it became the object of Sturdza's intense adulation 'in accordance with devotion, with perfect reverence and joy, [it was] kissed by a lip, humbled in prayer, and laid down, after being enfolded with submissive joy, befitting of the contents of deposited exalted grace . . .'[57] This statement encapsulates an elaborate presentable staging of the *voyvoda*'s personal reception of the long-awaited news. Its value lies not in describing what may have actually transpired, which would be hard to ascertain independently, but in reflecting what was acceptable within the contemporary discourse of power, both conceptually and linguistically. Also worthy of note is the *voyvoda*'s remark in passing that the imperial decree was 'this time addressing your most humble servant [that is, the *voyvoda* himself] (*bu defa abd-ı ahkarlarına hitaben*)'. This observation seems to register a novelty in the style of correspondence between the Ottoman centre and its appointed ruler of the principality. If so, it points in the direction of a more personal style of engagement of regional power holders in tune with the new objectives of bringing peripheries more closely in line with the centre. As if to confirm this hypothesis, the *voyvoda* expatiates on his measures for the wide dissemination of an exact copy of this imperial decree 'as an outward expression of gratitude on the wings of happiness (*şükran ala telek an-na'm*)'.

The second letter allows for a telling comparison of the same links in the respective chains of the processes of public notification regarding the royal births in 1840 and 1844. Thus, in 1844, on receiving the news, the *voyvoda* felt obliged to spread 'this public rejoicing (*bu feyz-i meserret-i amme*)' to the boyars and inhabitants of the Moldavian province, according to his 'entrusted duty of sincerity and devotion (*müterettib-i zimmet-i sıdk ve ubudiyetim*)'. In other words, whereas in 1840, there was still some spontaneity and personal leeway regarding the *voyvoda*'s response, by 1844 these had already been subsumed by an overarching 'duty (*zimmet*)', a term that had not been mentioned before. A quick look at the summaries of the two letters, probably prepared by scribes at the Sublime Porte for internal bureaucratic purposes, reinforces this impression of the direction of change over the intervening four-year period. Whereas the first summary contains no references to any duties the *voyvoda* may have to fulfil under such circumstances,[58] the second summary explicitly states that Mihail Sturdza's 1844 letter is about 'carrying out the requisite of greeting and felicitation and performing the incumbent duty of devotion'.[59] Significantly, this view from the centre contains yet another term for individual 'duty' – *vacibe*.

As for the group duty of ordinary people, it was explicitly laid out in the two letters in an identical and quite convoluted manner. In each instance, they had to see to 'the performance of the pomp of the requisites of dignity and majesty'.[60] In other words, an appropriate expression of the sultan's dignity and majesty was required of his subjects during these festivities. In each document, this phrase closely accompanies the list of activities on the ground. A feeling of joy, expressed through no fewer than ten different terms in the two letters, permeates the celebrating population. The dominant mode of popular engagement is invariably prayer for the sultan's and his progeny's health and prosperity. It comes through as a supreme unifier of the body politic along three main axes. The first is spatial. In his first letter, Sturdza continuously emphasises the fact that 'the totality (*kaffe*; *katıbe*)' of subjects partakes of prayer services. Thus, upon the arrival of the news of the prince's birth, 'benediction prayers from young and old were promptly evoked'.[61] The second axis is temporal. Not only does the first letter contain multiple references to separate prayer services, but their repetitive nature and habituating purpose with respect to the population cannot escape the reader's attention. Adverbs such as 'continuously (*aleddevam*)' and 'over and over again (*tekrar alettekrar*)' describe the manner of communal praying. The third, most intriguing axis is emotional-cum-spiritual. Towards the end of the first letter, the variations of subject joy escalate into 'a yearning with love and compassion (*henn*)' for God's blessing of the Ottoman house with many more princes in the future. With it, 'the eyes and hearts of the faithful subjects are continuously enjoined to action and joy'.[62] Despite being dated four years apart, the two letters reach remarkably similar culminations:

> The obligatory [lit. 'ordained by God'] prayers were performed over and over again, with tenderness of heart and tears of joy from the bottom of the heart, <u>an exalted site of acceptance by His Majesty God the Transcendent</u> . . .[63]

and

> As the benediction prayers were adopted as foremost among the sacred obligations of devotion, they were performed from the bottom of the heart and with a perfection of submission and humble supplication, <u>an exalted site of acceptance by His Majesty God the Transcendent</u> . . .[64]

The fact that Sturdza employed different terms in otherwise equivalent sections – '*merfu*' vs '*berdaşte*' to signify exaltedness, '*icabetgah*' vs '*kabulgah*' to signify the site of God's acceptance of prayers – may be an indication that these were more than strictly formulaic phrases. Behind these words, there was probably a real common contemporary practice of praying for the ruler and his family, informed by a common and stable conceptual framework.

Based on language alone, there is no way of distinguishing in these letters between Christians and Muslims celebrating sultan and dynasty, and no way of telling that a predominantly Christian body of subjects was in fact praying to God for a Muslim ruler. This may seem incredible to a reader today, yet it entirely conforms to the spiritually accommodating and integrating policies initiated by Mahmud II in the aftermath of the Greek Revolution for the purpose of forestalling future splintering of the Ottoman imperial populace along religious lines. The inclusive notion of God and like-minded practices of faith and prayer have both literal and symbolic dimensions in the letters. As mentioned above, the predominantly Christian Moldavian subjects are said to have put forth their hands in prayer for sultan and dynasty, a gesture typical of Muslim prayer services. Moreover, the term '*icabet*', discussed above, which in standard Ottoman parlance referred to Muslim believers, whose prayers God answered favourably, in the 1840 letter clearly signified a majority of Christian believers. This deliberate universalist trajectory clearly afforded the monarch a new range of strategies for both personal popularisation and regime perpetuation.

Abdülmecid's Public Image on the Eve of his 1846 Tour of Rumelia

The trope of love for the ruler, which grew out of public manifestations of joy and communal prayer sessions, was spelled out and immensely popularised by Abdülmecid himself during his tour of Rumelia in 1846, only two years after the writing of Sturdza's second letter. A year before that tour, an imperial decree (*hatt-ı şerif*) announced a few key features of the sultan's intended public image, which were lacking from the letters, analysed above. A translation of this decree, along with an address-commentary inspired by it, were printed side by side in Bulgar Slavic[65] on a leaflet meant for domestic distribution. This decree reveals what soon became the two cornerstones of Abdülmecid's *scenario* of power – education and public health.[66] In its penultimate paragraph, the edict specifically addressed the need for more schools and 'popular Enlightenment (*narodno prosveshtenie*)'. In addition, it envisaged the opening of a large hospital for poor people and strangers 'as a pious creation (*kato edno blagochestivo sozidanie*)'. Significantly, the decree presented both policies as originating from the sultan. The text portrayed him as intimately involved and emotionally invested in their success. Abdülmecid was concerned about institutions 'useful to the common good (*polezni za obshtoto dobro*) (1)'; he cared about 'the well-being of Our subjects (*dobroto byitie na Nashyite poddannyi*) (3)'.[67] Apparently, the alleged failure of his subordinates to turn these intentions into realities filled the sultan's heart with 'pity and grief' leaving him in peace 'neither day nor night (*ne denya ni noshtya*)'. This is a major departure from the aloof image of the ruler, which, according to the evidence previously examined, had been the norm. Moreover, this edict, dated 1 January 1845 (O.S.),[68] contains the earliest evidence of the sultan's title of 'tsar', deployed with respect to his Bulgar Slavic subjects.[69] In fact, this title appears, in some fashion or other, no fewer than eight times in the space of a single page of text, whereas 'sultan' does not appear even once. Paradoxically, just when it creates the impression of this being a Christian monarch, the tsarist reference is paired with a reference to 'the intercession of our St. Prophet (*hodataystvoto na nashego sv. Proroka*) (2)'.[70] This striking choice is an early indication of what quickly unfolded as a consistent policy of presenting the sultan as a rightful ruler to various non-Muslim communities along lines and with symbols familiar to them. Even though this chapter and the following one focus on a particular (Bulgar Slavic) subset of the largest (Christian) such grouping, there is evidence to suggest that this deliberate strategy cut across all non-Muslim faith-based communities of the Empire.

The theme of the caring ruler, with his priorities in education and public health, undergoes substantial expansion and complication in the address-commentary attached to the decree. This rich and strongly suggestive text, entitled 'Dear Bulgars of the same kin (*Lyubeznii mi edinorodtsi Bulgare*)!'[71], opens as follows:

> The generous and most merciful love, which today His Majesty, our Brightest Tsar, Sultan Abdul Medzhid [sic] pours fatherly on his faithful subjects through this beneficient **Hatti Sherif** [sic][72] of his hand, awoke my zeal (*revnost*) to popularise its translation in Bulgarian so that you may not remain without merriment and gladness of the universal joy, which this Tsarist course produces; you, I mean, who have dedicated your faithful hearts to His Tsarist love.

The Reign of Abdülmecid

This programmatic sentence opens and closes with the earliest direct reference to the trope of the sultan's love for his subjects. In doing so, it also picks up the thread of the fatherly metaphor Mahmud II deployed on his 1837 tour of Rumelia. There are further traits of Abdülmecid's moral portrait, such as generosity and mercy, which did not appear in the earlier sources. In addition, this sentence and the text it belongs to draw the reader's attention to the terms of engagement between the ruler and the ruled, adding in the process new details to the picture derived from the *Takvim-i Vekayi* issue and Mihail Sturdza's letters. The mention of the subjects' hearts, filled with joy, expressed via a repetitive, typically Ottoman phrasing is not new, but the strength and trajectory of enhancement of their bond to the object of their love – the ruler – is. So is the complexity of paternal-filial exchange between the two parties, which casts the social pact in a new light. The author reiterates the constancy ('day and night') of the sultan's interaction with and care for his subjects, comparing it to that of 'a natural father for his progeny (*kato edin prirodnyiy otets za svoyata rozhba*)'. This organic metaphor functions bilaterally. On the one hand, the father aims to give his progeny 'good upbringing, a development of the mental faculties, a moral education'; on the other, the child is thus 'good and useful, not only to itself, but capable of every aid to its father'. Therefore, if at the start of this address the subjects' hearts are 'dedicated' to the sultan's love, by its conclusion, they are 'perfectly dedicated' as well as being encouraged to 'strive in order to become already more deserving of His most generous mercy'. Several aspects of the relationship between the people and the monarch are particularly significant and deserve further attention. First, this call for a popular exertion in the name of the sultan is unequivocally a matter of duty (*niy sme dluzhni*). So is the act of prayer to God for the sultan's long life, prosperity and a peaceful 'tsardom'. Interestingly, this duty of supplication is invoked by way of an injunction to 'always pray to the almighty God with compassionate hands (*vinagi s rutse blagoserdnyi da molim vsevyishnyago Boga*)'. This vivid image is strikingly similar to the hand outstretched in prayer (like a beggar's) from the first of Sturdza's letters. It gives further credence to the earlier hypothesis regarding the existence of a prescribed physical posture of praying for the sultan, regardless of the supplicant's personal faith. In return, the subjects would have the hope of living quietly and prosperously 'under His mighty wing'. This metaphor would become permanently etched onto the public mind, reappearing, time and again, over the years in various texts of a similarly emotional, propagandising and mass-mobilising nature.

The close textual analysis of this address-commentary, composed by Ilar Stoyanov[73] and published with the financial support of Nikola

Tupchileshtov,[74] would be much less relevant and telling if this text remained an isolated act, the expression of a subjective individual attitude. However, there are a number of thematic links and striking similarities with another, formal text of state, which undeniably contains the sultan's own position. The text in question is the speech, read by Mustafa Reshid Pasha in the sultan's presence to representatives of the various Ottoman local communities in the courtyard of the government building in Edirne (in present-day Turkey) on 6/18 May 1846.[75] This speech officially opened Abdülmecid's 1846 tour of Rumelia. It explains early on the sultan's motive for the trip – 'to see with his own eyes and get to know the important needs of his various peoples, and thus complement all that is necessary for their happiness'.[76] This clarification comes on the heels of a fatherly metaphor laid out at the very beginning of the text – 'as a good father constantly caring for the well-being of his children'. The text then lists a number of immediate economic improvements, based on the royal inspection in and around Edirne, before returning to familiar topics, such as the social pact, the trope of love and the importance of duty. In most of these subjects, the speech starts with concepts, already expounded by Stoyanov, before charting new territory. For example, the recognition of the sultan's constant and extensive care for his subjects leads to the observation that 'such signs of magnanimity are very rare in the annals of the State'. In return, the popular end of the social pact reads as follows:

> Let <u>all of us</u>, subjects of <u>all ranks,</u> <u>dedicated</u> to our <u>Venerable</u> Tsar <u>get to know</u> them [the signs of magnanimity]! Let us thank God for having the best and <u>most righteous</u> Monarch, and let us <u>work</u> to show ourselves grateful and <u>worthy</u> of such superior <u>abundance (of goodness)</u>! Let us <u>unite</u> our <u>hearts</u> with <u>love</u> for the <u>fatherland,</u> and let us <u>hasten,</u> in accordance with the will of our most kind Tsar in the development and prosperity of <u>our fatherly place (otechestvennoto ni mesto)</u> where we first saw the sun.

This highly charged appeal reiterates the subjects' dedication to their ruler before taking their commitment to a higher level in a number of ways. First, there is a quick progression in the sultan's moral outlook. From a starting point of generosity and mercy (here, 'most kind (*preblag*)'), traits noted before – the sultan is portrayed as 'venerable (*pochitaem*)', 'most righteous (*nay-pravednyiat*)' and a source of 'superior abundance of goodness (*prevoshodna blagodat*)'. All of these divine/saintly attributes and prerogatives add an air of sanctity to the sultan's persona. As a result, the previously stated importance of duty to the ruler is here transformed into an imperative; the striving to please him is accelerated ('let us hasten') and intensified ('let us work to show ourselves grateful and worthy'). This escalating sense of urgency culminates in a profoundly new and quintessentially modern call for unification ('let us unite our hearts') and totalisation ('all of us', 'all ranks'). Unlike Stoyanov's address to the Bulgars, this call is much wider: it targets Muslims, Christians and Jews, as subsequent passages explicitly point out. The decree goes even further, however, in stating that 'the difference of faith and its law is a matter of everyone's simple conscience'. Perhaps even more astonishing is the rearrangement of the metaphors of 'love' and 'father' – what had heretofore been the sultan's fatherly love for his subjects – into the subjects' 'love for the fatherland' – a newly found basis for subject mobilisation. Paradoxically, the notion of fatherland in this text has not one, but two meanings. The above passage contains a clear definition of the first, *micro* sense, which must have had an instant resonance with the decree's target listeners in Edirne or elsewhere – 'our fatherly place where we first saw the sun'. The second, *macro* meaning, as well as the final articulation of the relationship between ruler and subjects, appears in the following passage near the decree's end:

> All of us are subjects of the same State (*istata Derzhava*), compatriots (*sootechestvennitsyi*) and children of the one and same fatherland! When this is so, it does not become us at all to scorn each other! But let us follow the same path which our Tsar has drawn for us. Let us imitate His respectable example! As you see, H.M. does not discriminate among any of his subjects in the distribution of his acts of mercy. Is it not then a sacred duty for us (*sveshtenna za nas dolzhnost*) to live in accord and to hasten with all our strength to everything that serves the well-being of our common fatherland (*obshtoto nashe otechestvo*)?

Here, finally, we have the complete transformation of the father-children metaphor of Ottoman society and the trope of love for the ruler into an appeal for a mass popular territorial bond with and love for an abstract *macropatria*. Since this conceptual novelty is far removed from the everyday lives of most people, however, it needs to be qualified. Therefore, it is constructed on the basis of the instantly recognisable and emotionally binding *micropatria*, the primary contemporary meaning of 'fatherland'. By a process of magnification capped by the boundaries of the Ottoman state, the new concept becomes 'a common fatherland'. The principles of uniformity ('the same path', 'let us imitate') and totality ('all of us', 'all our strength') get further confirmation and elaboration. As a result, this passage takes the imperative of duty a step further – to the realm of a sacred obligation.

In conclusion, the speech expressed a hope that the sultan's subjects would rely on help from 'the Divine providence (*Bozhiy promisal*)' to be able to reckon with 'His [the sultan's] Autocratic will (*Negovata Samoderzhavna volya*)'. The first reference comes through as a clear concession, compared to the Prophet's intercession of the previous year's decree, to the non-Muslim populace. This is a step in the direction of a composite heterogeneous image of the ruler in conjunction with the multiplicity of different religio-communal angles of viewing him. So is his title of 'autocrat (*samoderzhets*)' whose derivative forms appear no fewer than six times throughout the speech. Given that this text is shorter than the decree, its saturation with tsarist references (8) is even higher.

The Sultan's 1846 Tour of Rumelia

From Edirne, Abdülmecid proceeded to Eski Zağra (Stara Zagora), Kızanlık (Kazanluk), Gabrova (Gabrovo), Tırnova (Turnovo), Rusçuk (Ruse), Silistre (Silistra) and Varna.[77] The route of the 1846 tour followed closely Mahmud II's tour of 1837, except that it was in reverse order. According to witness accounts, along the way the sultan was greeted everywhere with poetic recitations and songs of praise and prayer, both in Ottoman and in Bulgar.[78] The pride of place among welcoming parties invariably fell on students, of all creeds, most clad in white uniforms, some in solemn church-going attire, with flowers and green branches in their hands. At every stop, ceremonial cannon salvos were fired during the day and elaborate firework illuminations were displayed at night. In the town of Kızanlık, known then as it is today as the producer of the most fragrant roses and the best rose oil, the sultan's visit coincided, possibly by design, with the rose harvesting season. So the locals sprinkled rose water and poured rose oil before the sultan's cavalcade. According to Hristo Stambolski,[79] no one harvested roses during the three days of the sultan's stay in town so that the whole area would be exquisitely scented.[80]

For his part, the sultan had doctors vaccinate all children against smallpox in public before sending each off with a small gift of money.[81] Even people with rare diseases were occasionally summoned to the sultan's presence so his doctors could cure them.[82] Needless to say, the sublime visit caused the locals, who were unaccustomed to direct contact with the centre of power, quite a stir. The fact that they were completely unaware of the sultan's looks produced, at least in one instance, a comic episode. In Gabrova, where the twelve-year-old Todor Burmov[83] was in the welcoming party of students lined up along the road several kilometres outside the town, the children commenced their solemn singing upon receiving the cue that the sultan was in the group passing by them, only to abruptly cut it short after being told it was not him. In the end, Burmov sang without knowing who, within the group of passing dignitaries, the sultan actually was. Apparently, the sultan's departing ceremony the following day did not help resolve the issue either.[84] Such ignorance of the sultan's visage would soon be radically ameliorated, with the wide, officially condoned, proliferation of royal portraits across the imperial domains, as well as abroad.

The most detailed account, albeit from a hostile source, relates the sultan's visit to Rusçuk, which, lasting four days, may have also been the longest. According to Nayden Gerov,[85] the greeting ceremonies proceeded on a communal basis, with the Jews being placed closest to the town walls, next to them the Armenians, then the Bulgars and finally the Muslims, situated the farthest from town, thus being the first to see and welcome the sultan. The front of each non-Muslim group consisted of schoolchildren, with candles and willow twigs, and priests in liturgical attire. Behind them stood other townsmen, some holding placards with words of praise for the sultan. The Muslim schoolchildren were also dressed in white, the difference being that some of them held green flags with white writing on them. A dervish presided over the Muslim group, holding a large green flag with a text in gold. Apparently, there was also a spatial separation by gender, with women remaining behind the town walls, while men formed two lines stretching for over a mile along the road outside. As the sultan approached, each group of youngsters would in turn sing for him, everyone else bowing profusely. It seems that Abdülmecid was dressed in a slightly more luxurious fashion than during state ceremonies in Istanbul, with his military coat sewn with gold, and diamonds around his neck harkening back to olden times. If so, this may have been an attempt to meet provincial expectations, which were still much less in tune with the fast-changing realities of sultanic power in the capital. As the sultan proceeded quietly, however, he followed none of his ancestors' protocol of restrained head movements and fixed sideway gaze in public, avoiding any eye contact. Instead, Abdülmecid opted to look around him constantly.[86]

Regardless of the memoirists' personal dispositions towards the unfolding sultanic spectacle – be it solemn (Stambolski), enthusiastic (Burmov) or sardonic (Gerov), all of them employed in their accounts the same titles of 'autocrat (*samodurzhets*)' and 'tsar', contained in the period documents analysed above.[87] In Rusçuk, the Bulgar students even sang to the sultan an anthem, entitled 'The Most Autocratic Tsar of Ours (*Samoderzhavneyshiy tsar nash*)'.[88] This is a testament to the wider relevance and popularity that these titles must have quickly gained among the non-Muslim Ottomans.

The Discourse of Reform and (Bulgar) Songs of Praise and Prayer for the Sultan

What provincial non-Muslim populations very quickly embraced, enriched and employed to their advantage was the discourse of the Tanzimat. Even though in substance, the Tanzimat reforms began at least a decade prior to 3 November 1839, the phrase '*tanzimat-i hayriye* (the auspicious Tanzimat)' promoted widely, both at home and abroad, after this date found resonance with the population, and created a substance of its own. Based on a Bulgar songbook, published in 1851 in Serbia, this process seems already to have been well under way during Abdülmecid's 1846 tour of Rumelia. This book opens with the texts of two prayers, recited by Bulgar schoolchildren to the sultan on his arrival at Tırnova on 14/26 May 1846. The first prayer appears in a highly formulaic cyrillicised Ottoman, a rare and fascinating occurrence in print. It seems identical to the one read at Kızanlık.[89] This may have been a standard reading at all schools across the imperial domains at the time, regardless of faith and denomination. Such was indeed the case with the second prayer, this one in Bulgar. Its title – 'A Hymn for Many Years (*Mnogoletstvenno vospevanie*)' – unmistakably points to its Orthodox liturgical origins, a familiar and comfortable zone for Orthodox Christian believers and hence an ideal platform for appealing to their sensitivities and directing their praises to the ruler. The publisher, Hadzhi Nayden Yoannovich,[90] who probably witnessed the event, explicitly indicated that the hymn was 'used in the Turnovo school (*supotreblaemoe v Ternovskoto uchilishte*)'.[91] This hymn, as well as the publisher's lengthy dedication to the sultan printed on the book's first page, contains an unusually high number of references to the ongoing reform process in the Empire. The dedication summarises in substantial detail, according to Yoannovich's understanding, the reform measures, broached by the Gülhane Rescript, twice mentioning it by name (*hattişerif*).[92] This seems an unusual subject matter for a songbook, especially in its opening lines. One would think that it would be a reflection of the decree's profound impression on and popularity among Ottoman non-Muslims. Judging by the hymn's text, this is indeed the case. In it, the Bulgars collectively thank the sultan for the 'acts of goodness (*dobrini*)' they received and continue to 'incessantly (*neprestanno*)' receive, as well as for the persistent service of justice in 'the time of the most resplendent, most serene, most peace-loving and most merciful ... Tsar and Autocrat'.[93] This titular phrase bears uncanny resemblance to medieval Bulgar and broader Slavic formulae. So does the prayer's repetitive, incantatory solicitation of peaceful and prosperous 'many years (*mnogaya leta*)'. It seems that the whole set of such notions was recently dusted off old books and brought back to public usage in the Ottoman Empire of the mid-nineteenth century.[94] It was then married to the discourse of reform. As a curious 1849 newspaper announcement shows, on the interface of these two main narratives, there was substantial room for improvisation, the expression of local sentiment and the advancement of local objectives. In this notice, the townspeople of Tırnova expressed their gratitude to the sultan for the dispatch of a certain Cemaali Paşa to govern the affairs of their town. The text opens with an exact reproduction of the hymn discussed above, before launching a praise of the above-mentioned bureaucrat's beneficial actions in *Tırnova*. Through him, the notice focuses on the ruler's upholding of justice, in line with 'divine justice (*bozhya pravda*)'. In the process, it twice refers to the Tanzimat reforms and once to the decree itself.[95] This newspaper announcement helps place Yoannovich's book in perspective. It serves as a preliminary indication that prayer texts such as this one were influential in a number of ways, going beyond the direct, short-term encounter with the ruler and into the realm of the long-term symbolic, with profound inculcating effects on the populace. Among them, the trope of love was central. The above-mentioned hymn calls the sultan 'the most peace-loving (*mirolyubiveyshago*)'. Yoannovich's book dedication reiterates this assessment and expands it to incorporate the sultan's subjects by referring to Abdülmecid's motivation for reform in the following terms – 'out of affection and a burning [lit. "hot"] desire for peace and the good livelihood of his subjects'.[96]

What is most remarkable about this book is that it also contains songs, which Davidov, inspired by the sultan's visit, composed in its aftermath for the purpose of creatively re-enacting and symbolically framing the encounter. Three of them merit closer attention and add important new dimensions to the symbolic interaction between the ruler and the ruled. Two of these songs appeared shortly after Abdülmecid's Rumelian tour in the 1847 Almanac also published by Yoannovich in Wallachia.[97] They contain what seems a largely factual account (with occasional metaphoric touches) of the sultan's visit. The first song explains to the people the purpose of the sultan's tour in the following terms:

> May there be peace and love
> And no violence
> Whoever has a need
> May tell him
> Give him a complaint
> And hope
> That somehow he will receive [it]

Ruler Visibility and Popular Belonging

> In his time
> Whatever one begs
> The tsar carries <u>in his pocket</u>
> Ready to bestow
> And to make good
> For this reason
> He passed here [Tırnova] too
> To <u>see</u> his reaya
> To go around his land[98]

These poetic lines reveal a close direct emotional connection between the (Muslim) ruler and the (non-Muslim) ruled, a radically new phenomenon in Ottoman history. This excerpt focuses on the top-down part of the relationship, painting the picture of a sensitive, highly accessible, benevolent and generous ruler, who is also omnipotent. The song continues with first-hand particulars of the sultan's visit to Tırnova, which largely fall in line with the memoirs relating other such visits from the tour. In the process, the motif of the sultan's larger-than-life stature gets a new dimension with the reverence Christian clergymen display for him. With a gospel in hand, they bow to the ground and stretch their hands up in a prayer to God for '[his] long life (*mnogaya leta*)'. The clergymen then accompany the sultan into town singing 'a song for many years (*mnogoletna pesen*)' along the way. Their enthusiasm infects the gathered multitude. That evening, everyone prays to God and performs animal sacrifice for the sultan's health.[99] In gratitude, the sultan bestows money gifts to all, ranging in value from five piasters (to boys) to twenty piasters (to clergymen).

The second song paints the whole encounter with the brush of folk fairy tales:

> <u>We</u> reached golden years
> We <u>saw</u> Sultan Midzhit [sic]
> Our fathers <u>have not seen</u>
> Our grandfathers <u>have not heard</u>
> Such a <u>serene</u> <u>tsar</u> (*hrisimo tsarche*)[100]
> Such a merciful sultan (*milostivno Sultanche*)

The choice of such an expressive medium and the mythic tone of the narrator's voice may perhaps be attributed to a combination of, on the one hand, the improbability of the above sequence of occurrences and, on the other, the high degree of common fervour it generated. Along these lines, the shift from third-person singular to first-person plural seems highly significant. So is the introduction of a temporal component via the blood connection to fathers (*bashti*) and grandfathers/ancestors (*dedi*), and the exponential hyperbolising deep into the past – the length of time during which the fathers have not seen anything like this pales in comparison to the length of time the grandfathers/ancestors have not heard anything like it. In its natural flow, this extreme popular excitement bridges divides based on strict interpretations of faith, leading to paradoxical results from our present-day point of view. The indications for a trajectory of religious and cultural syncretism, more or less subtle, are interspersed throughout the song.[101] At its very outset, the sultan is compared to a serene newborn lamb as well as a mighty lion.[102] Then, in the above passage, another word for 'serene' is used: *hrisim*. However, neither these nor the outbursts of ecclesiastic reverence for the sultan, detailed above, seem to adequately prepare the reader for the song's closing lines. They convey a popular rapture, which can be qualified as nothing less than a *personality cult*:[103]

> Wherever he stepped and sat
> And whichever way he looked
> We kiss that place
> And commemorate him
> With joy we were all weeping
> And on the trees we were climbing
> And for the sultan we watch
> Whence will we see him again
> Oh, will we prove worthy
> For him to twice appear to us
> In the year of 1846,
> He passed through Ternovo [Tırnova]
> Most merciful he appeared to us
> Inaugurated the land customs
> God [gave to] us to lord over.

The theme of visibility, the act of visual exchange between the ruler and the ruled, unobtrusively present in all of the above excerpts from this song and elsewhere, carries the gradually unfolding stages of popular embrace of the ruler as the people's own to such an intense conclusion.[104] As the poem makes clear, the cult of the monarch is centred on the space inscribed by the sultan's movement and vision. Perhaps most indicative of a cult is the shift from past to present tense in tune with the shift from the account of the sultan's visit to an account of popular behaviour afterwards. Whereas the visit is a one-time event, the response is a repetitive occurrence, unbounded in time – 'we kiss that place and commemorate him'. Based on this evidence, poetically enhanced yet largely grounded in reality, it may not be far fetched to state that the people treat the sultan as they would a saint. This impression is only made stronger by the use of the verb '*da se yavya* (to appear)' with reference to the sultan. This verb has a mystic, otherworldly connotation, often employed in relating supernatural, dream- or vision-like experiences. Thus, this song ends on a high point of ruler sanctity.

The same two songs by Davidov appeared in Yoannovich's 1851 songbook, with some highly suggestive changes, including an entirely new segment. The changes concerned several aspects of the relationship between the sultan and his subjects. Whereas in the 1846 version of the first song the sultan carried that which his subjects needed in his pocket, in 1851 he held it in his 'bosom (*pazva*)'. Thus, in symbolic terms at least, the ruler seems to be holding his subjects' needs in greater esteem in 1851. After all, the bosom is next to one's heart, where one would also carry a love letter. This sultanic gesture is then matched by a concession on the part of people – 'Only we should beg and implore him' – another novel addition. The subtle evolution of the social pact towards a shorter distance between the two parties and a more pronounced popular reverence for the ruler manifests in other ways as well. For example, the students welcoming the sultan in the 1851 text 'were sitting dutifully (*chinno sedyaha*)', a remark absent from the earlier version. Whereas the clergymen 'were bowing to the ground' in 1846, in 1851 they were 'all falling to the ground (*vsi na zemla padat*)'. The list of animals sacrificed for the ruler's health is longer in 1851. In addition to oxen, cows, lambs, kids and calves, it includes 'birds and sparrows, little pigeons'. That such an extensive description (a total of six poetic lines) should be included attests not only to the reality of the event of animal sacrifice (*kurban*), but possibly also to the wide range of social strata involved, with everyone contributing what they could afford. Perhaps in recognition of such a broad spectrum of devotion, an 1846 line – '[The tsar] Bestowed gifts on all of them (*Sichkite dari*)' – was sung twice in the 1851 version. More importantly, the first song received an entirely new ending, consisting of two parts. The first relates the sultan's didactic words to a gathering of local notables before his departure from Tırnova:

> From the saray he <u>looked</u> at them,
> And ordered them,
> To <u>look after</u> the <u>reaya</u>
> And not harm it
> To guide it,
> To instruct it
> From the saray he descends,
> And says to all:
> Turks of Muslim faith

The Reign of Abdülmecid

> Christian <u>reaya</u>
> I recognise alike
> And equal honour give
> Both Muslim faith
> And Christian
> Both Armenian
> And Jewish
> I recognise alike
> And equal honour give.

Once again, the visual exchange is prominent. It is a key element in the process of conveying the will of the ruler to his proxies, and ensuring the enforcement of that same autonomous omniscient will for the benefit of the populace. What is surprising, however, is the protagonist's choice to segment this heretofore faceless, malleable 'flock (*reaya*)' of non-Muslims on the basis of religious denomination. The text is deliberately repetitive in listing communities and insisting on their equal rights. It reveals an intense preoccupation with the Tanzimat's focus on equality. In short, what Davidov wrote and Yoannovich published and sold was more likely than not in tune with what people thought, felt, wanted to hear/read and were willing to pay for. In all likelihood, the act of naming in this excerpt reflects processes of acceleration of communal events and the gradual crystallisation of the communal frame of mind twelve years after the Gülhane Rescript. As the passage immediately following demonstrates, this choice in no way contradicts the overarching paternalistic role of the sultan in the familial metaphor of Ottoman society:

> In the coach he sat,
> To the <u>reaya</u> he <u>turned his eyes,</u>
> As <u>a father to</u> [his] <u>children,</u>
> That is how he <u>looked,</u>
> Outside of town he came,
> And told all of them:
> I hereby depart,
> To God I thee entrust,
> To God I thee entrust,
> My shadow I leave here,
> So you may not be sad
> And of me grievous

The last four poetic lines contain references to a universalised God and, just as striking, the invocation of the shadow of God (*zil-i allah*), a profoundly Muslim title of the sultan, in order to keep his Christian subjects

Ruler Visibility and Popular Belonging

from grieving his departure. One would be hard pressed to find a passage that better illustrates the syncretic nature of the integrationist project and the inclusive notion of faith on which it largely rested. This symbolic separation of the shadow of the ruler from his body is an early signal for a trajectory of abstraction in the terms of glorification of the sultan, which would gradually lead to a full-blown personality cult by the end of the nineteenth century under Abdülhamid II.[105]

Despite the protagonist-sultan's call, a final segment of the first song, not quoted here, captures in great detail the shared common sorrow accompanying his departure. Allegedly, the sultan's sheer physical presence gave people joy and allowed them to share their needs with him. Since the same segment also relates factual details of the sultan's departure from Tırnova and the people's return to town after seeing him off, it cannot be easily dismissed as a figment of Davidov's imagination.

The second song also displays changes along the path of ruler glorification. Whereas in the 1846 version the sultan, aged twenty-three, is treated lovingly as a youngster, the 1851 version casts the image of the older Abdülmecid (aged twenty-eight) with corresponding respect, in a more mature light. There is no trace of the diminutive form 'little tsar (*tsarche*)', his mercy is further emphasised ('merciful' becomes 'most merciful') and the epithet 'serene (*hrisimo*)' is replaced by the image of a ruler with some experience, 'a good master (*dobar gospodar*)'. At its end, the second song has two new lines, which serve as a thematic prelude to the entirely new third song.[106] The first of these lines replaces an earlier line – 'God [gave to] us to lord over'. This change acts to soften the notion of the sultan's control over his subjects, as imposed from above (by God), and instead shifts the emphasis to the theme of the ruler's reception by the people as their gift. Therefore, it serves as a perfect transition to the last song dedicated to Abdülmecid.

The new, third song grabs the reader's attention from its very title – 'Love for the sultan by his subjects (*Lyubov k sultanu ot poddannicite mu*)'. It carries in a most overt and intense form yet the call for individual mobilisation in the name of the ruler:

> Whoever loves the sultan,
> Runs to him,
> Loves him from the heart,
> Expends labour for him,
> Exhausts life,
> Does not leave the Tsar,
> Does not spare one's health,
> Always praises the Sultan,

<u>For the smallest need</u>
<u>Summons all the strength</u>
Serves him faithfully,
And remembers him.
<u>Prays for the Tsar</u>,
And slaughters kurban,
Rams and rams,
And fattened oxen
So <u>good-loving</u>
He is <u>God-loving</u>,
As he does not reject [the tsar]
So the tsar <u>loves</u> him,
(And) whoever hates the sultan,
He enters into sin
(And) whoever thinks ill of him
May God destroy him.

Unprecedentedly, this mobilisation unfolds in both prescriptive ('runs to', 'expends labour', 'exhausts life', 'always praises', 'serves', 'remembers') and proscriptive ('does not leave', 'does not spare one's health') lines of reasoning. Therefore, it inscribes a complete moral universe. As before, the individual behavioural model is based on love, though a love which is unequal. Of the five references to love in this segment, four originate with the individual and flow towards the sultan, and only one proceeds in the opposite direction. Moreover, the roots for 'love' in the original – '*obich*' and '*lyub*', a duality that the English translation does not reflect, are also employed in an asymmetric manner. For example, all of the '*lyub*' forms, the root carrying the more passionate type of love, centred on the sultan. However, the most remarkable aspect of this song is that it goes beyond love. The extreme call of popular duty to the sultan transforms what would otherwise be irrational behaviour into a normal regularity, thus creating a higher plane of activity ('for the smallest need summons all the strength'). Here, for the first time, the notion of *duty to* the ruler, traced above through a series of texts, enters the territory of *sacrifice for* the ruler. Once outlined with unusual detail, this higher plane is then taken a step further into the realm of the divine, which seals its legitimacy – the good-loving (*dobrolyubiv*) becomes God-loving (*Bogolyubiv*). Since Abdülmecid is both sultan (3) and tsar (3), the two terms being employed here on an alternating basis, he enters seamlessly into a Christian theological reference frame regarding the rightful universal ruler.[107] Therefore, actions against the tsar-sultan invoke notions of sin, with the ruler claiming divine protection.

The Rumelian Tour's Ripple Effects and the Beginnings of a Bulgar 'Feeling'

Far from being spurious or idiosyncratic, the themes pioneered by people such as Stoyanov, Davidov and Yoannovich on the micro level drew on parameters set by the macro frame of the Tanzimat. In fact, at least as far as the Bulgars are concerned, Abdülmecid's 1846 tour of Rumelia gave the vast majority of such works a jump-start.[108] The mental connection of provincial Bulgar populations to the sultan, forged single-handedly and vividly by the tour, was afterwards perpetuated by a nascent Bulgar periodical press. Barely a month after the tour, a eulogy of the sultan appeared on the pages of the only Bulgar periodical publication – the monthly magazine *Lyuboslovie* ('Love of Words') – published by Konstantin Fotinov[109] in Izmir. It was written by Stefan Izvorski,[110] a teacher in Şumnu, a town in the part of Rumelia the sultan had visited. The poem was dedicated to Abdülmecid 'as an eternal proof' of the good will of 'the Bulgar people (*Bolgarskiy narod*) to their August Master and Benefactor'.[111]

Izvorski played a key role in the institutionalisation of another of the tour's lasting legacies. Two issues later, in August 1846, *Lyuboslovie* published an account of the local school examination ceremonies, held on 11/23 August in Şumnu. The event drew so many spectators that the school building could not contain them and they spilled out all around it. The article explicitly noted that this was 'a custom which has never been held in their town, nor have their ancestors for so many centuries proved worthy and able to see [it]'.[112] The entry into the school building played out as a solemn public procession of the first order. Archbishop Porfiriy, surrounded by church cantors, led the way, followed by priests, town notables, merchants, artisans and everyone else. The archbishop performed a sanctification rite and delivered a speech in Ottoman highlighting the importance of education during the reign of Abdülmecid. Porfiriy reiterated the uniqueness of this open-door ceremony. His act was followed by a carefully choreographed song-dialogue between the teacher (Izvorski) and his students. It was a song of praise and prayer for the sultan, capped with religious formulae – 'for ages and ages (*vo veki vekov*)' and 'amen (*amin*)'. Afterwards, Izvorski, in turn, delivered a speech of his own, with education as the primary focus yet again. Apparently, this speech had profound effects on the multitude, leading some to 'deep silence', causing others to adopt 'absorbed expressions' or 'irrepressible tears'. Finally, all students, dressed in white shirts, with little red fezzes, seated in twelve groups of twelve, stood up and began reciting poems of praise. They proceeded in a strict order, group after group, with each student uttering four lines. The recital culminated in the turn of a very young child with a strong voice, seated in the sixth group amidst all students and spectators.

In its entirety, this two-part teacher-student performance was more intricate than anything the sultan witnessed during the tour itself. The theme of education, a central component of Abdülmecid's *scenario of power*, announced with the 1845 *ferman* and its accompanying address-commentary, analysed above, hereby found some of its earliest grass-roots resonance. Rather than an outlier, the Şumnu ceremony is a telling example of the sort of activities the sultanic tour inspired across Rumelia. *Lyuboslovie*'s very next (September) issue contains an account of a strikingly similar ceremony, involving all five schools of Kotel (in present-day Bulgaria), a Rumelian town not very far from Şumnu. Moreover, the same archbishop Porfiriy presided over that event as well. In this instance, the high cleric's speech explicitly acknowledged the importance of the sultan's 'humane' (lit. 'people-loving (*chelovekolyubiv*)') wishes with respect to his 'flock (*stado*)'. Tsarist references proliferate yet again throughout this account, becoming ever more firmly embedded into the contemporary discourse of Ottoman rulership.

In a rare demonstration of the all-imperial, trans-communal nature of Abdülmecid's image-making policies, the same page of the June issue of *Lyuboslovie* on which Izvorski's eulogy appeared also related the story of a choir of twenty-five Hellene-minded Rum schoolgirls greeting the sultan with 'God Save the Tsar' upon his exit from Friday prayers in the Bebek neighbourhood of Istanbul. The article explicitly acknowledges the song's roots – 'and there they sung to the Tsar a song, after an English Tsarist song, which began as follows: "God save our Tsar Abdul Mecid [sic]"'.[113] Once again, in less than two lines of text, the tsarist reference appears twice with reference to the sultan. While future research will clarify the exact relationship between Western and Eastern Christian hymns in informing the origins of such celebratory practices among Ottoman non-Muslims of the mid-nineteenth century, one thing seems clear. These practices quickly became an integral component of a wider drive for the consolidation of subject loyalty at home as well as recognition by and symbolic reciprocity with the West.[114]

With the publication of the first major Bulgar newspaper[115] (*Tsarigradski Vestnik*) in the Ottoman Empire commencing in 1848, a major new medium compounded the sporadic decentralised influence of songbooks.[116] By bringing to its readers all across the far-flung imperial domains events and high personages from the capital on a weekly basis, the paper enhanced their awareness of an Ottoman centre, personalised by the sultan, his family and government ministers. A quick review of the contents of various articles over a period of several months from the year 1851 provides a sort of cross-section of the ways in which the above-analysed themes defining the ruler-ruled interaction were further developed and anchored in the public mind. This snapshot reveals both top-down and bottom-up conceptions of the relationship between the sultan and his subjects. To begin with, the fatherly metaphor flourished. For example, one finds references to 'the fatherly Sultanic wishes', as well as to a sultan 'who watches equally over all of his subjects and cares for all of them as a humane and good-natured father'.[117] In a letter from the Bulgars of Tulcea, a town in present-day Romania, one even finds the image of a sultan who 'loves (*lyubi*) his subjects as his own adopted children'.[118] This is the earliest characterisation thus far retrieved of the sultan's emotional connection to his subjects, employing the more passionate and intense form of the verb 'to love'. It thus continued the trend whereby the perceived distance between the ruler and the ruled only got shorter over time.

Education ostensibly remained among Abdülmecid's topmost priorities in 1851. There are at least two reported cases of his personal attendance at student exams in this narrow stretch of time – once at the school (*medrese*) of the Fatih Mosque, and once at the Imperial Military School.[119] Apparently, the sultan's initiative made waves across the domains and inspired local adaptations. A letter from Razgrad (in present-day Bulgaria) relates the visit of a number of local dignitaries, which included the sub-district governor (*müdür*) Adil Bey, the religious judge (*qadi*) Mustafa Efendi and the chief jurist (*müfti*) Hüseyin Efendi to a Bulgar school on the sultan's birthday. Much to the guests' delight, upon their entry the students instantly stood up and sang a hymn, entitled 'May God Give Many Years to the Most Peaceful, Most Serene and Most Nobly Born Tsar Sultan Abdul Medzhid [sic]'.[120] As the article made clear, this hymn was at that time sung in schools on a daily basis. Afterwards, the governor delivered a didactic speech to the students. The judge then addressed the town notables with words of advice and guidance, which included the expression of 'the tsar's burning [lit. "hot"] desire for the enlightenment of the peoples in all of His State'. Leaving little doubt that such events did indeed solidify communal consciousness, the article's author concludes by saying that 'this visit is a sign of the prosperity of our town, and of the Bulgarian kin (*roda Bolgarskago*)'.

As the Bulgars saw themselves increasingly in terms of belonging to a greater, supra-regional group, they phrased their gratitude to the sultan for his reform movement and the functionaries dispatched locally to administer it in broader terms. Thus, if, in 1849, in the case outlined above, a group of Bulgar residents of Tırnova had thanked the sultan on the pages of *Tsarigradski Vestnik* on behalf of their townspeople, two years later, a group of merchants from the same town wrote a similar letter in gratitude for 'the people-saving Tanzimat (*narodospasaemyiy Tanzimat*)'.[121] Six months earlier, an identical attitude had already emerged in an editorial piece on the cover of the same paper. It praised 'the people-saving (*narodospasitelnyiy*) writ of the Tanzimat'.[122]

The process of intensifying popular infatuation with the ruler often took on dimensions that from a present-day vantage point seem paradoxical. In this respect, one of the most fruitful grounds for symbolic syncretism was the realm of regalia. Soon after the discourse of the sultan as tsar got under way, it became insufficient to refer to the sultan simply as 'tsar'. Instead, the public imagination was stimulated with regalia-driven metonymic referents. Some, such as the 'throne (*prestol*)'[123] are common to the Ottoman Muslim and Bulgar Christian symbolic systems, but others, such as the 'sceptre (*skiptur*)' are Christian only. Yet, repeatedly, newspaper articles placed a sceptre in the hand of the sultan, thus producing a factually incorrect image but one that was powerfully resonant with readers. For example, one published text spoke of 'peoples, whom the Lord God has subjected to the Lord-protected sceptre of His Majesty the Sultan', while another asserted that the sultan 'has no other goal apart from the prosperity and tranquillity of all people (*lyude*) who are placed under his most glorious sceptre'.[124] References such as these made the ruler's image intelligible and appealing to his non-Muslim subjects in a dual, mutually reinforcing fashion. On the one hand, they invoked vivid symbols of secular power; on the other, and even more importantly, they often carried subtle interwoven signs of a corresponding, higher sacred plane the sultan also inhabited. Examples include the above-mentioned 'Lord-protected sceptre (*bogohranimyiy skiptr*)' as well as the sultan's 'Lord-endowed state (*Bogodarovanna derzhava*)'.[125] They gave the sultan a crucial (universal) divine stamp of approval in the eyes of his subjects. Consequently, as with the final additions to Davidov's poetic account of the 1846 encounter between the people and the ruler, sacrality could and did emanate from the sultan's persona itself. A speech by the Grand Vizier Mustafa Reshid Pasha, which appeared on the cover of *Tsarigradski Vestnik* in 1851, the same year Davidov's songbook was published, included a term as abstract as 'the truthful Tsarist mind (*istinnyiy Tsarskiy razum*)'. Aiming at a synopsis of the accomplishments of the sultan's reign, the speech contains in a remarkably condensed form the motifs of Abdülmecid's scenario of

Ruler Visibility and Popular Belonging

power and the interrelation of concepts and symbols central to his popular appeal:

> [the sultan] then condescended to open an easy road towards the dissemination of the arts and an education which leads the human being towards prosperity and salvation in this world and the next (*spasenieto na toyze i na onze svet*), and teaches everyone their duties (*dolzhnosti*).
>
> Truly prosperous are we . . . And more fortunate (*blagoschastlivi*) are our children for, partaking of such acts of kind goodness (*blagosti*), they find through the Tsarist grand endowment (*velikodarovanie*) and doing good (*blagodeyanie*) ready, pre-arranged ways to learn, be guided and improve. May the Lord God give us in alms the beneficent shadow and canopy[126] of H. I. Majesty for many years! Amen.[127]

These lines paint the sultan's road to educational reform as the road to personal 'salvation in this world and the next' – the most intense syncretic sacred element yet. The shift to a forward thrust in the temporal continuum, a novelty in the discourse of the ruler-ruled relationship, is reaffirmed by a juxtaposition of the lives of the sultan's present subjects and their children. Whereas earlier comparisons involved people of the present ('we') and the past ('our fathers and grandfathers'),[128] this is a first encounter with an image of posterity in a 'present-future' comparative setting. Posterity is hereby placed within a didactic paternalistic scheme ('ready, pre-arranged ways to learn, be guided and improve'), which draws attention yet again to the ruler as the fountain of overarching goodness and overwhelming generosity. The former attribute of the ruler, in fact, operates even on a subconscious level as this passage of only three sentences contains as many as seven words sharing the root 'good (*blago*)'.

The theme of the ruler as the conduit of goodness from God to the people evolved further in songs of prayer and praise for the sultan dating from the last years of Abdülmecid's reign. An 1857 songbook, published by two Bulgar teachers – Spas Zafirov and Tsani Zhelev – contains a prayer-song for the sultan, which was clearly composed for the purpose of being performed at Bulgar schools on a daily basis. Two of its stanzas are worthy of note:

> To our Fortunate Tsar,
> Our Father, and Lord[129]
> Abdul Mezit [sic], oh Lord,
> Extend your Protection
> Grant [him] extreme health,
> Create [protection] for many years.

. . .
Oh, you, Tsar of heaven,
Protect our most kind
Tsar Abdul Mezit [sic],
Extend Him many days,
For our prosperity,
And heavenly protection.[130]

In yet another demonstration of religious syncretism, these lines describe the stages via which divine blessings reach the people. First, the students implore God to extend his protection to the sultan-tsar. Second, the latter's long life and well-being in turn guarantee the people's own prosperity and celestial protection. Thus, the sultan-tsar is an indispensable link in the chain of bounty descending from heaven to earth. By echoing in period Bulgar eulogistic poetry and polemic prose alike, this notion became a widely held truism. For example, an 1859 'Prayer-Song for Many Years (*Mnogoletstvie*)', accompanied by an explicit note that these lines were 'sung in every Bulgar church (*peyat se u seka Bulgarska Tsurkva*)', commences by urging 'our people (*nash narod*)' to rejoice, glorify God and thank the tsar for its peaceful life.[131] In the same vein, an essay appearing on the pages of *Tsarigradski Vestnik* that same year appeals to God in the following terms: 'Glory to You God our Lord, who supports on the throne our Autocrat Sultan ABDUL MEDZHID [sic] and *pours through him your mercies on us*!'[132]

The 1850s mark progressively higher levels of popularity for such conceptual formulations of Ottoman sultanic authority. The main vehicle for their dissemination remained the songs of praise and prayer. With all of the above analysis in mind, it becomes easier to situate the following statement by Ivan Vazov, one of the best-known Bulgarian writers and widely regarded as 'the patriarch of Bulgarian literature': 'In the school of my little hometown [Sopot] one would glorify Sultan Abdul Medzhid [sic] in Turkish hymns before one heard about and glorified the [Bulgarian] Enlighteners St Cyril and St Methodius . . .'[133] The period Ivan Vazov (1850–1921) had in mind probably encompassed the mid- to late 1850s when he himself was a schoolboy. By the end of the 1850s, these songs infiltrated a growing number of festive occasions and cultural settings. For example, they were performed at ceremonies for the completion of the annual school exams, such as the one in the town of Gabrova in 1859.[134] Apparently, that same year they were also an integral part of a large welcoming ceremony for the sultan at Saray Burnu in Istanbul. Worthy of note is the fact that 'children from the Muslim, Christian and Jewish schools' all came together to welcome, with their songs and chants, Abdülmecid back from a sea voyage.¹³⁵ Extant poetic texts from that year, if not that particular occasion, confirm the uniformity and stability of some symbolic perspectives on central authority, analysed above. Consider the following excerpts from two eulogies, which appeared in an 1859 Rum publication in Ottoman (written in the Greek alphabet):¹³⁶

> (A)
> God the Protector, let the Sublime Porte <u>shine</u> with the glory of reign!
> A thousand years to Our Lord Sultan Abdülmecid, the <u>Refuge of the Universe</u>!
> Let his sons, the princes and the light of his eyes, inherit the reign according to God's will!
> <u>Pray cheerfully for him</u>, servants of God all over <u>the universe</u>!
> . . .
> (B)
> Certainly my sultan knows
> How <u>happy</u> all the servants are.
> <u>The face of the earth</u> <u>lightens</u>
> And <u>the world</u> is <u>devoted to you</u>!
> . . .
> You are so beautiful, my Lord,
> That the souls <u>sacrifice themselves</u> for your manners!
> . . .
> With the scarlet locks of the hyacinth
> You are like the red <u>roses in the garden</u>! . . .¹³⁷

The metaphor of light ('shine', 'lightens'), the organic metaphor of the rose garden and the grand spatial order ('the face of the earth', 'the world', 'the universe' (2)), combined with the concepts of subject happiness and prayer, devotion, and even sacrifice are all eerily reminiscent of the language of Sturdza's letters of the early 1840s and Davidov's songs of the turn of the 1850s. They delineate a discourse of rulership that transcends any particular religio-cultural point of origin or framework. What is even more remarkable is the transplantation, within a decade and a half or so, of this discourse from the elite to the mass level, a move that, needless to say, would open vast opportunities for popular absorption.

New Avenues for Macro-communal Identification and Macro-territorial Attachment

Throughout the 1850s, the Bulgars began to develop a more explicit and elaborate abstract sense of communal belonging transcending any particular locale or any familiar zone of microregional real-life habitation. Following in the footsteps of sultanic celebrations, one of the major mechanisms facilitating this process was the invention and popularisation of a celebration of their own (imagined) community. On the initiative of Nayden Gerov, the same hostile observer of Abdülmecid's visit to Rusçuk in 1846, the day of St Cyril and St Methodius was marked on 11/24 May 1851 for the first time with a secular celebration at the 'St Cyril and St Methodius' school in Filibe (Plovdiv), where he taught.[138] The date was borrowed from the Christian feast of the two Byzantine theologian and missionary brothers who are credited with creating the first Slavic (Glagolithic) script in the ninth century.[139] In 1856, Yoakim Gruev,[140] a teacher, suggested that the day be marked as a holiday of the Bulgar schoolchildren. The next year, its annual celebration commenced in Istanbul, Filibe, Şumnu and Lom (in present-day Bulgaria).[141] The public prominence of educational and religious motifs in Abdülmecid's *scenario* of power made the launching of this holiday possible and acceptable. By establishing a connection to a mythic distant Slavic and Bulgar past, 11 May stimulated a sense of cultural specificity in the minds of participants, which would flourish in the 1860s, as the next chapter will demonstrate.

The process of enhancement of communal belonging was further aided by the cultivation of a new and correspondingly abstract territorial attachment. The most obvious harbinger of this shift was a change in the dominant image of the land itself. Until the mid-nineteenth century, one's relationship to the land was overwhelmingly construed from a local, microregional vantage point. This construction stemmed from lived realities where property was accumulated and perpetuated through the male line. So one's place of birth and the land nearby were overwhelmingly viewed through the prism of 'patrimony (*bashtiniya*)'. Hence, the term 'fatherland (*otechestvo*)', signifying above all one's place of birth, a sense which the 1845 *ferman*, analysed above, skilfully attempted to extend to the macro level of the entire imperial domains on the basis of the fatherly metaphor of the sultan. By the 1850s, however, both of these versions of 'fatherland' began to yield ground to an alternative (abstract, macro) concept – 'the land of the Bulgars, Bulgaria'. On the surface of it, the name alone did not set a historical precedent. In the dedication to his 1847 Almanac, mentioned above, Nayden Yoannovich had already introduced himself to his readers as, among other things, 'a book vendor across all of Slavic Bulgaria (*Slavenobolgaria*)'. Moreover, one of Davidov's poems in the Almanac about Abdülmecid's visit to Tırnova did mention the sultan's crossing of Thrace (*Trakia*) and Bulgaria (*Bolgaria*) on his way. These terms were both lacking in substance, however, and they denoted different things. The former was a loose cultural marker, referring to all the lands where Slavic Bulgar people lived. The latter was a loose geographical marker, denoting the lands north of the Balkan range (with Thrace lying to the south, respectively), which clearly contained only a fraction of all Bulgars.[142]

The new, momentous development in the 1850s was the trend towards the representation of Bulgaria as 'mother'. It strengthened the notion of a blood connection among the Bulgars, and opened the door to a more intense emotional appeal and group mobilisation via the creation of accompanying images of Bulgaria's personification and victimisation.[143] At the same time, these novel processes were also inextricably linked with the rise of axiomatic antagonistic images of 'the other' used as rallying points. Once again, the seeds of these parallel developments were sown by the cyclical popular celebrations and the syncretic discourse of sultanic power, introduced a decade or so earlier. By the late 1850s, motherly metaphors of the land, with elements indicative of the above-mentioned processes, appeared in polemic articles on the pages of Bulgar newspapers. Todor Burmov's 1859 essay, mentioned above, was one of them. Entitled 'The Feelings of the Orthodox Bulgar in the Days of Sultan Abdul-Medzhid [sic]', it was an address to God, which laid out the motherly metaphor and its attendant imagery in the following dramatic terms:

> According to Your holy will our reigning [lit. 'reigning as tsar' *tsarstvuyushtiy*] Sultan vouchsafed to have the name of our mother Bulgaria, buried for many centuries, resurrected . . . You [Bulgaria], though long held in the black heart of earth, for dead and breathless, at the slightest move cruelly confined by your spiritual sister torturer, you stayed alive, survived and rebelled in order to serve with your typical fidelity the tsar and lord (*vlastelin*), appointed by God, under your present name: BULGARIA. We, orphaned children of yours, not without tenderness, are cordially watching your troubled look; however, cheered by the generosities of our most merciful Lord, we are fully convinced that you will acquire your typical liveliness and joy, when you come fully to your senses from the subterranean sufferings, gathering under his monarchic protection your lawful children as a hen gathers its chicks under its wing (Matthew 23:37).

These lines paint the picture of a harmonious triadic relationship between the Bulgars, Bulgaria and the sultan. The intensity of Bulgaria's portrayed victimisation is startling ('buried', 'dead', 'breathless', 'cruelly confined', 'troubled', and so on). However, so are the syncretic religious, highly charged terms of the sultan's own involvement: he is instrumental in Bulgaria's resurrection, and is even placed in the same phrase with a reference to a Gospel of the New Testament! Another section from this text captures in a most succinct manner the relationship of this Bulgaria to the ruler: 'under [his] protective wing'. This expression, first mentioned in Stoyanov's 1845 address-commentary, becomes a catchphrase. It

The Reign of Abdülmecid

already appeared in identical symbolic circumstances in another polemic article several months earlier, entitled 'Which of the Living Tongues to Study'.[144] This piece also contains another novel personification, that of the Bulgar people (*narod*) as a group: 'It now resembles a young human being (*chelovek*) who for the first time enters the world'. The author, most likely the newspaper's editor, Dragan Tsankov,[145] firmly insists on the need for education so this young person can make the right choices. In his effusive enthusiasm, he speaks of Bulgar letters (*knizhnina*), even of a Bulgar natural world (*priroda*). It seems that by the following year, such practices of naming and claiming had already spilled over into the perennial songbooks. A song in one such publication, penned by another teacher, Nikola Gerov Belchev,[146] invokes the image even of 'Bulgar forests (*dubravi bulgarski*)'.[147]

The redefined close communal relationship of the Bulgars to the monarch, forged by the 1846 tour, the cultural production and celebratory practices it inspired, and the abstract communal public space/sphere these spawned, only grew stronger over the years. This relationship gradually became the central legitimating component in an increasingly politicised process of voicing communal concerns, in the crystallisation and manifestation of communal agendas, and in the clash of communal rivalries. In this sense, the textual evidence drawn from songbooks and other sources points to a direct proportional relationship between the rise of Bulgar group consciousness and the emergence and evolution of negative images of 'the other', a vital antithesis solidifying Bulgar group boundaries.

A quick look at the early sources analysed in this chapter shows that they contain few, if any, deployments of 'Bulgar' or references to a negative 'other'. The few that appear often do so in titles (Ilar Stoyanov's 1845 address-commentary), postscripts (the same source) or accompanying commentaries (Stefan Izvorski's 1846 poem) rather than in the main bodies of their respective texts.[148] For example, the 1849 open letter to the sultan identifies its authors simply as 'Turnovo residents (*turnovski zhiteli/ Turnovtsi*)'. Remarkably, despite all the changes they underwent from 1846 to 1851, Davidov's various texts make no references to 'Bulgar' whatsoever. Instead, the non-Muslim group is invariably referred to, in the customary Ottoman parlance, as 'flock (*reaya*)'. In fact, following the above-mentioned 1845 title of Stoyanov's impassioned address, the term 'Bulgar' does not appear again in any of the examined sources until 1857.[149] Terms denoting an antagonistic 'other' appear more frequently in the sense of 'enemy of the sultan', which gradually becomes identical to 'sinner'.[150] Only at the very end of the 1850s, commensurate with the rapid ascent of the image of a personified and victimised Bulgaria, does a shift in emphasis occur away from enemies of the sultan towards enemies of Bulgaria and the Bulgar people. Hence, the startling image of a 'spiritual sister torturer' in Burmov's 1859 text.[151] Dragan Tsankov's article, analysed above, contains a passage which best illustrates the mutually reinforcing evolution of Bulgar vs antagonistic 'other' terminology and rhetoric:

> the whole Bulgar people, ten centuries under Phanariot[152] yoke, begins to feel its weight. Let us repeat from the whole heart: what a precious time for the Bulgar! Our second golden age comes out from the thick darkness as the joyous nature tears away from the austerity of winter.

This excerpt charts a Bulgar-centred temporal continuum both backward ('ten centuries') and forward ('our second golden age'). The equivalent dichotomies 'winter-spring ("the joyous nature tears away")' and 'darkness-light ("golden")' give additional depth and clarity to the author's evocative vision. Finally, the elements of totalisation and unity ('the whole Bulgar people', 'the whole heart') are integral to the text's mobilising message. While occasionally present in earlier texts, usually of limited readership, by the end of Abdülmecid's reign, these motifs came to affect a much larger audience via the songbooks. The theme of education and the trope of love by and for the ruler also retained their centrality, while the distance between ruler and ruled continued to shrink. Even a conservative text such as the popular 1859 'Prayer-Song for Many Years (*Mnogoletstvie*)', which downplays group identity,[153] focusing exclusively on education (three out of six stanzas) and metaphors of light, breaks new ground in its portrayal of the sultan:

> With a strong voice he cries,
> In order to fire up a zeal (*revnost*)
> For learning in us
> And again to praise us.

This stanza assigns a more active role to the sultan vis-à-vis his Bulgar subjects than ever before. For a ruler, who until relatively recently had been neither seen nor known, to engage in this vocal ('with a strong voice he cries'), unprecedentedly reciprocal ('to praise us') and highly emotional ('to fire up a zeal') manner is an unmistakable sign of rapport with the mass of his subjects. At the same time this is also a subtle indication of a loss of status that the mystic *aura* detachment confers. What this odd poetic scenario only alluded to – the growing Bulgar group self-confidence – was fast becoming evident at the grassroots level. Here are the opening lines of Belchev's songbook published only a year later:

The Reign of Abdülmecid

Sing, oh, <u>Bulgars</u> <u>in consent</u> (*suglasno*)
Exclaim <u>all of you</u> today <u>vociferously</u> (*veleglasno*)
Glorify <u>all of you</u> the good Sultan
May he hear this song of <u>praise</u>.

From a position of marginality, the theme of unity suddenly jumps to the centre of the discourse of community. This call enjoins the Bulgars to make themselves heard, quite literally.[154] Even more fascinating in its thematic accents and overall symbolic structure is the final item in this songbook. It reproduces the 1859 *Mnogoletstvie*, with the following highly significant additions:

For many peaceful years
To our Strong Master
Sing, oh, <u>brothers</u> <u>little Bulgars</u> (*Bulgarcheta*)
<u>All of you, all of you</u> <u>in one voice</u>
Long live, long live
Tsar Abdul Medzhid [sic] Sultan
May his high Divan
<u>Shine</u> like <u>the sun</u>
May he live and <u>not spare himself in giving</u> (*da sya razdava*)
In <u>all</u> of <u>bulgaria</u> [sic] today
May <u>the Black Sea, the Danube, the Sava</u>
<u>Jump to the skies</u>
May <u>all</u> countries <u>listen</u>
May it be <u>heard across the world</u>
How our dear <u>tsar</u> <u>father</u>
Is <u>loved</u> and glorified
And you, God! Gentle God
<u>Protect</u> him with invisible <u>shield</u>
And <u>under his feet</u>
<u>All</u> his <u>enemies defeat</u>
And His <u>shining</u> <u>Diadem</u>[155]
<u>Preserve</u> Glorious and honest
<u>For as long as there are</u> in <u>the world</u>
<u>Sun, moon and stars</u>.
. . .
May he <u>overwhelm his enemies</u>[156]

This poetic sequence, which did indeed have a lasting impact, as the next chapter will demonstrate, spans the full spectrum of previously analysed motifs – the act of naming oneself and the other, the personification of Bulgaria, the cluster of fatherly tsarist, syncretic regalistic ('diadem'), light, love and cosmic/grand-spatial metaphors. In most of these aspects, however, this song goes beyond anything previously seen. The new spin on the blood connection ('brothers') and the centrality of Bulgar children ('*Bulgarcheta*') at the popular level signals a new level of group solidarity, which immediately translates into a new level of group mobilisation ('in one voice'). Despite sharing the diminutive form with its common nuance of genuine endearment, 'the little Bulgars (*Bulgarcheta*)' (1860) could not be more different from 'the serene little tsar (*hrisimo tsarche*)' (1846) as the focus of attention in a eulogy to the (same) sultan.[157] The scale of change is further accentuated by the specific territorial macro-mapping and personification of Bulgaria ('May the Black Sea, the Danube, the Sava jump to the skies'), accompanied by a parallel personification of the rest of the world ('May all countries listen'). This unusual juxtaposition draws attention for the first time to the nascent competitiveness of the 'us'-group ('May it be heard across the world') and the corresponding self-assured assertion of its own exceptionalism.

The sultan's part of the social-pact equation also undergoes substantial alterations. The old role of the antagonistic 'other', as the sultan's enemies, is still present, but it no longer takes centre stage despite the inclusion of images of defensive ('shield') or aggressive ('under his feet', 'defeat/ overwhelm enemies') militarism. If anything, this motif of belligerence acts as yet another subtle agent for group mobilisation. Not surprisingly, the sultan's aura is further diminished by the introduction of the radical notion of *sultanic sacrifice* for his subjects ('May he ... not spare himself in giving (*da sya razdava*)').

Finally, all of these developments culminate in the majestic image of a grand-spatial order ('the sun', 'sun, moon and stars'), etched into eternity ('for as long as there are in the world'), of the type first observed in the Sturdza letters about two decades earlier.[158] This cosmic re-enactment, however, takes place with a very different agenda in the background, namely with a niche carved out for the Bulgars 'under the sun'.

Conclusion

From the outset of his reign, Abdülmecid adhered closely to a number of Mahmud II's image-making policies. First, he perpetuated the ruler's high direct visibility, making it palatable to foreign and domestic audiences alike. Second, he regularised the distribution of medals and orders on sultanic occasions as symbols of prestige in a burgeoning field of open competition for royal favour. Third, he firmly established the trope of love for the ruler, broached by his father, as the mainstay of his own scenario of power. In part, he did so through sultanic tours of the type Mahmud II had embarked on. Evidence from one of them, the 1846 tour of Rumelia, perhaps the least researched, demonstrates the avenues for the creation of a lasting image of the ruler in the minds of multitudes of ordinary people, where, in most cases, none had existed before. Among them, the songs of praise and prayer, frequently tied to the discourse of Tanzimat reform, occupied a central place. With their effusive, increasingly complex metaphoric ornamentation, and standardised, repetitive, incantatory performances, the songs were converted into a powerful, large-scale medium for letting a heretofore distant ruler into the hearts and minds of his subjects across the imperial domains.

Over time, the sultan's image became subject to contradictory influences. On the one hand, its symbolism and level of abstraction grew in the direction of a personality cult; on the other, an equally powerful trend of humanising the ruler and shortening the vertical distance between him and his subjects was also at work. In this complex repetitive interplay of image, rhetoric and practice, a key factor in the creation of a modern public space/sphere, Ottoman subjects developed and reinforced new, more abstract ties of allegiance and experiences of groupness, both real and imagined. The chapter illustrated this phenomenon by dwelling on the case of the Bulgars, which is by no means unique, and the changing lyrics of their songs of praise and prayer for the sultan. It demonstrated in minute detail the ever so subtle stages of transformation of the notion of a common Ottoman fatherland, envisaged by the centre on the eve of the 1846 tour, into, in this case, a notion of a common Bulgar motherland, with its attendant images of personification, victimisation and unification vis-à-vis a negative 'other'. This transformation, the by-product of a deliberate project of mental and spiritual centralisation around the figure of the sultan, signalled a paradigm shift. This chapter revealed its opening phase; the next one completes the task. Chapter 3 culminates in an examination of the apogee of Bulgar enthusiasm for the sultan in the mid-1860s and the growing disparity between Bulgar attachments to the ruler on the one hand and the macro-community on the other, in the late 1860s and early 1870s.

Notes

1. This is a dual concept designed with an integral connection to the average person in the provinces in mind. It is a gradually evolving public space/sphere, which starts from a zero point (the ruler has no presence physically and minimal presence symbolically). Its expansion is dictated in the first place by the sultanic tours of the countryside (a major, if sporadic effect helping jumpstart the phenomenon) and then, much more significantly and

lastingly, by the annual ruler celebrations. Thus, it commences quite literally as a public space, where the people welcome the ruler or gather and organise in groups to celebrate him annually (at the town/village square or a specially designated area outside). By way of recurrence, a growing scale and a rising ritual complexity over time, these celebrations gradually tipped the balance towards a public sphere of wider boundaries of the desirable/permissible/acceptable symbolic interaction between the ruler and the ruled, which ultimately set the stage for a modern type of belonging. For a different conceptualisation of public space/sphere, based on a different notion of socialisation and social control, see Kırlı, 'Surveillance', *Publics, Politics, and Participation*. For a similar approach, see Brophy, *Popular Culture*. For the most influential formulation of a concept of public sphere, see Habermas, *The Structural Transformation of the Public Sphere*.
2. I have deliberately rendered the controversial term '*millet*' as 'community of co-religionists' – its historically accurate meaning. Today, needless to say, '*millet*' means 'nation', but such a translation, with reference to a pre/non-national past, is simply untenable. If one's starting point and way of historical conceptualisation relies on the axiom that nations are primordial entities, an exploration of the kind I attempt here would be impossible.
3. In my subsequent analysis, I purposefully avoid present-day ethnonational markers, as these were not used in a consistent, standardised manner during the period under consideration here. In the case of the Bulgar(ians), with the creation of the Principality of Bulgaria by the Congress of Berlin in the aftermath of the 1877–8 Russo-Ottoman War, what had previously been a loose religious (mainly Eastern Orthodox), linguistic (South Slavic) and cultural marker became firmly ethnic and national. Therefore, for purposes of historical accuracy, I prefer to use the term 'Bulgar' (the Ottoman designation) and 'Bulgarian' (the modern nation-state designation) with the dividing mark being the year 1878. In this vein of thought, I use the terms Rum and Greek to denote group identifications before and after modern nation-state formation, as well as without and within state borders where the frame of reference is centred on the modern Greek nation-state, formally founded in 1832.
4. As noted earlier, Rumelia is the common Ottoman name for the European part of the Empire. The vast majority of settlements the sultan visited on this particular tour are located in present-day Bulgaria.
5. *Takvim-i Vekayi*, 27 July 1839: '*icra-yi nevaziş ve iltifat-ı şahane'ye rağbet ve himmet buyurulmak hasebiyle*'.
6. '*izhar-ı kemal-ı şadi ve mefharet*'.
7. '*Musadakat*' ('mutual sincere friendship'); '*muhalasat*' ('mutual sincere friendship'); '*muhadenet*' ('mutual friendship'); '*musalemet*' ('mutual peace/reconciliation').
8. *The Times*, 14 December 1839. François d'Orléans, prince de Joinville (1818–1900) was the third son of Louis Philippe, duc d'Orléans (1773–1850)

who became king of France (1830–1848). The prince was an admiral of the French navy.
9. Ibid.
10. Ibid.
11. See HAT 1622/66.
12. Ibid., '*merasim-i tehniyet ve levazım-ı ubudiyetin ifa ve icrasına vechle*'.
13. See Zürcher, *Turkey*, p. 45, pp. 59–60, and Findley, *Turkey, Islam*, p. 97. Zürcher also mentions the Hüdavendigar and Gelibolu experiments (p. 43).
14. '*vaz ve icra buyurulmuş olan tanzimat-ı hayriye usulünce muhassıl nasb ve tayin kılınan . . .*', HAT 1424/58246.
15. Ibid., '*Gerede ve Marmara ve Tırnova ve Karamürsel ve Bandırma ve Antalya ve Adapazarı ve Zağferanbolu ve Bartın ve Lefke ve Nevrekob ve Bolu kazalarıyla İstanköy ceziresi . . .*'.
16. Ibid., '*sürur ve mefharet olarak kemal-ı teşekkür ve mahmedetle dua . . .*'.
17. Ibid., '*kelimat-ı taltifiye iradıyla memleketleri cihetine iadelerinde . . .*'.
18. On *teb'a*, see Mardin, *The Genesis of Young Ottoman Thought*, p. 189.
19. See Braude, 'Foundation Myths', in *Christians and Jews in the Ottoman Empire*, vol. 1, especially pp. 71–2.
20. Findley's textual analysis of the Gülhane decree is an exception to this pattern.
21. See Lyberatos, 'The Application of the Tanzimat', in *Power and Influence*, p. 115.
22. Ibid., pp. 113–14.
23. The above-mentioned document already contains the following organic metaphor of the community: 'we are all in common obliged, *as one body in one soul (hreostoumen oloi koinos, os en soma en mia psyhi)* . . . We are all obliged as a Body to sympathise and care for the other, as the body cares for its parts; likewise, the parts shall help and protect the Body'. I am thankful to Andreas Lyberatos for sharing his reflections and the original Greek text with me. Italics are my own.
24. '*ed'iye-yi tezayüd-ü ömür ve ikbal-ı şahane ve hüsn-ü muvaffakıyet-i padişahane tekrar ile zibzeban ihlas ve ubudiyet*', *Takvim-i Vekayi*, 27 July 1839.
25. See Redhouse, *A Turkish and English Lexicon*, p. 46 and Sami, *Kamus-i Türki*, p. 82.
26. See Eldem, *Pride and Privilege*, p. 21.
27. Ibid., pp. 66–7.
28. I.DH. 16/770 (30 June 1840).
29. Ibid.
30. This may to some degree be due to the short-lived practice of direct central tax collection (*muhassıllık*) itself, which lasted only one or two years. Yet the more fundamental reason may be the prevalent lack of proper scientific recognition and study of the intimate connection between socioeconomic and sociocultural policies in the late Ottoman Empire.

31. On the Naqshbandi sheyhs' influence on the young sultan, see Abu-Manneh, 'The Islamic Roots', *Die Welt des Islams*, 173–203.
32. Most likely, this number derived from the number of daily prayers in accordance with Muslim precepts.
33. See HAT 742/35091.
34. See I.DH. 51/2544. Even though the document dates from 7 February 1842, it most likely refers to the previous year's royal birthday celebration.
35. See A.DVN. 5/9. The document could only be approximately dated.
36. See A.MKT. 140/44 (17 July 1848).
37. Hobsbawm defined this term as follows: 'both "traditions" invented, constructed and formally instituted and those emerging in a less easily traceable manner within a brief and datable period – a matter of a few years perhaps – and establishing themselves with great rapidity'. See Hobsbawm and Ranger, *The Invention of Tradition*, p. 1. The overarching purpose of such 'invented traditions' is to legitimate the monarchy by presenting it as ancient, rooted in the natural order of things and therefore worthy of existence.
38. See I.DH. 67/3303 (23 September 1842). In a testimony to the unifying function of the event, this audience brought together both the cream of the capital's elite and 'ministers to the provinces (*taşra vüzerası*)' who happened to be in Istanbul at that time.
39. See HR.SFR.3 2/63 (28 September 1842). See also HR.SFR.3 9/72 (27 November 1844).
40. See *Takvim-i Vekayi*, 1 October 1836.
41. I.DH. 51/2544.
42. In addition to I.DH. 51/2544, see I.DH. 98/4934 (23 February 1845).
43. Turnovo in present-day Bulgaria.
44. See I.DH. 5/195 (1).
45. Ibid., '*cümle islam ve reaya kullarına zuhura gelen inşirah-ı derun ve kemal-ı mesruriyetlerimiz iktizası*'.
46. Mihail Sturdza (1795–1884) was a prince of Moldavia from 1834 to 1849. A man of liberal education, he did much for his province's internal development, from infrastructure to industry and education. In 1848, he quelled the attempted revolution without bloodshed.
47. I.HR. 7/365 (1).
48. '*mevaki-yi lazimede top ve tüfenk endahtı ve musanna fişenk şenlikleri resminin icrasıyla*'.
49. This is a traditional Near Eastern stringed musical instrument.
50. '*uğur-u şahanede zebh-i karabin ve acize ve fukaraya taksim-i nukud ve denanir*'.
51. I.HR. 28/1301 (1), '. . . birkaç gece bütün Yaş kasabası ve boyar haneleri ve esvak ve dükkan (?) ve maslahat yerleri hüner ve . . . ile tertib ve telvin olunmuş şümu ve kınadil ile münevver olarak . . .'
52. '*müeyyid min atr-ı Allah olan devlet-i aliye-yi ebedi ed-devamın bir fehva-yı asaleten sabit ve fer'a fi's-sema devhat-ı adalet sayesinde müstazıl ümem ve milel-i mütenevvi* . . .' The underlining is mine.

The Reign of Abdülmecid

53. I.HR. 7/365 (1), *'emn ve asayiş ve ezher cihet-i refah, hal ve aramiş halati istihsal ve istikmalı'*.
54. Each letter was written on a single sheet of paper.
55. Other popular attitudes towards the sultan, such as submission, humility and reverence, are also tinged with joy and piety.
56. I.HR. 7/365 (1), *'destkeşa . . . da'vatına muvazebet ile can ü gönülden husul-u umniyye-yi hayriyeye muntazır ve nigeran'*.
57. Ibid., *'hasbel'ubudiyet kemal-ı ta'zim ve behcet ile buside leb-i ibtihal ve nihade sürr-ü inqıyad iştimal kılındıktan sonra mazamin-i inayetrehin-i münifesi ala mayelik'*.
58. See I.HR. 7/365 (3).
59. I.HR. 28/1301 (2), *'icra-ı lazime-i tebrik ve tehniyet ve ifa-ı vacibet-i ubudiyet'*.
60. *'hunna levazim-i şan ve şükuh saltanatı ifaye . . .'*, I.HR. 7/365 (1) vs *'levazim-i şan ve şükuh saltanatı icraya'*, I.HR. 28/1301 (1).
61. I.HR. 7/365 (1), *'sagir ü kebirden isticlab-ı da'vat-ı hayriyeye müsaraat kılındığı'*.
62. Ibid., *'uyun ve kulub-u ibad-ı sadakat-ı i'tiyad aleddevam reviş ve mesru buyurulmak'*
63. Ibid. *'ed'iye-i mefruzesi tekrar alettekrar riqqat-ı kalb ve eşk-i sürur ile an samim el bal <u>merfu icabetgah</u>-ı cenab-ı rab el-müteal kılındıgı'*. Underlining is my own.
64. I.HR. 28/1301 (1), *'ed'iye-i hayriyesi akdem feraiz-i ubudiyetten ittihaz kılınarak an samim el bal ve kemal-ı huzu ve ibtihal ile berdaşte kabulgah-ı cenab-ı rab el-müteal kılındıgı'*. The underlining is mine.
65. This is a loose umbrella term for the various dialects spoken and written before the creation and codification of a formal Bulgarian literary language following the establishment of a modern Bulgarian nation-state.
66. I have not been able to locate the Ottoman original, but in this case, the translation seems to be even more important, since it was the chief medium for direct impact on the target subject audience.
67. Numbers in parentheses hereafter refer to the frequency with which certain words and phrases appear in the text.
68. 13 January 1845 (N.S.). The text of the edict and that of the address-commentary can be found in Georgov, *Sbornik za Narodni Umotvoreniya*.
69. Lyberatos has demonstrated the use of a very similar sultanic title – *'anax gen. anaktos* (king)' – in the case of the Hellene-minded Rum of Filibe (Plovdiv) as early as 1841. See Lyberatos, 'The Application of the Tanzimat', p. 115.
70. The abbreviation *'sv'*, which stands for *'sveti'* (holy) is identical to the one preceding the names of Christian saints in modern Bulgarian.
71. Unless otherwise specified, the capitalisation and punctuation are in accordance with the original.
72. Worthy of note is the larger font of the decree's title, here faithfully reproduced, which is superior to any other in the text, including the sultan's own.

73. Ilarion Stoyanov (later, Makariopolski) (1812–75) was a Bulgar priest and leader of the Bulgar community in Istanbul.
74. Nikola Tupchileshtov (1817–95) was an affluent Bulgar merchant and a leader of the Bulgar community in Istanbul.
75. To date, I have only been able to locate a Bulgar translation of the text of the speech.
76. Apparently, this was also a central motif behind the sultan's tour of Crete that same year. See Karateke's 'From Divine Ruler to Modern Monarch', *Comparing Empires*, p. 293.
77. All of these towns are situated in present-day Bulgaria.
78. In Gabrova, the rehearsals, led by the Metropolitan of Tırnova's chief cantor, lasted for several days prior to the sultan's arrival. See Burmov, *Spomenite Mi*, p. 22.
79. Hristo Stambolski (1843–1932) later became a professor of anatomy and histology at the Imperial Medical School in Istanbul, as well as an important figure in the affairs of the Bulgar community of Istanbul. After 1878, he settled in Eastern Rumelia (present-day South Bulgaria), where he became a successful politician.
80. See Stambolski, *Avtobiografiya*, p. 31.
81. This took place in Kızanlık, Gabrova, Tırnova, Rusçuk and probably elsewhere. See Stambolski, *Avtobiografia*, p. 31; Burmov, *Spomenite Mi*, p. 23; Gerov, 'Dnevnitsi', in *Vuzrozhdenski Putepisi*, p. 72.
82. See Gerov, 'Dnevnitsi', p. 72.
83. Todor Burmov (1834–1906) was a Bulgar teacher, journalist and intellectual, later a Bulgarian politician and the first prime minister of Bulgaria.
84. Burmov, *Spomenite Mi*, p. 23.
85. Nayden Gerov (1823–1900) was a Bulgar teacher, ethnographer, writer, book publisher and, later, Bulgarian lexicographer.
86. This description is based on Gerov, 'Dnevnitsi', pp. 67–70.
87. The word '*samodurzhets*' at that time had little, if any, of the negative associations the word 'autocrat' instantly conjures up today. Instead, as its constituent morphemes suggest, it signified a ruler of an independent state.
88. Ibid., p. 70.
89. See Stambolski, *Avtobiografia*, p. 31.
90. Hadzhi Nayden Yoannovich (1805–62) was a Bulgar poet, publisher and travelling book salesman.
91. Yoannovich, *Novi Bulgarski pesni*, p. 4. The hymn's author was Penyo Davidov (1799?–1860), head teacher in Tırnova. See Kisimov, *Moite Spomeni*, pp. 30–1.
92. Here is an excerpt: 'May trade be free everywhere . . . and the tax with good measure; may life be lived with a fear of God, without difference among persons and faiths, and may all people be equal before the law . . . may everyone keep his father's faith, without changing it by force . . .'
93. '*vo vremeto na svetleyshago, krotchayshago, mirolyubiveyshago i milostiveyshago . . . Tsarya i Samoderzhtsa*'.

The Reign of Abdülmecid

94. The exact circumstances of this major transformation have yet to be clarified. It remains unclear whether there was an explicit order to this effect from the Ottoman centre or whether the initiative came from below in the aftermath of the Gülhane Decree. One way or another, as this chapter and the next one demonstrate, this new discourse of the ruler gained prominence in the mid-1840s and lasted for several decades thereafter.
95. *Tsarigradski Vestnik*, 5 November 1849. The text is signed 'P.D.', most likely the initials of the above-mentioned Penyo Davidov. 'Tsar City' (Tsarigrad) is still a widespread nickname for Istanbul in modern Bulgarian and other Slavic languages. Ironically, it seems to have outlived its Ottoman counterparts – Dersaadet, Asitane and others.
96. '*ot obich i goreshto zhelanie za mirut i dobriy pominok na poddannitsite si . . .*'.
97. *Almanac or Calendar for the Year 1847*. Perhaps in an intended gesture of added solemnity, both this publication and the 1851 songbook were printed in old Church Slavonic letters, as if these were liturgical texts. Such was also the case with Stoyanov's 1845 edict translation and address-commentary.
98. The notable lack of punctuation is in accordance with the original.
99. The Balkan folk practice of '*kurban*' in Bulgarian and '*kourbania*' (in Greek), from the Hebrew '*qorban*', survives today. Its roots remain contentious. Whether it originated in pagan times or not, Muslims and Christians alike shared this ritual, perhaps with overlapping justification. For a lengthy discussion on this topic, see McClelland, 'Sacrifice, Scapegoat, Vampire'.
100. The diminutive form '*tsarche*' can be literally rendered as 'tsarlet' or 'little tsar'. For a moment one might suspect this of being a derogatory term, yet the author's intention here is clearly different. This diminutive form was probably justified by the sultan's young age (twenty-three in 1846) and it shows fondness for the ruler, the sort of gentle attitude one would normally exhibit to a youngster.
101. For the purposes of this study, I define 'syncretic' as follows: of a mixed nature, combining heterogeneous, potentially conflicting elements into a seamless harmonious whole.
102. Serene (*krotuk*) as a lamb
    Upon its birth
    Strong as an aslant (a profanation of the Ottoman Turkish word '*aslan*' (lion)).
103. For the purposes of this study, I define 'personality cult' as follows: a set of ritual practices and attendant rhetoric signifying an extreme power/status differential between the celebrant/ruled/subject and the celebrated/ruler/object channelled through acts of homage, related to the object's body and persona, especially in his absence, and involving higher degrees of creative abstraction over time.
104. Interestingly, throughout the song there are more references to Abdülmecid as 'tsar' (7) than 'sultan' (6, including the title).

Ruler Visibility and Popular Belonging

105. See Chapter 4.
106. 'May God continue (his) days
And upon us bestow him'.
107. It is worthy of note that this text lacks explicitly/exclusively Christian or Muslim markers of faith.
108. As evidence of the type evaluated here, which was long conveniently ignored and/or suppressed by national(ist) historiographies, re-surfaces, future research will allow a more complex, multi-communal evaluation of this, in my view, landmark sultanic tour. At present, I have no reason to believe that the effects studied here did not influence all Rumelian non-Muslims in similar ways and with similar force.
109. Konstantin Fotinov (1790–1858) was a Bulgar literary man, educator, journalist and translator.
110. Stefan Popnikolov Izvorski (1815–75) was a Bulgar teacher, poet and priest.
111. *Lyuboslovie* ('Love of Words', a literal translation of 'philology'), June 1846, p. 85. Interestingly, this magazine ceased publication a few months later due to, in the words of its editor, K. Fotinov, 'a listless popular commitment (*narodna sklonnost neuserdna)*'. See its last issue, dated December 1846.
112. Ibid., August 1846, p. 125.
113. '*I tamo peyaha na Tsaria pesn' spored Angliyska Ts. pesn', koia nachnuvashe taka: "Tsaria nashego Abdul Medzhida spasi Bozhe"*' (original capitalisation), *Lyuboslovie*, June 1846, p. 85.
114. Note that the third occurrence of 'tsar' here refers to the English Queen (Victoria).
115. The first Bulgar newspaper, *Bulgarski Orel*, edited by Ivan Bogorov (1820–92), appeared in 1846–7 abroad (Leipzig), for only three issues.
116. *Tsarigradski Vestnik* was a Bulgar weekly newspaper published in Istanbul by Ivan Bogorov, Alexander Exarch (1810–91) and Todor Burmov. It was the longest running (1848–62) and arguably the most influential Bulgar newspaper.
117. See *Tsarigradski Vestnik*, 12 May 1851 and 13 January 1851, respectively.
118. Ibid., 19 July 1851.
119. Ibid., 31 March 1851 and 16 June 1851, respectively.
120. '*Tishaishago, Krotchaishago, i Blagoutrobneishago Tsaria Sultan Abdul Medzhida, Bozhe sohrani na mnogaia leta*', *Tsarigradski Vestnik*, 12 July 1851.
121. Ibid., 19 July 1851.
122. Ibid., 13 January 1851.
123. Ibid., 19 May 1851 and 18 August 1851.
124. Ibid., 13 January 1851 and 12 May 1851, respectively.
125. Ibid., 19 July 1851.
126. This is yet another piece of regalia, shared by Muslim and Christian cultural systems.

The Reign of Abdülmecid

127. *Tsarigradski Vestnik*, 18 August 1851.
128. See the analysis of the 1846 version of Davidov's text above.
129. Whereas in English, the word 'lord' may refer to both God and an earthly ruler, Bulgar has words for both God/Lord (*gospod*) and ruler/lord (*gospodar*). In this case, both are employed.
130. Spas Zafirov (?–1885) and Tsani Zhelev (1828–1907) were Bulgar teachers. Curiously, the songbook was entitled 'Bulgar Rebec' (*Blugarska Gusla*).
131. Addendum to *Tsarigradski Vestnik*, 29 August 1859. The songwriter is anonymous.
132. Ibid., 24 October 1859. Capitalisation is original; italics are mine. The author's initials – 'T.S.B.' – most likely point to Todor Stoyanov Burmov. This is the same Todor Burmov who, at the age of twelve, had witnessed Abdülmecid's 1846 tour in his hometown of Gabrova, and was inspired by the grandeur of the sultan's retinue and procession to go and study in Istanbul, which he indeed accomplished.
133. Vazov, *Subrani Suchinenia*, p. 356. I wish to thank Nadezhda Alexandrova for procuring a copy of this speech for me.
134. *Tsarigradski Vestnik*, 18 July 1859.
135. Ibid., 25 July 1859. Most likely, the voyage in question was Sultan Abdülmecid's five-day visit in late July 1859 to Selanik (Thessaloniki in present-day Greece) where he was greeted by all local communities in much the same manner as Bulgars had welcomed him in 1846. For a memoir containing a detailed description of the welcoming ceremonies as well as songs of praise and prayer for the sultan, composed by the author, Penyo Davidov's Jewish counterpart in Selanik, see Halevi et al., *A Jewish Voice*, pp. 68–76, 142–8.
136. Cf. the cyrillicised Ottoman prayer from Yoannovich's 1851 book.
137. Sia Anagnostopoulou and Matthias Kappler first translated these texts. See the Appendix of their article 'Bin Yaşa Padişahımız!', *Archivum Ottomanicum*, pp. 70–1. The above translations have only minor stylistic alterations.
138. One of the earliest sources documenting the event is Rilsky's *Hristomatia*.
139. St Cyril the Philosopher (826–69 CE) and St Methodius of Thessaloniki (815–85 CE). For their symbolic significance in the modern Balkan context, see Rohdewald, 'Nationale Identitäten', in *Beyond the Balkans*, pp. 357–76.
140. Yoakim Gruev (1828–1912) was a Bulgar educator, pedagogue and translator. Later, he became a member of the Bulgarian Literary Society (today, the Bulgarian Academy of Sciences) as well as a politician in South Bulgaria.
141. Radev, *History of the Bulgarian Literature*, p. 208.
142. This was a traditional usage, based on the geographical heartland and base of expansion of the first (681–1018 CE) and second (1185–1396 CE) Bulgar kingdoms. In the West, this term survived the Ottoman expansion and the end of the second Bulgar kingdom, appearing on Western maps throughout the entire period leading up to the nineteenth century.

143. Interestingly, 'fatherland' was never personified.
144. *Bulgaria*, 6 May 1859. *Bulgaria* was 'A Newspaper for the Bulgar Interests', which was published several times a week in Istanbul from 1859 to 1863.
145. Dragan Tsankov (1828–1911) was at the time a Bulgar journalist and public intellectual. He later became a Bulgarian politician and served twice as prime minister of Bulgaria.
146. Nikola Gerov Belchev (?–1876) was a Bulgar teacher and priest. He was later sentenced to death and executed by the Ottoman authorities for his participation in the 1876 April Revolt.
147. Belchev, *Pesnopoyche*.
148. The memoirs relating the 1846 tour are a different story, but they were published much later, with the editing process probably including anachronistic acts of (sub)conscious 'auto-nationalisation'.
149. Zafirov and Zhelev's songbook contains references such as 'the Bulgar' (*Blugarina*) and 'the Bulgar tribe' (*blugarskoto plemia*). Note the lack of standardisation of the term – *Slavenobolgaria, bulgar, blugar* – were all legitimately deployed.
150. Izvorski's 1846 poem contains the following reference to the sultan: 'Tsar and Master over all enemies'. Less than two months later, the students' song at the annual school exams in Şumnu reiterated this line, and added another one – 'Long live the true champion over enemies'. On the enemy as 'sinner', see the last four poetic lines on p. 71.
151. See the passage on p. 80. The 'spiritual sister torturer' in this case is the group of the Helene-minded Rum, whose members dominated the Rum Orthodox church hierarchy in the Ottoman Empire, continuously denying the Bulgars a separate church organisation. In 1860, this conflict reached boiling point when the Ecumenical Patriarch's name was not mentioned during Easter services at the St Stephen Church in Istanbul, but it would be another ten years before the Bulgars were formally granted the right of a separate ecclesiastical institution.
152. This is a synonym for the Helene-minded Rum, derived from the district of Phanar, their powerbase in Istanbul.
153. This text never calls the Bulgars by name and contains no markers for totalisation or unity whatsoever.
154. The next four lines, which complete the stanza, contain two more repetitions of the address form 'all of you' (*vsi*).
155. A diadem is a piece of Roman (and, later, Byzantine Christian) regalia, which had no Ottoman equivalent.
156. Capitalisations are in accordance with the original.
157. See p. 66 and endnote 100.
158. See p. 54.

3

Further Stimuli for and Patterns of *Millet* Accentuation and Differentiation: the Reign of Abdülaziz (1861–76)

The Accession of Abdülaziz in the Provinces and the Capital

On 14/26 June 1861 Abdülmecid passed away and his brother Abdülaziz rose to the Ottoman throne. The accession of Abdülaziz was celebrated on an unprecedented scale both in the capital and across the Empire's far-flung provinces. A closer look at some of these celebrations, detailed in archival reports and on the pages of newspapers from the period, shows a remarkable degree of continuity from the previous reign. What is more intriguing and significant is the even higher level of communal engagement in a ceremony which was more complex and had a correspondingly higher degree of organisation and coordination than ever. Here is an example from Sivas, a medium-sized town in east-central Anatolia where 'a welcoming ceremony and stipulations of honour and respect (*merasim-i istikbal ve şerayit-i ta'zim ve ibcal*)', occasioned by the news of the accession, took place. It drew various groups of schoolchildren, both Muslim and Christian, along with their teachers, to a vast open plain outside the town called Kabak Square.[1] The multitude gathered there included everyone from commoners to regional notables, council members and district heads. In addition, Armenian bishops and monks as well as *millet* notables (*mu'teberan-ı millet*) and elders were in the crowd.[2] Finally, mounted police, regular imperial troops and a band of musicians were also present.

The ceremony commenced with much pomp at a carefully chosen auspicious time and with the district governor (*mutasarrıf*) at the head. A seat of honour (*kürsi*) was placed before numerous pitched tents. Above it, the substitute judge (*naib efendi*), standing up, read, 'in perfect observance of custom (*kemal-ı adab ile*)', the sublime decree announcing the new accession. The empty seat of honour probably stood for the absent sultan. As Douglas Brookes has shown, according to Turkic royal mythology, the throne signified power by way of distinguishing the one sitting on it in a group setting in which everyone else stood up.[3] So this ceremonial

Ruler Visibility and Popular Belonging

Figure 3.1 Photograph of Sultan Abdülaziz (partially painted in oil) by anonymous author (Viçhen Abdullah?). Ayşe Orbay, *The Sultan's Portrait: Picturing the House of Osman* (Istanbul: Iş Bank, 2000), p. 525.

element, the only one of its kind so far identified, may point to a higher degree of abstraction in the provincials' experience of the ruler. According to this logic, a simple seat of honour would be enough for everyone's imagination to recreate a higher, hypothetical scene in the presence of the monarch and thus establish a temporary but vivid connection to the centre of power.

The Reign of Abdülaziz

Here is an account of the reaction this ceremony elicited from the local Muslim spiritual leadership:

> Present there and listening, with delight and just pride, the eminent ulema and exalted dervishes, on behalf of the esteemed sheikhs, with <u>conviction</u> and <u>sincerity of heart</u>, God's omnipotence as <u>the exalted site of acceptance (of prayers)</u> by the divine consummate greatness, performed a prayer for the enduring everlasting continuation of the days of life and might of His Majesty the Padishah . . .

This passage highlights some continuities between the two reigns in the rhetoric of power and the acts of popular appeal for divine intercession in its name. About twenty years after Abdülmecid's accession and Mikhail Sturdza's letters, two of the terms of emotional bonding to the ruler remained the same – 'sincerity of heart (*ihlas*)' and 'conviction (*sıdk*)'. So did the abstract visualisation of 'an exalted site of acceptance (of prayers) (*berdaşte icabetgah*)'. Moreover, these terms remained constant irrespective of the subject-supplicant's age or religious affiliation. In 1861 Sivas, the Muslim and Christian schoolchildren had the same 'sincerity of heart (*hulus el-kalb*)' and raised their 'Amen (*amin*)' to 'God's site of acceptance (of prayers) (*icabetgah-ı hüda*)'.[4] As before, the object of these popular manifestations of devotion to the ruler was 'the sublime heart's desire (*dilhah–ı ali*)'.[5]

One of the most obvious novelties compared to Abdülmecid's reign was the public's compliance with higher standards of discipline and order in 1861. Not only were the classes of Muslim and non-Muslim subjects arranged in lines, but public criers (*münadiler*), dispersed among them, directed the waves of popular acclamation. In recognition of the emotional sublimity of this sight, the report's author compared the crowds to 'the surge of the Assyrian sea (*mevc-i derya-ı asuri*)'. This grand-spatial metaphor also seems to be a novel usage. More remarkable still is the fact that it is centred on the people rather than the ruler or the dynasty. What this metaphor conveys is a newfound wonder at the power to assemble and control the crowds, the power of a modern state. This power was further manifest in a military review of the imperial troops and the band, which coincided with 'a great prayer of "Long Live the Sultan" (*büyük büyük padişahım çok yaşa duası*)'. Against the background of this sequence of well-choreographed and well-timed ceremonial motions, the themes of unity and totality that first surfaced in Abdülmecid's latter years only become more pronounced. The Sivas report emphasised unity in at least two ways. First, it stressed the synchronous recitation of the prayer for the sultan by adults and children alike, irrespective of faith. The former did so 'from one mouth (*bir agızdan*)', the latter 'in one voice (*yekzeban*)'. Second, the report also emphasised the strength of the crowds' chanting. Once again, both adults and children acted alike. As the former uttered the prayer 'with a loud voice (*avaz-ı belend ile*)', so the latter produced their 'reverberating Amen (*zemzeme amini*)'. When everyone present had performed 'the obligation of gratitude (*vecibe-yi teşekkuri*)', all returned to their quarters. That night the candle illuminations were limited to the imperial barracks and the government building only. This exclusive focus probably intended to elevate the status of the military and civilian administrations as the two main pillars of the Ottoman state. For the following three days and nights, the entire population of Sivas partook of the candle illuminations. The exact manner in which the author of the report conveyed the sense of everyone's involvement is worth pointing out: 'Muslims and non-Muslims, and all the rich and poor, and the other classes (*müslim ve re'aya ve kaffe-i bay ü geda ve esnaf-ı saire*)'. Despite the earlier usage of *millet* with reference to non-Muslims, here the author reverted to the traditional word for non-Muslims – '*re'aya*'. It is quite likely that both were in public use at this time, perhaps interchangeably. What is also interesting is that this phrase describing the local Ottoman subjecthood totalises it for the first time based on class. Further analysis of ceremonial settings dating from this period will shed light on the significance of this novelty.

Apparently, accession celebrations across the Dardanelles, in Rumelia, were no less impressive. The extant descriptions create the impression of a nascent standardisation of protocol. For example, a report from Samakov (Samokov in present-day Bulgaria) confirms the enforcement of three-day popular illuminations (only without setting military and civilian institutions apart).[6] A report from Sofya (Sofia in present-day Bulgaria) shows that a public crier (*glashatay*) announced the accession there, enjoining all communities – Muslims, Bulgars and Jews – to the main town square for the reading of the imperial decree.[7] In Sofya, as in Sivas, schoolchildren from all communities 'cried out vociferously (*vyikaha gromoglasno*)' their 'Amen' for the sultan. In both of these locales, the imperial troops were present and the military bands played. Garrison cannons across major towns of the Empire invariably roared their twenty-one-gun salutes. Provincial correspondents of Bulgar newspapers also reflected the emotional sublimity felt by their fellow townsmen in similar ways. Compare the following two excerpts from Sofya and Tırnova reports, respectively:

> Bulgar Brothers! Hereby commences an even brighter epoch for the future (budnina) of our people (*narod*), because our new tsar-father . . . will turn his

fatherly eye to our dear little kin (*rodets*) as well . . . and will condescend to pour his sublime mercy over us, Bulgars . . .⁸

Dear Mr. Editor, I cannot describe to you the feeling (*chuvstvovanieto*) of the gathered people (*narod*). It was a true exultation (*edno tselo torzhestvo*).⁹

These heartfelt addresses clearly inherit many long-standing elements of the Abdülmecidian discourse of power – the tsarist title, the metaphors of light and fatherhood, the images of a visual exchange between ruler and ruled ('his fatherly eye') and a sultanic outpouring of mercy onto the Bulgars. In addition, they absorb some much more recent innovations, such as the identification of a communal Bulgar 'feeling' and 'brotherhood'. As a result, these addresses point towards a new conceptual stage. The ever more frequent transplantation of terms, such as 'kin (*rod*)' and 'people (*narod*)', from their native local/regional settings onto an imaginary macro canvas of Bulgar-ness, signals the rise of a putative blood connection as the basis for an abstract macro belonging. Even more fascinating is the practice, evident in the first passage, of placing one's imagined macro community within a temporal continuum which is sanctified. Unlike the common Bulgar word for 'future' (*budeshte*), the word '*budnina*' is tinged with a solemn poignancy. It carries the notion of a fateful unfolding and would best be rendered in English as 'times to come'. The use of the word 'epoch' (*epoha*) with its legendary connotations lends further support to such speculations.

Beyond the increasingly standardised protocol and the rhetorical accretions, there was still room for local variation and improvisation. In Samakov, uninhibited popular celebrations dominated the scene: 'Everywhere bagpipes, rebecs (*kemencheta*), songs played, at every bazaar [people] danced the horo'.¹⁰ In Tırnova, on the other hand, the news of Abdülmecid's death and Abdülaziz's accession led the Bulgars to 'pay their last respects to their late Tsar and protector'.¹¹ That day all shops and other commercial establishments closed in remembrance of the deceased sultan. In the evening, the town churches' clappers¹² sounded as they would for a funeral. The following morning, a special dual commemorative-cum-congratulatory service was held in the Holy Mother of God (*Sveta Bogoroditsa*), the town church. The churchwardens, along with the entire clergy, led holy services. After the Gospel, they announced in a short speech the reason for this 'extraordinary holiday (*izvunreden praznik*)'. Afterwards, a teacher (I. Shivarov) delivered a speech to the congregation, laced with startling Christian eschatological motifs:

Let us offer warm prayers to the almighty for the pacification (*upokoenie*) of the soul of our blissfully resting (*blazhenopochivsh*) Autocrat in the dwellings of the righteous (*zhilishtata na pravednite*), in eternal and unending bliss and let us say: May God pacify [his soul] in the Tsardom of heaven (*Tsarstvo nebesi*).

This is the most remarkable syncretic inclusion of the sultan, a Muslim ruler, into the moral universe of his devout Bulgar Christian subjects.[13] The solemnity of this act is further underscored by the predominant use of Old Church Slavonic, the sacred language of Slavic Orthodox liturgy. In addition to the higher-register language of this passage, towards the end the speech encourages the congregation to pray 'so that God may safeguard him [the sultan] as the apple of one's eye (*yako zenitsu oka*)'. This is yet another peculiar reference signifying an intimate embrace of the ruler. The most impressive aspect of the above passage, however, is the symbolic action it relates – the sultan's entrance into heaven as if he were a veritable Christian tsar.

The latter part of the teacher's speech turned the audience's attention to the accession of Abdülaziz. Shivarov encouraged his fellow townsmen to turn to the new sultan 'unanimously [lit. "with one soul"] and with love (*edinodushno i s lyubov*)'. This expression combined the theme of unity with the trope of love. The latter was instantly transferred to the new reign and registered as a natural expectation from the new ruler. Shivarov also invited his listeners to 'pin their hopes' on the new ruler 'by showing most clearly [their] zeal (*revnost*) and devotion to his throne'. What had begun as zeal to popularise the will of the ruler in 1845 then became zeal for education, pronounced throughout Abdülmecid's reign and captured in an 1859 song. Here, in 1861, it was undergoing yet another transformation into zeal for the Ottoman state.

The spontaneous Bulgar Christian ceremony of remembrance of the late sultan and celebration of the newly installed one culminated in a performance of 'the song for many years of the new Tsar Sultan Abdul Aziz' by schoolchildren, lined up on both sides of the congregation, joined by the priests from the altar. As the author of the report put it, the Bulgar people did this 'out of their own volition, as grateful sons to their father, as faithful subjects of the state'. As he wrote this, he pointed in passing, not without satisfaction, that the Bulgars did all this without having among their ranks a certain Grigor, 'the Phanariot hornet'. This spiteful remark hints at a major theme underwriting most, if not all of these Bulgar celebrations – the theme of the communal 'negative other', the Hellenised Rum. It was present in the Sofya report and even more so in reports about the Bulgar celebration in the imperial capital, where the largest and most vocal Bulgar community resided.

In Istanbul, the Bulgars took advantage of their church's favourable location in the Balat quarter on the Golden Horn. So for the day of Abdülaziz's sword girding they prepared a special ceremony to honour the sultan during his passage to Eyüp, further up the Golden Horn where the investiture ceremony traditionally took place. The church-wardens erected two columns, draped in white cloth, connected by an iron semi-circle on top that was decked with flowers and greenery. These columns supported three marble slates with Ottoman writing in gold, which read: 'May Our Sultan Abdülaziz Live for a Thousand Years!'.[14] In the shadow of this decorative arch stood the Bulgar clergy in their Sunday best. Lined up on both sides were schoolchildren dressed in white, along with acolytes. The ceremonial roar of the cannons announcing Abdülaziz's departure for Eyüp drew the attention of the numerous crowds gathered on the church grounds. Five minutes later, the sultan was greeted by the navy personnel from the imperial fleet stationed on the Golden Horn. When the sultan approached the Bulgar church, the acolytes and the students began to sing a song, specially composed for the occasion, accompanied by the loud cheering of the crowds. While passing, the sultan's attention was drawn by this 'popular ceremony (*narodna tseremoniya*)', and he returned the greeting by ordering his thirteen rowers to hoist their oars in the air. The Bulgar clergy bowed and the people cried out in the midst of the imperial batteries' continuing thunderous salvos.

This ceremonial description, distilled from several extant sources, is centred on an article from *Dunavski Lebed*. Its author, Yosif Daynelov,[15] interspersed his narrative with snapshots of the collective communal excitement at the opportunity to engage, however fleetingly, with the ruler. These range in focus, intensity, and scope. In terms of focus, organic metonymies, such as 'Bulgar heart(s)' (4) and 'Bulgar soul' (2) dominate the article. In terms of intensity, one notices the progression from 'Bulgar feeling' (1) to 'Bulgar joy' (1) to 'Bulgar fervour (*plamennost*)' (1). In terms of scope, the gamut runs from 'extreme Bulgar esteem (*pochitanie*) for the sultan' (1) to 'the wide horizon of Bulgarness (*bulgarshtina*)' (1). In all, there are eighteen such markers, where few or none had appeared in pieces of similar content just a decade earlier. Scattered throughout the text are signs of the Bulgars' emergent communal agenda:

> On this important day our <u>people of the one/same kin</u> (*ednorodtsi*) wished to <u>distinguish themselves</u> as always by <u>their great devotion to the throne</u> . . . This [the church's location] the Bulgars considered a good fortune for the expression, from close quarters, of <u>their feelings for their tsar</u> . . . This very charming decoration was perfect in its execution, and <u>unique in its existence</u>, since <u>only the Bulgar people</u> resorted to such a beautiful expression of <u>their love for their master</u> . . . And let's be glad that we could <u>pour our devotion</u> before <u>the eyes</u> of

<u>our very own</u> Sultan, and at the same time hope that H.I.M.[16] will not tolerate at all <u>the oppression and mistreatment</u> of the <u>Bulgar people</u>.

The term '*ednorodtsi*', centred on the blood connection, quite common in the private correspondence of Bulgar intellectuals, captures the communal spirit in a much more credible fashion here.[17] However, this passage goes beyond the limits of a particular term and provides some of the texture of the communal experience as a whole. It allows a rare glimpse into the mechanism that transformed a sultanic ceremonial occasion into an occasion for communal self-celebration. Finally, this passage also conveys the workings of embryonic concepts, which would soon become entrenched as permanent features of the ethnonational mental universe – the group's competitive spirit, leading to a sense of superiority and uniqueness vis-à-vis other groups, and, in a parallel line of expansion, the group's perception of its own victimisation, used as a rallying point. Not surprisingly, the article's very next sentence suggests that the Bulgar representatives in Istanbul should act with 'patriotic audacity (*patrioticheska derzost*)'. This is the earliest appearance to date of this West-imported word in a ceremonial setting. A quick look at the other accounts of the Bulgar celebration in Istanbul reveals that the communal agenda, analysed above, was not a mere figment of this particular author's imagination. One of them even went a step further and added an element of sacrality by characterising the communal celebration as a 'sign of the Bulgar awe [lit. "awe of God (*bogogovenie*)"] of the throne'.[18] In addition to the short-run impulse of ceremonial events themselves, such strong terms were also made possible by the syncretic long-term thread, traced in the last two chapters. If Abdülmecid had become 'tsar' in the mid-1840s, gradually acquiring proper Christian (imaginary, not necessarily real) regalia, as explained earlier, the rise of Abdülaziz to power in 1861 created perfect conditions for the further enhancement of the sultanic portrait in the minds of Bulgar subjects. In consequence, the Bulgar press presented the new accession as an act of 'becoming tsar (*vutsariavanie*)' and the Ottoman Muslim investiture ceremony of sword girding as its universal Christian counterpart, a coronation (*koroniasvanie*; *koronovanie*).[19] Thus far the practice does not seem so unusual, given that many Western travellers depicted the sword girding, otherwise utterly incomprehensible to their home audiences, in identical ways. What is highly unusual, however, is the creative reconstruction of the extremely private sword-girding ceremony in a different issue of *Dunavski Lebed*: '[Sultan Abdülaziz] who was even solemnly crowned [lit. "married to tsardom"] . . . at the Eyüp Mosque, in this case girding the sword of Osman, and with the flag of the Prophet in his left hand swore on the Qur'an, which was offered him by the Sheyhulislam'.[20] This fascinating syncretic excerpt clearly does not describe truthfully what transpired behind closed doors in Eyüp.[21] As a matter of fact, Abdülaziz did not gird the sword of Osman, but caliph Umar's; he did not hold the flag of the Prophet in his left hand, and there was no transaction between him and the şeyhülislam involving the Qur'an. What the passage does do successfully is explain the sacred procedure to which a mere handful of top-echelon Ottoman statesmen were privy to a loyal Christian audience eager to know about it, using a frame of reference familiar to them.[22] Ironically, this frame of reference has contemporary Russian tsarist overtones. 'A marriage to tsardom (*venchanie na tsarstvo*)', a concept entirely absent from the Ottoman symbolic system, was clearly imported from Alexander II's coronation in Russia five years earlier, which was copiously reflected in the Bulgar press too.[23] As for the flag of the Prophet and the Qur'an, their symbolic function in this description of an investiture ceremony is identical to that of a gonfalon or a flag of a sovereign Christian state and the Bible. This creative 'Ottomanisation' of an essentially Western ritual of public swearing an oath of office still in use today adds new brush strokes to the picture of changing popular (in this case, non-Muslim) perceptions of central Ottoman authority pointing to a more informed and expectant public.

The Standardisation of Annual Royal Accession and Birthday Celebrations

Several months into the new sultan's reign, the decision to celebrate the royal accession day and royal birthday on a regular basis as public holidays was announced.[24] According to Ahmet Cevdet Pasha, a leading late Ottoman statesman and historian, this was Fuad Pasha's decision.[25] The goal was to gain ceremonial reciprocity with the West in the aftermath of the Ottoman Empire's inclusion into the Concert of Europe.[26] As Cevdet Pasha pointed out, this goal had heretofore eluded the Ottomans, since theirs were religious holidays.[27] What this meant was a difference in calendars – the Western holidays were fixed to particular solar dates whereas the Ottoman lunar-calendar dates had solar equivalents that shifted from year to year, thus making it impossible for Westerners to keep track. As explained earlier, despite Mahmud II's best efforts to implement the solar calendar from the outset of annual Ottoman royal accession and birthday celebrations in 1836, the undertaking remained a short-lived experiment. For reasons not entirely clear, Abdülmecid did not achieve this either. Domestic resistance must have been strong, since even in 1861, with the lasting regularisation of these holidays, the shift was not complete – it affected the accession but not the royal birthday, which continued to be celebrated in the Muslim (lunar) calendar.

Over the course of the next few years, the annual sultanic celebrations grew, though their timing remained inconsistent. In Halep (Aleppo in present-day Syria), the first accession anniversary was celebrated in much the same way as the accession itself had been in Sivas.[28] The resident troops were drawn at the Imperial Barracks Square to a mixed crowd of about 4,000–5,000 Muslims and Christians, the standard chant 'Long Live the Sultan' echoed three times, amongst prayers, 'in one voice (*bir ağızdan*)' and military music. Afterwards, there were mass-scale town decorations and illuminations for days on end, as well as twenty-one-cannon salvos five times a day. However, these particular festivities commenced on the Muslim calendar date (17 Zilhicce 1278), which corresponded to 3 June (O.S.), instead of 14 June (O.S.), the solar date of the accession a year earlier. Still, this spectacle unfolded before the eyes of most consuls of friendly states residing in Halep, an act that clearly reflected its foreign-policy objectives too. Regarding the locals, the announcement of 'the outward sumptuous marks of public joy (*sürur-u umumiyenin asar-ı zahire ve fahiresini*)' was an imperative of the first order. Based on adaptive expectations from year to year, a preoccupation of this kind became a major factor driving the cult of personality, as the analysis of subsequent celebrations will demonstrate.

A second reason for the inconsistent timing of sultanic celebrations had Christian rather than Muslim considerations at heart, as the 1863 accession festivities in Tırnova demonstrate.[29] In this town, a public crier (*telalin*) announced on Wednesday, 12 June (O.S.) that the accession celebrations would be held on Sunday, 16 June (O.S.). Apparently, this choice was not based on the Muslim calendar date for that year (4 June), as it had been in Halep the previous year. Instead, it seems that the solar date (14 June, O.S.) was pushed back two days so the '*dunanma* [sic]'[30] could fall on a Sunday, by far the most significant day in the Christian liturgical week. This accommodating gesture from the Ottoman authorities to the local Christians is an early example of what I call *cross-dating* – later a widespread practice during the reign of Sultan Abdülhamid II (1876–1909).[31] In this way, the Orthodox Christian Bulgars could more readily embrace the annual sultanic holiday and its attendant spectacle. Perhaps as a balancing countermeasure, the first cannon salvos that Sunday roared during the Muslim morning prayer (*sabah namazı*).

After the completion of church services, the town notables, along with the teachers and students from all the schools in town, paid the head district official (*kaymakam*) Ali Bey a visit at his summer residence (*köşk*) on the outskirts of town to greet him on the occasion of the royal accession. The students, lined up outside, said 'their habitual prayer (*obyuchnata si molitva*)'. Afterwards, one of them recited a poem of praise in Ottoman, followed by the performance (in Bulgar) of 'the song for many years [*mnogoletstvenata pesen*] for the sultan, the tsar's ministers *Vyukyulya-Efendilerimis*, and, finally H.H.,[32] the Kaymakam of Tırnova'.

Several aspects of this ceremony merit further attention. First, in contrast to the above-mentioned example from 1851 Razgrad on Abdülmecid's birthday,[33] in Tırnova in 1863, it was the students who visited the local representative of central Ottoman power to pay their proper homage on the anniversary of Abdülaziz's accession. Second, whereas in 1851 Razgrad *several* local dignitaries had visited *one* school, in Tırnova twelve years later, *all* teachers and students visited *one* local dignitary, the *kaymakam*. Third, when they sang and prayed, the students in Tırnova did so not only for the monarch, but also for his ministers, coming all the way down to the head district official, the local embodiment of central authority.[34] Anagnostopoulou and Kappler mention a similar practice by the Hellene-minded Rum on the Aegean island of Midilli (Lesvos in present-day Greece) during the reign of Abdülaziz. In that case, one can actually see how the lyrics changed in accordance with the rank of the dignitary being feted.[35] Such songs were performed by students from all communities in their languages as well as in Ottoman, and the occasions only multiplied. In addition to birthdays and the anniversaries of royal accessions, they included school exam ceremonies and even spontaneous, wholly improvised events. Thus, in September of the same year, 1863, Hellene-minded Rum poets organised a public reading by schoolchildren in honour of the sultan in Yanya (Ioannina in present-day Greece). The act prompted the Muslim and Jewish communities in town to follow suit. In addition to Ottoman, the Jewish schoolchildren sang not in Ladino, the everyday language, but in Hebrew, the higher-register language of prayers and eulogies. In addition to 'sultan', the children hailed Abdülaziz as their 'king (*melech*)'.[36]

This gradual process of vertical extension of the number of feted celebrities in a decreasing formal ranking order but in an increasing order of familiarity from the local perspective illustrates the workings of two opposite processes. On the one hand, it shows a higher degree of cultural penetration and indoctrination of provincial populations, and their corresponding activation along lines acceptable to the centre. Simultaneously, however, such ceremonies create a host of novel opportunities for intra- and inter-communal interaction, (re)drawing boundaries and clarifying the nature and essence of group belonging in the process. In this regard, the speech delivered by one of the younger students at the 1863 Tırnova festivities provides a fascinating, one-of-a-kind example, worth quoting at length:

> We cannot remain silent about the <u>unremitting labours</u> of H.E. [His Excellency] our <u>good-natured</u> Kaymakam. Since setting foot in our town, he has not ceased <u>caring, day and night,</u> for the observance of <u>the righteous tsarist laws</u>. And as [a] <u>peace-loving</u> [person] he always declares <u>peace, love</u> and <u>accord</u> across the district, always <u>labours</u> for the common <u>tranquillity</u> of the subdistrict and <u>ponders everything which is good for our town</u>. Apart from all these [things], H.E., as [a] <u>virtuous</u> [person], wished to leave behind in our region <u>an eternal trace and an immortal name for himself</u> with <u>the repair of the roads</u> and the renewal of the town discussions about <u>the cleanliness of the streets</u> and other such [matters]. <u>Once upon a time</u> His late Deceased Father Süleyman Pasha left <u>an unforgettable name for himself</u>, through <u>his good works</u> regarding the regional fountains. So did too H.E. Kaymakam Bey Efendi, who among <u>his other good works</u>, in this year's dearth of water in our town, has already taken good measures for <u>the renewal of his father's above-mentioned good works</u>. We therefore hope that our town will receive from H.E. <u>many other acts of goodness</u> as well for as long as it is the district's fortune that he should stay here . . .

This text demonstrates the high degree of sophistication with which one Bulgar community played the centre at its own game in 1863. It shows how skilfully the frame of the royal occasion could be used to stretch the canvas of local objectives (street cleaning, road improvement, water supply and so on). The method at work is even more impressive. A closer look reveals that in the symbolic space delineated by this speech, Tırnova is a microcosm of the Empire and the *kaymakam* has taken over core sultanic qualities. He labours 'night and day'.[37] He is good-natured, peace-loving and virtuous.[38] So, it turns out, was his late father. In a bizarre sense, the temporal continuum of the ruler's dynasty has thus effectively shrunk to a span of barely two lifetimes – the *kaymakam*'s and his father's. Apart from a vague passing reference to 'the righteous tsarist laws', the present sultan himself is entirely absent from this long excerpt. This is not nationalism yet. There are no Bulgar references, apart from two technical ones referring to the tongue in which the majority of ceremonies were performed. The communal references are 'townsmen (*grazhdani*)', '(Ottoman) Turkish-speaking Muslims (*turtsi*)'[39] and 'Christians (*hristiyani*)'. As in Sivas two years earlier, the 1863 Tırnova text totalises the local population's involvement in the imperial holiday, based not only on age ('old and young') but also on class ('from the first to the last').

The type and content of celebratory proceedings analysed above were not unique to Tırnova. The Ottoman Archives in Istanbul hold a rare cache of song and prayer texts penned by a provincial Bulgar teacher by the name of Toma M. Birovski, which sheds light on similar activities in the towns of Vidin and Lom (in present-day Bulgaria) on the occasion of the sultan's birthday that same year, 1863.[40] As in Tırnova, the students of Lom and Vidin paid a visit to the local authorities, this time at the government building (*konak*) in order to sing their songs and chant their prayers. As it turns out, their song of praise to the ruler is an exact reproduction (with only the sultan's name changed) of the 1860 Belchev text analysed in the previous chapter, itself a substantially revised version of the 1859 *Mnogoletstvie*. This lineage demonstrates the wide scope of contemporary sultanic song circulation and its lasting capacity to penetrate and shape public consciousness at different levels. A quick look at the prayer text reveals continuity with the symbolic headway made by the previous reign, as well as the appearance of further metaphoric accretions. For example, the theme of education ('science' (3)) and enlightenment ('the freedom of enlightenment' (2)) dominate the text and by themselves justify the common call for prayer in the name of the ruler. Variations of the organic and cosmic metaphors, as well as images of syncretic regalia and sultanic dominance over a negative 'other', are all present. The analogy between the effect of the life-giving sun on all 'earthly products (*zemleni proizvedeniya*)' and the effect of 'the imperial mercy and compassion' on 'the tranquillity, prosperity and advancement of the sciences' exemplifies the former. A reference to Abdülaziz's 'High Prosperous [lit. "God-saved (*Bogospasaemyiy*)"] New Throne'[41] and a wish for the sultan to be 'an eternal victor over his enemies' illustrate the latter. The students concluded their prayer with a joyous triple chant of 'Long Live the Sultan!'.

The Apogee of Bulgar Enthusiasm for the Sultan in the Mid-1860s and the Gradual Shift towards a Centrality of their Own Group

As the opportunities for symbolic ruler-ruled interaction multiplied in the mid-1860s, the field of learning provided the stage for some of the most evocative expressions of the changing social pact. A visit of the Ottoman Minister of Education, Ethem Pasha, to Bulgar schools in *Rusçu*k in 1864, for example, prompted a teacher's speech, which contained the following segment worth quoting at length:

> In requital for these tsarist acts of grace (*tsarski milosti*) what must we presently do? We must sacrifice ourselves, spilling even the last drop of our blood in his

name. Not because H. I. Maj. will want this now from us, we must sacrifice our hearts and turn our thoughts to him, so we can better recompense him! Let us show him both with thoughts, and with words, as well as actions that we are his most faithful subjects attached to his throne. Let us hate (*mrazim*) everyone, who may wish (*poishte*) to insult, with word and action the glory of our tsar! Let us prove with our deep devotion that there is not [another] tsar so good for us on Earth. Let all of Bulgaria cry out: Long live! Long live! Our people-loving (*narodolyubiviya*) tsar Sultan Abdul Azis [sic]! Let him be glorified immensely [lit. 'from the earth to the sky/heaven (*nebeto*)']! Let his tsarist throne be strong and invincible![42]

Evidently, this passage, unmatched in its intensity by any of the texts so far analysed, employs many symbolic concepts initiated and elaborated at various points in time over the course of the previous two decades. Examples with relatively more distant precedents include the organic metaphor of the heart, the grand-spatial metaphor ('from the earth to the sky/heaven'), the trope of love ('people-loving'), the syncretic regalistic metonymy of power ('his tsarist throne') and the tsarist title itself. Others, such as the military motif ('strong and invincible'), the intergroup competitiveness ('there is not [another] tsar so good for us on Earth') and the principles of totalisation, personification and unification ('Let all of Bulgaria cry') are more recent developments. However, the most fascinating aspect of this segment lies in the call for sacrifice in the name of the ruler. While by itself the call is not new, the context of most extreme mobilisation in which it is placed, is. Its building blocks are several. First, the use of novel terms of obligation of the ruled to the ruler – 'requital (*vuzdayanie*)' and 'recompense (*vuzblagodarenie*)' – seems to frame a highly skewed relationship between the two parties. Second, a passing reference to 'the tsarist acts of grace'[43] is hardly a matching counterweight for a popular self-sacrifice to the last drop of blood. Third, in a step reminiscent of the earlier analysis of the third song of Yoannovich's 1851 songbook,[44] but even more extreme, the call of popular duty to the sultan transforms what would otherwise be irrational behaviour into an acceptable norm, thus creating a higher plane of activity ('Not because H. I. Maj. will want this now from us, we must sacrifice our hearts . . .'). Fourth, this higher plane interacts for the first time with the realm of thought ('turn our thoughts to him'; 'both with thoughts and with words, as well as actions'). Fifth, this unprecedented state of popular euphoria culminates in a bizarre depiction of a negative 'other' and a common call against him or her – 'Let us hate everyone, who may wish to insult . . .' Herein lies another novel paradox. Even though this call addresses a hypothetical situation – the triggering cause (an insult to the ruler) exists only in principle – the response (a popular hatred) is already under way.

A close look at this passage leads to the surprising conclusion that it has more or less laid out, albeit in disguise, the main coordinate axes of the ethnonational mindset. The permanent (open-ended) state of popular agitation ('let us prove with our deep devotion') is certainly among them. So is the higher level of attempted symbolic intervention into the lives of ordinary people and control of the popular psyche. The image of the last drop of blood, which makes a first appearance here, is indicative of a wider pattern of group emotional self-flagellation without a precedent in the local tradition. It has long since become self-evident, a modern cliché. One need only switch the focus of attention from the imperial monarch to the religio-cultural community, in order to harness these newly realised energies for the cause of nationalism, as they are to this very day.

As the duties to the ruler increased, so did the duties to the group in the mid-1860s. A sifting through ceremonial descriptions of 11 May – the new Bulgar communal holiday touched upon in the previous chapter – allows for a unique look at the intersection of the two types of duties. References to 'a popular duty (*dolzhnost narodna*)' had appeared in the Bulgar periodical press since Abdülaziz's accession in 1861.[45] By 1866, there was already talk of 'popular duties (*narodni dluzhnosti*)' and accusations of 'neglect (*nemarenie*)' thereof. In response to the latter, according to an anonymous provincial correspondent of Vremia,[46] fellow Bulgar townsmen from Tatar-Pazarcık (Pazardzhik in present-day Bulgaria) put together their best 11 May celebration to date.[47]

The portraits of St Cyril and St Methodius graced a school wall. Church services in their name as well as a holy ceremony of 'blessing of the waters (*vodosvet*)' took place at a specially erected stand bearing the saints' icon in the middle of the local schoolyard. The head teacher delivered a speech, which, among other things, dispelled the 'deception (*zabluzhdenie*)' of some fellow townsmen that 'only with the Greek learning and the Greek language could people educate themselves and advance'. Two (all-boy and all-girl) choirs performed songs which 'delighted the devout (*blagochestivoto*) and kin-loving (*rodolyubivoto*) heart'. The conclusion of the letter amounts to a vehement diatribe against the Hellene-minded Rum. All the while, the anonymous author maintained that the Bulgars would always remain 'devoted to the teachings of the orthodox Church and faithful subjects of the Sultan'.[48] The event's legitimacy in the eyes of local Ottoman authorities was further assured by the very visible presence of a number of symbols of monarch and state. First, a triumphal arch made of 'entire pine trees' and decorated with a golden crescent and star was erected in front of the school gate. Second, a portrait of the sultan, painted by local artists (Stefan and Toma Antonov) and decked with roses and other flowers, was hung on a wall. Third, the prayer-song 'for our merciful tsar and father the Sultan' was also performed following church services.

Protestations of subject loyalty notwithstanding, this letter contains discreet indications that the centre of popular attention was by this time beginning to shift from the monarch to the Bulgar group. The 'heart', a symbol long monopolised by the sultan-tsar, was starting to engage in 'kin-loving (*rodolyubie*)' on a wider scale. The townsmen's solemn mood that day was indicated by a passing reference to their attire – 'dressed up as they would be at Easter'.[49] Moreover, on the wall between the portraits of the two brothers and Abdülaziz's image, there was yet another picture – of the baptism of tsar (and saint) Boris in Preslav.[50] With the subtle inclusion into the ceremonial setting of a medieval tsarist figure the Bulgars could claim as their own, a visual temporal continuum was being established which facilitated the advancement of communal consciousness under the guise of a faith-based holiday.

Other 11 May celebratory accounts from the provinces provide additional details for a more complex and credible picture of this process of transformation. A letter from Kotel relates the communal excitement about the 11 May festivities in the following terms: 'As great as the desire for this popular ceremony (*narodno turzhestvo*) was, with which the people (*narod*) burnt, the outcome was even more brilliant (*blyaskav*)'.[51] This sentence reveals changes in other long-standing symbolic motifs. The capacity to 'burn' with 'desire' hitherto solely attributed to the sultan[52] is hereby given to 'the people' and directed towards a 'popular ceremony'. In addition, *light*, another time-honoured prerogative of monarch and dynasty, now emanates from this popular ceremony ('the outcome was even more brilliant').

In Kotel, 11 May festivities included a large procession of the saints' icon from the local church to the school, headed by the clergy. The author twice noted the unprecedented solemnity with which proceedings unfolded. As in Pazarcık, portraits of the saints and the sultan were on display. Instead of the baptism scene, these were accompanied by a portrait of Midhat Pasha, the provincial governor, and, notably, the portraits of (unnamed) Bulgar Metropolitans. Still more remarkable is the fact that the author chose to refer to the latter figures as 'our people's *holy*[53] leaders (*narodnite ni sviashtennonachalnitsi*)'. The motif of 'holiness' in connection to the people is another complete novelty for any ceremonial setting so far examined. At first sight, this usage could be attributed to the peculiar nature of the spiritual realm invoked whenever clergy were involved. It might therefore be easily dismissed as inconsequential. However, another 'holy' reference, this time quite unambiguous, appears in yet another letter on the same page of *Vremia*. Apparently, in Balçık (Balchik in present-day Bulgaria), due to an altercation with the Hellene-minded Rum, church services could not be held in Old Church Slavonic on 11 May. So the Bulgars stepped out, thereby remaining without religious service 'in this *holy* (*sviat*) and *great* (*velik*) [for all of them] day'.[54] The event prompted the indignant anonymous author to seek measures to safeguard 'the *holy rights* of the Bulgar population (*sviashtennite pravdini na bulgarskoto naselenie*)'.[55] The issue did not leave *Vremya*'s editor, Todor Burmov, indifferent, either. He responded below by providing practical advice on 'solving the Bulgar question and doing *right* by the Bulgars (*da sya reshi bulgarskiyat vupros i da sya otdade pravoto na bulgarete*)'. As the case of the 11 May celebration in Izmir that year shows, however, there was still room for local accommodation and traces of syncretism of an inter-communal nature.[56] According to another letter on the same page of *Vremia*, on the request of the Bulgars living in that town, the Metropolitan of Izmir and his deacon read prayers and sung chants in Old Church Slavonic, a language which both knew a little, during services at the church of St John.[57] The Bulgars then treated the Metropolitan to refreshments in a room set aside for the purpose before taking him to the Bulgar all-girls school, where an antiphon (*tropar*)[58] to 'the Slavic apostles and teachers, St Cyril and St Methodius', was sung, along with 'the song of H. I. M. the Sultan and another one in Greek'. It seems that with the latter song, the Bulgars returned the Metropolitan's favour. That day not a single Bulgar shop opened for business. The Bulgars were very eager to explain to the genuinely curious members of other local communities 'this holiday unknown to them'. In the author's words: 'on 11 May, the <u>memory</u> of the Slavic apostles, earliest teachers (*purvouchiteli*) and enlighteners, St Cyril and St Methodius, is solemnly celebrated <u>across all of Bulgaria</u> (*po vsichka Bulgaria*) and <u>the other Slavic lands</u>'. The introduction of a concept of 'group memory' and the reference to a pan-Slavic connection are fresh indicators of an enhanced communal consciousness, not to mention the presence of a reified 'Bulgaria'. Such motifs would only become more pronounced in the years to come.

    Finally, it is worth looking at 1866 celebrations of the sultan proper in order to gain a more balanced perspective on the 11 May festivities. A letter about accession day activities in Filibe, which appeared on the pages of *Vremia* about a month later, contains just the right information and level of detail for such a comparative purpose.[59] From the outset, this letter stated, as did virtually all 11 May accounts, that this accession day was celebrated 'with a higher solemnity than any other time'. According to it, the district governor (*kaymakam*) of Filibe, Atta Bey, received and shook hands with officers and representatives 'belonging to each people (*ot vsiaka narodnost*)'[60] from sunrise to sunset. The latter were accompanied by schoolchildren from their respective community performing songs 'for the tsar'. The governor listened to them with great attention and gave each group 100 kuruş for sweets. First were the Bulgars, followed by the Muslims, Armenians, Hellene Rum and others. As the author proudly observed, the two songs of the Bulgar students, specially composed in Ottoman, touched Atta Bey's heart to such an extent that 'his eyes began to fill with tears'. In the evening, the governor invited all foreign consuls and two or three leading members 'belonging to each people' to a banquet and entertainment in the local government building (*konak*). In the courtyard, a crowd of 5,000–6,000 men, women and children marvelled for many hours at the wonderful illuminations and fireworks, while also enjoying refreshments of 'sweet drinks of various kinds, ice creams and other things'. Apparently, such 'common merrymaking (*obshto uveselenie*)' on accession day took place in Filibe for the first time. In conclusion, the letter complimented Atta Bey for the cleanliness with which he 'made happy (*oshtastlivi*)' the inhabitants of Filibe. The good works in question – the elimination of stagnant pools of water along the streets in the town's lower quarters, helped eradicate cases of fever. In essence, what the Tırnova townsmen had hoped for in the 1863 speech analysed above, the Filibe townsmen managed to accomplish by 1866.

The juxtaposition of the two types of ceremony shows a remarkable degree of symbiosis. Each combined motifs of centre and community in a free-flowing, seamless manner. Each engaged the popular attention and generated a substantial amount of genuine fervour.

The Growing Disparity between Bulgar Attachments to the Sultan and the Macro-community in the Late 1860s and the Early 1870s

In 1867, on his return from a trip to Western Europe, the only such sultanic event in all of Ottoman history, Abdülaziz made a stop in Rusçuk, the capital of the Danubian province of Ottoman Rumelia. The welcoming ceremony, attended by the top echelon of Ottoman government, including the Grand Vizier, Ali Pasha; the Minister of War, Mehmed Rüşdi Pasha; and the governor of the Danubian Province, Midhat Pasha, was spectacular.

The Reign of Abdülaziz

Figure 3.2 Photograph of Şahzade (Prince) Abdülhamid (1867) by W. & D. Downey Photographers, probably taken in Balmoral Castle, Scotland (Wikimedia Commons).

Ruler Visibility and Popular Belonging

Here is how the official provincial newspaper *Tuna/Dunav*, published in both Ottoman and Bulgar, described the visual exchange between ruler and ruled from the Bulgar perspective: 'The admiration and joy, which showed on the merry face of the <u>tsar</u>, was indescribable, and satisfied with the <u>unanimous</u> cry of the <u>people</u> (*narod*) – 'Long Live our <u>Tsar</u>!' – [he] was raising his hand and greeting the spectators'.[61] This is easily the highest point of the ruler-ruled public exchange so far observed, undeniably under the influence of the sultan's foreign visit, which had ended barely a few days earlier.[62] On his way to the provincial administration building, the sultan encountered welcoming parties from the local communities in the following order – Muslims, Bulgars, Armenians and Jews. In the midst of the processionary street, in a manner reminiscent of the 11 May celebrations in Tatar-Pazarcık a year earlier, the Bulgars had erected a triumphal gate, decked with flowers and topped by a crescent. The triumphal gate also displayed the imperial monogram (*tuğra*), with slogans in Ottoman and Bulgar flanking it:

Millet-i Bulgar hemişe itmede böyle dua,
devletinle şevketinle padişahım bin yaşa.

and

Slavno-dulgovechno tsarstvo i zhivot,
Za tsaria si moli Bulgarskiy narod.

In English, the Bulgar text reads as follows: 'The Bulgar people (*narod*) pray for a glorious and long-lasting tsardom and life for their tsar'.[63] Perhaps the most noteworthy aspect of these slogans is the act of calling the Bulgars a *millet*, in black and white, for the sultan and everyone else to see. Apparently, less than nine years after its first alleged use in a sultanic decree with reference to the Bulgars, the term had gained public currency.[64]

Within and around the triumphal gate stood Bulgar clerics, 'in a most reverent manner (*nay blagogoveyno*)', dressed in liturgical attire, with the Gospel and crosses in hand. Next to them were the town's most notable Bulgars, followed by Bulgar schoolboys and schoolgirls, clad in white clothes with narrow bands of red cloth,[65] especially sewn for the occasion, and with flowers in their hands. Their teachers stood in front of them, in five symmetrically arranged groupings. Behind the students, and immediately preceding the lines of 'all the local and outside (*vsichkite mestni i vunkashni*)' Bulgars, including women and children, stood twenty Bulgar peasants dressed in their Sunday best, each holding a sheaf of wheat from his field. Although precise event planning information has

The Reign of Abdülaziz

yet to surface, it is quite probable that the idea to include peasants, a novel idea at sultanic ceremonies, was quietly borrowed from the coronation procession of the Russian emperor Alexander II eleven years earlier, which for the first time in history featured a peasant elder from each province of the Empire.[66] As part of the multiple coronation activities, these peasant elders also presented Alexander II with bread and salt, an alleged ancient Slavic tradition.[67] The Bulgars instead opted for the sheaf of wheat (July being the harvesting season), a symbol of fertility, as well as their productive labour and use to the Empire. The important point to take away, as in contemporary Russia, especially after the Emancipation of the Serfs in 1861, is the trend towards the inclusion of a wider range of participants in imperial ceremonies.[68] In other words, this is yet another manifestation of the principle of totalisation.

Upon his approach, the sultan 'raised his eyes' and read the Ottoman slogan with 'a merry face'. When his horse stepped into the triumphal gate, Abdülaziz looked at the Bulgars 'tenderly (*umilno*)'. The latter unanimously cried out 'Long Live!' with 'an indescribable enthusiasm (*vuztorg*)'. The sultan then raised his hand and greeted them. At this time, the students commenced singing a Bulgar song for him. Surprisingly, a close look at its text reveals a picture quite different from the above description of an almost ecstatic interaction between the Bulgars and their ruler. This text contains barely a few of the symbolic motifs employed earlier – a grand-spatial metaphor (the sun), metaphors of light ('shine', 'enlighten') and the principle of totalisation ('Let all of us cry out'). Metaphorically, it is far inferior to most of the earlier songs of this type analysed above. Instead, the anonymous poet introduced a frequent repetition of content-poor refrains:

> Yasha – hello (*da zdravey*)!
> Yasha – long live (*da zhivey*)!
> Yasha-Yasha-Yasha![69] (4)
> May God protect
> The munificent (*blagodaten*) guest,
> The autocratic (*samovlasten*) Tsar! (2)
> Let all of us cry out:
> May God save Sultan Azis! (2)

So the avowed Bulgar enthusiasm for the ruler seems to be more a matter of form than content. There is evidence to suggest that a leading motif for such extensive ceremonial preparations for the ruler's visit was the opportunity to celebrate the community itself. Moreover, contrary to earlier examples from the 1840s and the 1850s, the community in question consisted in this case not so much of fellow Bulgar-speaking Rusçuk townsmen, but of Bulgars broadly conceived. This clearly points to the diminution of the local identity, formerly dominant. Throughout the article, there are no fewer than nine separate Bulgar group references (excluding language), but not one distinctly local marker.[70] All of them are capitalised, including the one in the Bulgar-language slogan. If the slogan's original text was truthfully reflected in the article, then a truly remarkable situation arises whereby the reference to Bulgar people (*Bulgarskiy narod*) is the only capitalised non-opening expression in a slogan, in black and white, which also features the words 'tsar' and 'tsardom'. Finally, the article's authors refer to 'a popular duty (*narodna dluzhnost*)' to their 'dear compatriots (*mili suotechestvennitsi*)' as the driving motivation to provide detailed descriptions, especially of the climactic encounter between the ruler and the ruled at the triumphal gate.

In anticipation of the sultan's visit to Rumelia, preparations for welcoming ceremonies were also under way in other towns, in accordance with central directives. In his memoir, Todor Ikonomov,[71] then a teacher in Şumnu, mentions in passing that Muslim and Bulgar students were lined up in exercise at the local government building (*konak*) and the local governor's residence (*saray*).[72] Ikonomov was angered by cases of mistreatment of his students at the hands of local Ottoman clerks during these ceremonial exercises. Some of them would be pinched, others slapped. In another memoir, Atanas Iliev,[73] then a student in Eski Zağra, reported similar preparations for the sultan's upcoming visit in greater detail.[74] As in Rusçuk, the Eski Zağra students were expected to wear white clothes. As in Şumnu, they mixed in with Muslim students – in this case, singing for several days at the local middle school (*rüşdiye*) under the guidance of Hoca Hacı Raci Efendi, a popular and much respected local Muslim teacher. Unlike Rusçuk, these students were learning an Ottoman song, whose opening words Iliev still remembered. They contain standard motifs, such as the sultan's title of 'ruler of the world (*şah-ı cihan*)' and his provision of 'justice (*adalet*)'. Much like Ikonomov, Iliev had some unpleasant memories regarding these activities. He reflected on the overbearing, supercilious manner with which Muslim students received their 'infidel (*gyaurski*)' counterparts.

In the end, the sultan decided to head straight to Istanbul. From Rusçuk, he took a train to Varna on the Black Sea where he boarded a ship to the capital. Not all rehearsals came to naught, however. Some ten days after the projected visit of the sultan to Eski Zağra, the provincial governor, Hurshid Pasha, arrived instead. On orders of the local governor, he was received 'with honours worthy of a tsar (*s tsarski pochesti*)' outside the town by the entire civilian population. So Iliev and the other students, lined up in the courtyard of the local government building by their teacher, daskal Stoyan, had a chance to perform the song they had learned after all.

In the following years, a number of factors combined to weaken the Bulgar loyalty to the sultan and respect for Ottoman authority as a whole, in tandem with the growth of their own macro-communal consciousness. Among them were mismanagement of local affairs, intensifying attempts to limit the flow of people and ideas to and from the Russian Empire, and tightening censorship, to name a few. The effects of these factors are clearly visible on the ceremonial plane.

In July 1868, the same Hurshid Pasha, governor of the province of Edirne (Adrianople), toured the countryside in the aftermath of a Bulgar rebel incursion from Wallachia, which was crushed.[75] According to Nayden Gerov, a Russian subject and at that time the Russian consul in Filibe,[76] judging by the governor's route, his probable goal was finding out which way the Bulgar population leaned.[77] To this end, Hurshid Pasha collected 'addresses of fidelity and devotion'. This was a foreign diplomatic tool, first implemented by Midhat Pasha in Rusçuk the previous year. Along the way, the governor stayed with both Muslim and non-Muslim hosts in order to demonstrate the equality of the two collectivities. In Filibe, he stayed with Mihail Gümüşgerdan, a controversial local (Hellene-minded Bulgar) notable.[78] The Slavic-minded Filibe Bulgars took this as an affront and refused to pay Hurshid Pasha the customary visit at this address. They did not change their minds even after the governor visited their newly built school, 'St Cyril and St Methodius'. Finally, the standoff was resolved a day before the governor's imminent departure when the latter made a second concession and invited them to visit him at the local government building, which they did. According to Gerov, this persistent position of the Bulgars, 'formerly so timid (*robkiy*) before the Turkish-speaking Muslims (*turki*)', made a strong impression. The consul also added:

> But they <u>recently</u> became <u>so invigorated</u> that, along with this, they <u>refused</u> to submit addresses of fidelity and devotion, all under the excuse that the governor did greater honour to this notorious <u>scoundrel</u> and inveterate <u>enemy</u> of <u>their people</u> [lit. 'of their belonging to a people (*narodnost*)'] than them.

The pages of Gerov's personal archive are full of similar instances of defiant Bulgar communal conduct regarding the addresses of fidelity and devotion, which the Ottoman authorities apparently continued to solicit until the eve of the Russo-Ottoman War of 1877–8.[79] By carefully sifting through the Russian consul's correspondence, one can get a sense of, on the one side, the increasingly ideological, and on the other, increasingly reactive nature of the symbolic interaction between the ruler and the ruled in the early 1870s. The resulting perception of the public space/sphere in those years is one of much tighter regulation than ever before. A main set of restrictive measures targeted the Russian Empire as the source of disruptive pan-Slavist ideas. For example, one of the things Hurshid Pasha did on his 1868 tour of the countryside was to inquire whether the Bulgars had local teachers educated in Russia, as he passed through towns and large settlements. In towns where they did have them, such as Kalufer (Kalofer in present-day Bulgaria) and Karlova (Karlovo in present-day Bulgaria), the locals often gave disingenuous answers.[80]

In June 1870, the Filibe police confiscated Russian liturgical books from a Bulgar book vendor (Hristo G. Danov)[81] on the grounds that some prayer texts contained in them mentioned the name of the Russian emperor. This was the first instance known to Gerov whereby books were taken from the interior of a bookshop rather than simply being stopped at customs upon their entry into the Empire. The case was all the more remarkable since identical literature, only in the name of the Habsburg emperor, Franz Joseph I, printed in Vienna by the Patriarch of Karlovac in Old Church Slavonic, was left undisturbed. What is more, during the confiscation, the subprovincial governor (*mutasarrıf*), Ali Bey, apparently recommended their use in lieu of the confiscated ones.[82]

In March 1875, Gerov wrote to his superior, Count Nikolay Ignatiev, the Russian ambassador to Istanbul, about another matter concerning Bulgars and the Russian Empire. The letter detailed an earlier chain of communications between the Ottoman Consul in Odessa (in present-day Ukraine), Vehbi Efendi, the Ottoman Ambassador to St Petersburg, Mehmed Kamil Pasha, and the then Ottoman Foreign Minister, Ahmed Arifi Pasha,[83] regarding the studies of up to thirty Bulgar students in Odessa, without Ottoman permission and the procurement of proper passports for travel abroad. According to Gerov, Kamil Pasha's report to Arifi Pasha in particular expressed concern that upon return to 'their old fatherland', these young people 'devote themselves to pan-Slavic ideas which disturb the internal peace of the Ottoman Empire and create disturbances'. In consequence, the report recommended that this flow be stemmed and young people seeking studies or employment in the Russian Empire dissuaded from doing so.[84] In Gerov's opinion, provincial authorities already knew well that 'the [Ottoman] government did not wish for local Christians and Russians to get to know each other, and in order to prevent their rapprochement would not have failed to erect a Chinese wall between them, had it only been possible'.[85]

Other restrictive measures concerned the content of circulating literature. The same 1870 government raid on the Bulgar bookshop in Filibe led to the confiscation of a book entitled *Istoricheski Pregled na Bulgarskata Tsurkva ot Samoto i Nachalo i do Dnes* ('*A Historical Review of the Bulgar Church from its Inception to Today*') by Marin Drinov.[86] The reason, in Ali Bey's view, was a particular expression the author used while describing the appearance of the Ottomans on the political scene in [medieval] Bulgaria (on pp. 100–1): 'this terrible adversary (*strashen nepriyatel*) appeared at a very bad time for Bulgaria'. Ali Bey's charge was that instead of the word 'adversary (*nepriyatel*)', its synonym – 'enemy (*vrag*)' – was employed, which could also mean 'devil'. To Gerov, this was a clear case of nitpicking, especially given the fact that the Ottoman language also had a word with these identical two meanings. The real reason, in the consul's mind, was that 'the Ottoman government could not have the Bulgars studying their history prior to their subjugation by the Ottomans'.[87]

Ali Bey's concern does not seem misguided. Drinov's book certainly allowed for the establishment of a temporal continuum back, whose medieval link could potentially be converted into a sacred mythological kernel and communal rallying point much like the figures of St Cyril and St Methodius. Despite the best of such censoring efforts, however, the image of the sultan continued to recede. The 1873 celebration of 11 May at Istanbul's Robert College,[88] which had a large number of Bulgar students, and the 1875 celebration of accession day in Rusçuk, which turned out to be Abdülaziz's last, provide good examples of this trend. The account of the former, which appeared on the pages of the *Levant Herald*, relates the texts of speeches delivered on the occasion.[89] These contain references to 'memory' and 'nation', 'honour', 'right' and 'holy duty'. What they do not contain is a single mention of the sultan. In a parallel fashion, they contain multiple references to 'Bulgaria' and 'Bulgarian'. What they do not contain is a single marker of regional belonging.

Finally, the printed Bulgar account of the 1875 accession day in Rusçuk enthused over the Western-style ball held by the governor of the Danubian Province, Mehmed Asim Pasha, rather than its august occasion. Whereas the feted monarch was mentioned only once in passing, sentence after sentence was devoted to the mixed-gender dancing at the ball and the popular fashion of wearing a red flower on one's chest.[90]

The imperial decree for the establishment of the Bulgar Exarchate[91] (28 February 1870) and its subsequent unilateral promulgation (11 May 1872) in the Bulgar church of St Stephen in Istanbul signalled the end of the paradigmatic dominance of (syncretic) Ottomanism in the life of this non-Muslim imperial community and the beginning of the rise of the national idea among its members. A shift in the common outlook is palpable in the memoirs of some members of the Bulgar leadership in Istanbul. For example, Marko Balabanov[92] spoke of 'that common intoxicating wind for political freedom, which was blowing almost everywhere in our fatherland in the third quarter of the last [19th] century'.[93] The 1870s did indeed witness a rise in Bulgar revolutionary activity ranging from sporadic rebel incursions of the type touched upon earlier to systematic internal preparations, such as those led by Vasil Levski and Dimiter Obshti's Internal Revolutionary Organisation.[94] In 1870, the Bulgarian Revolutionary Central Committee was founded in Bucharest for the purpose of uniting various radical groups within and without Bulgaria. Its goal was the formation of an autonomous or independent state and a possible federation with Serbia, Greece, Montenegro and Romania. The Committee organised the abortive Stara Zagora Uprising of 1875 and the April Revolt of 1876.[95] The latter resulted in many thousands of casualties, a fact much publicised in the West and Russia under the title 'the Bulgarian Massacres', sparking a public outcry. The April Revolt thus precipitated the Russo-Ottoman War of 1877–8, which led directly to the establishment of modern Bulgaria.

Conclusion

This chapter opened with the analysis of a wide range of celebrations of Abdülaziz's accession to the throne by both Muslims and non-Muslims in the capital and the provinces in order to demonstrate the high degree of penetration, organisation, coordination and overall sophistication of such festivities by 1861. This analysis confirmed, yet again, the remarkable degree of continuity, from reign to reign, of the principles of staging central Ottoman authority. It also shed light on what amounted to an increasingly complex apparatus of ruler glorification and subject loyalty creation. The chapter then drew the reader's attention to the process of standardisation of the sultan's accession day as an annual solar secular public holiday a quarter of a century after its introduction by Mahmud II. With this background in mind, the focus of attention shifted back to the Bulgar songs and eulogies of the sultan, whose themes and lyrics in the early part of Abdülaziz's reign borrowed heavily from Abdülmecid's legacy. The chapter then demonstrated the intricate interweaving of motifs of sultanic and Bulgar communal (self-)celebration as well as the gradual intersection of the more established duties to the ruler with the newly arising duties to the group. This relationship, for a while mutually reinforcing, was illustrated via a cross-section of celebrations of 11 May, a recently invented

The Reign of Abdülaziz

Bulgar communal holiday. The concept of group memory, the discourse of communal rights and their sanctification, not to mention the more visible and commanding presence of a reified 'Bulgaria' were all clear indications of a novel, macro-communal consciousness. Gradually, the stream of popular excitement for the ruler was diverted towards communal causes, at first slightly and subtly, then more substantially and assertively. The centrality of the ruler even in core ruler celebrations was at first dulled, then altogether displaced.

The next chapter constitutes a break with substantial portions of the foregoing analysis. It details the second shift in modern ruler visibility, under Abdülhamid II, and the sultan-caliph's peculiar yet persistent and successful symbolic policies aiming to re-energise the Ottoman monarchy and dynasty in the aftermath of a series of destabilising shocks. Consequently, the chapter is centred on a different target audience – the Muslim imperial populace – which by this time has firmly emerged as the main pillar of the Ottoman state.

Notes

1. See A.MKT.UM. 484/63, dated 16 July 1861.
2. One of the peculiar features of this sultan's reign was the common usage, from its very outset, of the term '*millet*' (a community of co-religionists) and *millet*-based phraseology, such as 'for state and communitay' (*din ü devlet içun*). In all likelihood, this novel implementation was a natural consequence of communal processes discussed in the previous chapter. It seems to have merely acknowledged what was by that time fast becoming a social reality.
3. See Brookes, 'Of Swords and Tombs', *Turkish Studies Association Bulletin*, 10.
4. A.MKT.UM. 484/63.
5. Ibid.
6. *Tsarigradski Vestnik*, 08/20 July 1861.
7. *Dunavski Lebed*, 04/16 July 1861. *Dunavski Lebed* was a weekly newspaper published in Belgrade in both Bulgar and French in 1860–1. Its chief editor, Georgi Rakovski (1821–67), was a Bulgar radical thinker and revolutionary.
8. Ibid.
9. *Bulgaria*, 12/24 July 1861.
10. *Tsarigradski Vestnik*, 08/20 July 1861. *Horo* was a popular Bulgar folk dance.
11. *Bulgaria*, 24 July 1861.
12. A clapper is a wooden plank or a metal plate, used in lieu of a church bell.
13. Interestingly, the speech commences with the address form 'devout Bulgar brothers (*blagochestivi bratya Bulgari*)'.
14. '*Sultan Abdülaziz Efendimiz yaşa yaşa binler yaşa*', *Dunavski Lebed*, 11/23

July 1861. See also *Tsarigradski Vestnik*, 24 June/6 July 1861 and *Blugarski Knizhitsi*, 5 June 1861.
15. Yosif Daynelov (1839–91) was a Bulgar merchant, journalist and public intellectual. Although closely associated with Rakovski, for whose paper he served as correspondent, Daynelov generally adhered to a moderate political line in terms of the advancement of Bulgar affairs. Later, he served as a district judge in Bulgaria.
16. His Imperial Majesty.
17. On the term's use among Bulgar intellectuals, see Stephanov, 'Bulgar Milleti Nedir?', in *'Istanbul' – 'Kushta' – 'Constantinople'*.
18. See the article in *Blugarski Knizhitsi*, 5 June 1861. *Blugarski Knizhitsi* was 'a journal of the Bulgar letters (*spisanie na Blugarskata knizhnina*)', published in Istanbul by Dr Dimitar Mutev (1818–64) from 1858 to 1862.
19. See *Dunavski Lebed*, 11/23 July1861. See also Blugarski Knizhitsi, 4 June 1861.
20. *Dunavski Lebed*, 27 June/9 July 1861.
21. For details of the actual proceedings, see Karateke, *Padişahım Çok Yaşa!*, p. 70.
22. On the highly restricted access to this ceremony, see Karateke, *Padişahım Çok Yaşa!*, p. 60.
23. Some Bulgars witnessed the event in Moscow. At least one, Nayden Gerov, even composed an ode to the emperor on this occasion. For a description of the coronation in the Bulgar press, see *Tsarigradski Vestnik*, 22 September/ 4 October 1856.
24. There are scores of archival reports documenting this step at the Turkish prime minister's Ottoman Archives in Istanbul. For a small sample, see A.MKT.UM 516/61, A.MKT.UM. 521/77 and A.MKT.UM. 574/85.
25. Protégés of the famous reformer Mustafa Reshid Pasha (1800–58), Fuad Pasha (1814–69) and Ali Pasha (1815–71), who alternated between the posts of Foreign Minister and Grand Vizier, dominated Ottoman decision making during the first decade of Abdülaziz's reign.
26. This was accomplished with the Treaty of Paris, which concluded the Crimean War (1853–6). In this war, the Ottomans sided with England and France against Russia, and emerged victorious.
27. For Cevdet's argument, see his *Ma'ruzat*, p. 41. For an influential interpretation of it, see Deringil, *Well-Protected Domains*, p. 172.
28. See A.MKT.UM. 573/88.
29. See *Suvetnik*, 1/13 July 1863. This was a weekly Bulgar newspaper published in Istanbul from 1863 to 1865. Its editors were Todor Burmov and Nikola Mihaylovski. Mihaylovski (1818–92) was a lawyer and man of letters. After 1878, he served as vice-chairman of the State Council.
30. A public merrymaking with fireworks. This definition draws on the entry for '*donanma*' in perhaps the most comprehensive contemporary Bulgarian dictionary, compiled by Nayden Gerov. See Gerov, *Rechnik na Bulgarskiy Yazyik*, p. 334.
31. Later cross-dating refers to the act of combining one ceremonial occasion

(such as the inauguration of a building) with another (such as the royal accession anniversary) on the same day for an accumulated effect on the public mind. This was a major strategy for autocratic legitimation in many late empires. For a panoply of such examples, see Chapter 4.
32. His Highness.
33. See Chapter 2.
34. As the text shows, there was even a term for this sequence of separate personalised acts of well-wishing by the community, an indication that this was a stable practice. It was called '*mnogoletstvuvanie*' (a wishing for many years).
35. See Anagnostopoulou and Kappler, 'Bin Yaşa Padişahımız', 66–7.
36. See A.MKT.MHM. 280/86. The document was dated 24 September, a date of no apparent significance. I am thankful to Julia Cohen for looking into the Hebrew texts and for her illuminating remarks.
37. Cf. the 1845 *ferman* in Chapter 2. Apparently, eighteen years later, this metaphor of the constancy of sultanic care for his subjects survives and ruler proxies fully partake of it.
38. This set is Abdülmecid's legacy.
39. Even though the correct literal translation is 'Turks', it has the potential to create a serious misunderstanding today. When this article was written, the marker '*turtsi*' was chosen for its loose religio-cultural content in the same way 'Bulgar' was deployed, as explained in the previous chapter. It referred to Ottoman Muslims whose mother tongue was Ottoman Turkish. This marker made no reference to an ethnonational group, with a claim to its own state of Turkey, as it does today. In order to forestall the process (conscious or not) of retroactive nationalisation in the mind of the reader, and thus avoid a major historical inaccuracy, I have chosen to render *turtsi* as '(Ottoman) Turkish-speaking Muslims'.
40. See I.DH. 504/34313. In Vidin and Lom, festivities apparently followed the Muslim calendar date of the sultan's birthday (15.Şa'ban). The texts are dated 22 January 1863 (O.S.), that is, on the eve of the sultan's birthday of 15.Şa'ban.1279 (23 January 1863 (O.S.)/5 February 1863 (N.S.)).
41. These capitalisations are in accordance with the original.
42. See *Suvetnik*, 12/26 September 1864.
43. The preceding paragraphs of the speech speak of the high visit's stimulating effects – a gift of Ottoman books and a map of Europe to the Bulgar schools of Rusçuk as well as a monetary gift of 1,000 kuruş. It also alludes to the admission, a few years earlier, of ten Bulgar students to study in imperial schools in Istanbul (a fact also corroborated by Stambolski, *Avtobiografiya*, pp. 45–7).
44. See p. 71 ('for the smallest need, summons all the strength').
45. See *Tsarigradski Vestnik*, 16/29 June 1861. In fact, this reference was made on the same cover page that announced Abdülmecid's death and Abdülaziz's accession.
46. This was a Bulgar weekly newspaper, published in Istanbul by Todor Burmov from 1865 to 1867.
47. See the letter, dated 17/29 May 1866, *Vremia*, 28 May/9 June 1866.

Ruler Visibility and Popular Belonging

48. Capitalisations are in accordance with the original.
49. Easter is by far the most significant feast in the Eastern Orthodox liturgical calendar.
50. Tsar Boris I converted his subjects to Christianity in the years 863–4 CE in Preslav, then capital of the kingdom of Bulgaria.
51. This letter, dated 11/23 May 1866, was printed on the same page of *Vremia* as the Pazarcık letter. See endnote 47 above.
52. See the previous chapter – p. 65, with respect to 'peace and the good livelihood of his subjects' and p. 74, with respect to 'the enlightenment of the peoples in all of His State'. Both references date from 1851.
53. Italics are my own.
54. Here is another allusion, conscious or not, to Easter, which in Bulgarian literally means 'Great Day' (*Velikden*).
55. This letter, dated 17/29 May 1866, was printed on the same page of *Vremia* as the Pazarcık and Kotel letters. See endnote 47 above.
56. The large divergence in size between the Hellene-minded Rum and Bulgar communities in Izmir (in favour of the former) was probably also a major factor behind the engineering of this amiable compromise. This was certainly not the case in most, if not all, of the other towns involved.
57. Ibid. The letter was dated 19/31 May 1866.
58. A verse or a series of verses sung as a prelude or conclusion to some part of the holy service.
59. See the letter dated 24 June/6 July 1866, *Vremia*, 2/14 July 1866.
60. The word '*narodnost*' is rendered in English as 'nationality' today. However, in the context of the 1860s, such a translation is, in my view, inappropriate and historically inaccurate. Therefore, I have opted for a literal translation – 'a belonging to a people'.
61. *Tuna/Dunav*, 26 July/7 August 1867. This official newspaper was edited by Ismail Kemal Bey (1844–1919), who later became the founder of the modern Albanian state, and Ahmed Midhat Efendi (1844–1912), a writer, journalist and publisher, in Rusçuk from 1865 to 1877. Its Bulgar translators were Stefan Popov (1840–93), a teacher and writer, and Ivan Chorapchiev, an educator and public intellectual.
62. In Pest (the Pest side of present-day Budapest), Abdülaziz boarded a steamboat which took him to Vidin and then Rusçuk.
63. There is a slight divergence in meaning between the two slogans. Accepting the Ottoman one as primary, its more exact rendition would be 'The Bulgar people (*millet*) always say this prayer – a thousand years to you, my padishah, and your empire, and your imperial majesty'.
64. According to Hristo Stambolski's memoirs, in the spring and summer of 1858, a group of Bulgar dignitaries petitioned the Grand Vizier to have fifteen to twenty Bulgar students admitted to the Imperial Medical School in Istanbul. Their request was eventually granted in September that year.

65. It would not be far-fetched to read in the colour red a gesture of loyalty to the Ottoman flag.
66. See Wortman, *Scenarios of Power*, vol. 2, p. 39. As noted earlier, many Bulgars travelling to and from the Russian Empire for educational and business purposes had witnessed the 1856 coronation in Moscow. Over time, the number of such travellers increased exponentially.
67. Ibid., p. 43.
68. For the Russian case, see Wortman, *Scenarios of Power*, p. 13.
69. This orthography and capitalisation are in accordance with the original.
70. The two local markers that do appear are tied to the Bulgar designator – 'Bulgars of Rusçuk (*Ruschushkite Bulgari*)'. This brings the total of Bulgar group references to eleven.
71. Todor Ikonomov (1835–92) was a Bulgar educator, later a Bulgarian politician and leader of the Conservative Party.
72. Ikonomov, *Memoari*, p. 98.
73. Atanas Iliev (1852–1927) was a teacher and later headmaster of the All-Girl High School in his native Stara Zagora.
74. Atanas Iliev, *Spomeni*, pp. 73–4.
75. This was the detachment (*cheta*) of rebels led by Hadzhi Dimitur (1840–68) and Stefan Karadzha (1840–68), which crossed into the Ottoman Empire in early July 1868.
76. Filibe was a major town, capital of an Ottoman subprovince (*sancak*).
77. Popruzhenko, *Arkhiv na Nayden Gerov*. Understandably, most of the consul's correspondence is in Russian.
78. Mihail Gümüşgerdan (1800–81) was a Bulgar merchant and entrepreneur.
79. Popruzhenko, *Arkhiv na Nayden Gerov*, vol. 2, pp. 278–85, 288–9.
80. Ibid., vol. 1, p. 472.
81. Hristo G. Danov (1828–1911) was a Bulgar teacher and man of letters, later the founder of book publishing in Bulgaria.
82. Popruzhenko, *Arkhiv na Nayden Gerov*, vol. 1, p. 544.
83. Arifi Pasha was relieved of his duties as Foreign Minister in January 1875.
84. Ironically, Gerov's own career presented a case in point as to why the Ottoman authorities should try to prevent Bulgars from going to Russia. In 1839, at the age of sixteen, he left for Odessa in order to study at the Richelieu Lycée, where he completed his studies in 1845. After obtaining a Russian passport, Gerov returned to the Ottoman Empire and became a teacher in his hometown of Koprivshtitsa, from 1846 to 1850. In 1851, he initiated the 11 May holiday in Filibe, which slowly gained traction. In 1857, Gerov became Russian vice-consul in Filibe, an office he held until 1876.
85. Popruzhenko, *Arkhiv na Nayden Gerov*, vol. 2, pp. 109–11.
86. Marin Drinov (1838–1906) was a Bulgar historian and philologist who studied at the Kiev Seminary and the Moscow Imperial University. Later, he was among the founders of the Bulgarian Academy of Sciences.
87. Popruzhenko, *Arkhiv na Nayden Gerov*, vol. 1, p. 545.

88. Robert College was founded in 1863 by Dr Cyrus Hamlin, an American Protestant missionary, educator, inventor, technician, architect and builder, and Christopher Robert, a wealthy merchant and philanthropist from New York.
89. See *Levant Herald*, 14 June 1873. This Istanbul daily newspaper appeared in English and French.
90. See *Napreduk*, 21 June 1875. This weekly Bulgar newspaper appeared in Istanbul from 1874 to 1877. Its chief editor was Ivan Naydenov (1834–1910), a journalist and public intellectual.
91. The Exarchate was a separate Bulgar ecclesiastical institution with its own hierarchy.
92. Marko Balabanov (1837–1921) was a Bulgar lawyer and journalist in Istanbul. He later moved to Bulgaria where he worked as jurist and politician, serving as Foreign Minister and even Chairman of the Bulgarian National Assembly.
93. See Balabanov, *Bulgarska Kolonia v Edin Ostrov*, p. 369. The island in question is Heybeliada (Halki) of the Princes' Islands near Istanbul where a large number of influential Bulgars formed a tightly knit community from 1850 to 1876.
94. Vasil Levski (1837–73) and Dimitur Obshti (1835?–73) were Bulgar revolutionaries, co-founders of the Internal Revolutionary Organisation. The former subsequently became enshrined as Bulgaria's ultimate national hero. For the most comprehensive study of Levski's mythological status within the canon of present-day Bulgarian nationalism, see Todorova, *Bones of Contention*.
95. See Jelavich and Jelavich, *The Establishment of the Balkan National States*, pp. 138–40.

4

The Second Shift in (Modern) Ruler Visibility: the Reign of Abdülhamid II (1876–1909)

Overview

Sultan Abdülhamid II's reign (1876–1909) was one of the longest and most influential in all of Ottoman history. He steered the Empire through one of its most tumultuous and transformative periods. Until very recently, most scholars viewed this sultan's reign quite critically, largely in isolation from his predecessors and successors, almost as an aberration in the general pattern of Ottoman reform and modernisation in the last century of the Empire. This is probably due in part to the sultan's autocratic style of ruling and the loss of much territory and international prestige, which marked both the outset of his reign and its aftermath.[1] Other reasons for such harsh treatment include long prevailing perceptions of the late Ottoman Empire as a stagnant environment, its modernisation as a strictly secular egalitarian process and its nationalist movements as progressive incontrovertible forces. Most of these stances have been substantially revised in the past two decades, which has prompted a general re-evaluation of this sultan's legacy too.[2] Recent scholarship has restored some balance to his portrayals, by pointing out some of the positive linkages, through education, correction, philanthropy and other areas of modernisation, between the Abdülhamidian reign, the Young Turk period and, in some ways, even the early Turkish Republican period.[3] Others have improved our understanding of his accomplishments, by focusing solely on his life, reign and ideology. Among them, the most influential research has come from Selim Deringil.[4] This chapter aims to complement the work of these scholars in several ways.

First, it will relate more systematically Abdülhamid II's style of ruling and discourse of power to those of his predecessors, emphasising both continuities and discontinuities. This comparison will be organised around the concept of *ruler visibility*, vis-à-vis the following binary opposites – target audiences at home and abroad, majority and minority audiences, and the use of notions of *past* and *future* in the moulding of the ruler's public persona. Second, this chapter will shed light, in chronological order, on the range and effect of techniques of royal image making, employed by this Sultan in order to support and perpetuate his personal autocratic regime. As it turns out, this range was wider, more complex and arguably more successful than any other Ottoman sultan's before or since. Therefore, this chapter will examine types of ruler visibility, created directly – through staged public appearances or lack thereof – and indirectly, by resorting to material objects and abstract metaphors as ruler proxies.

The value in studying Abdülhamid II's propaganda tools lies in gauging not only their immediate effect but also some of their long-term implications, which have been long ignored. In the final analysis, this chapter aims to contribute towards our understanding of the dynamic and eclectic nature of late imperial rulership in the Ottoman Empire and beyond. It will examine the channels through which royal power responded to the rising legitimacy of the principle of popular sovereignty, deliberately resisting and inadvertently assisting centrifugal national causes in the process. The ideological underpinnings of this reign, revealed through the prism of ceremony, can give us fresh insights into the rise of ethnicity to the realm of conscience and politics, which was rather more tentative and fitful than is generally assumed. As I hope to demonstrate in this chapter and the rest of the book, the modernising/nationalising effects of the various ceremonies of the monarch transcended the boundaries of Turkish-speaking or even Muslim subject populations. These ceremonies for the first time conditioned various imperial groups for a sort of collective cult of a national monarch,[5] the likes of which flourished long after the disintegration of the Empire.

Abdülhamid II's Position within the Line of his Predecessors

One of the main premises of this book is that the evolution of royal ceremonies reflects in a condensed form important sociocultural and sociopolitical change. In the case of the nineteenth-century Ottoman Empire, this relationship was clearly very strong. Mahmud II (1808–39) and Abdülhamid II (1876–1909), the two sultans who oversaw periods of most intense political upheaval, combined with territorial and population loss, were also the most committed ceremonial innovators. The carefully planned abolition of the Janissary Corps in 1826 availed Mahmud II the political opportunity to reform the Empire and revolutionise his own image in ways that would have been inconceivable to his predecessor Selim III (1789–1807). As we saw earlier, this first successful shift in late Ottoman ruler visibility entailed the initiation of annual royal birthday and accession day celebrations both at home and abroad.⁶ The sultan thus reached out, in an unprecedented manner, to Muslims and non-Muslims alike. The terms of glorification of the ruler, however, were more reserved and less abstract than they would become later, especially under Abdülhamid II. Nonetheless, Mahmud II did symbolically employ the past in an attempt to anchor the legitimacy of his autocratic regime and reforms. This practice of *invented traditions* would flourish under all subsequent sultans. It was indeed common to all late empires. Yet the stressed elements of the past, which were integrated into this sultan's mythology of power, were Islamic and not yet dynastic. For example, he called the new corps of troops which took the Janissaries' place 'Victorious soldiers of Muhammad (*Asakir-i Mansure-yi Mohamediye*)'.

Under Mahmud II's sons, Abdülmecid (1839–61) and Abdülaziz (1861–76), the changes in the monarch's mythology of power were more subtle, but still quite significant. Following in Mahmud II's steps, they cast their images in the mould of Western rulers by making themselves more directly visible than any other sultan before.⁷ They accomplished this despite the fact that, unlike their father's, their reigns were dominated by powerful bureaucrats, first Mustafa Reşid Pasha, and then the famous Fuad Pasha and Ali Pasha. Excepting his son Murad V's three-month reign in 1876, Abdülmecid went further than any other Ottoman sultan in presenting himself as a benevolent ruler of Muslims and non-Muslims alike, thus garnering the latter's most enthusiastic response.⁸ Having been spared confinement in the Cage for Ottoman Princes (*Kafes*), Abdülmecid treated his relatives with similar leniency after coming to power. For the first time, the image of the royal family and a gradually accelerating interest in dynastic history came to the foreground of ceremonial activity. In this respect, Abdülaziz's reign became a watershed in Ottoman history. Upon his rise to power, the new sultan reinstituted Mahmud II's short-lived practice of solar ruler celebrations, this time making it permanent.⁹ Thus, he continued the trend towards a personality cult of the ruler, which Abdülhamid II then brought to full fruition. Under Abdülaziz, the wave of enthusiasm for all things foreign, so characteristic of the previous two sultans, began to be tempered by a turn to the native. Whereas Abdülmecid had chosen to restore Aya Sofya (*Hagia Sophia*), Abdülaziz turned his attention to ancestral tombs in Söğüt, the cradle of the Ottoman dynasty. His interest in the past culminated in a veritable *Ottoman Renaissance* showcased both at home and abroad – at the Vienna World Fair in 1873, the Ottomans' first such participation.¹⁰ Abdülhamid II maintained the Ottoman presence at such venues, with a preponderance of historic imperial themes. He continued to draw inspiration for his own projects from landmark Ottoman monuments, fusing various architectural elements in a style typical of his own time. Abdülhamid II expanded tremendously his uncle's tomb restoration work and became fascinated with the roots of the dynasty more than any other sultan. He engaged the names of some dynastic personages of mythic status, beginning with Ertuğrul, Osman's father, in an unprecedented range of ceremonial ways. In the tendency to go further back in time in an attempt to capture his subjects' fancy and shore up his own legitimacy, Abdülhamid II was no different from other late imperial rulers, such as Franz Joseph I (1848–1916) of the Habsburgs or Nicholas II (1894–1917) of the Romanovs. The role of Ertuğrul was equivalent to that of Rudolf or Mikhail Romanov, respectively.[11]

Abdülhamid II also continued the trend whereby a new Ottoman sultan would reverse his predecessor's *scenario of power*. In some respects, he fitted rather well the long-term pattern of alternating rigidity and gentleness of character conveyed by the Ottoman ruler in public throughout the nineteenth century. As I will demonstrate below, from the outset of his reign Abdülhamid II's image was quite aloof, in a way reminiscent of Mahmud II's and Abdülaziz's, and quite unlike the accommodating images of Abdülmecid and Murad V. In one key aspect – *ruler visibility* – however, Abdülhamid II orchestrated a radical change, thus breaking away from the philosophy and practices of all four of his predecessors.

Once he was able to consolidate power, a few years into his reign, Abdülhamid II began to deliberately withdraw from public view[12] and withhold the propagation of his portraits. This was a bid not so much for security as for status – both personal and caliphal. Therefore, a unique split in the sultan's mythology of power took place, which determined how the sultan interacted with domestic and foreign, Muslim and Christian parties. With foreign dignitaries he would interact with little restraint, on one usually unspoken condition – that the meeting took place behind closed doors. Domestic Christians were allowed to celebrate Abdülhamid II as they would a Western ruler, including the use of his portraits. To Muslims, both at home and abroad, however, he invariably proscribed his likeness, encouraging in its stead non-visual calligraphic renditions, such as his monogram and the slogan 'Long Live the Sultan! (*Padişahım Çok Yaşa!*)'. So in the course of a few years, Abdülhamid II began to phase out his direct visibility[13] in favour of rounds of intensifying indirect (symbolic) visibility.

The direct visibility of the Ottoman royal male line followed the same trajectory in this period, from a peak in the 1850s and 1860s, with one important exception. The portraits of the Ottoman princes still circulated freely; clearly, they could not partake in the sultan's new aura. The implications of this overall shift are as significant to the shaping of the image of the monarch and dynasty as those overseen by Mahmud II more than half a century earlier. In comparison to his grandfather, however, Abdülhamid II managed to be more powerful, while at the same time being much less visible. What follows is an inquiry into many of the symbolic channels from which Abdülhamid II's autocratic power emanated and defined ties of subject allegiance in the last quarter of the nineteenth and (roughly) the first decade of the twentieth centuries.

The Early Reign. The Sultan's First 'Look' and Acts, and their Public Reception

The year 1876, 'the year of the three sultans',[14] which witnessed the bureaucrat-led depositions of, first, Abdülaziz, and then Murad V over a period of three months, became one of the most traumatic years in Ottoman history. The fact that the deposition of the increasingly autocratic Abdülaziz was followed several days later by his death under mysterious circumstances added further fuel to the fire. All of these events profoundly weakened the image of the Ottoman dynasty, which had been remarkably stable for most of its long history.

Commenting on the late Abdülaziz, a *Levant Herald* journalist noted that he 'never recognised or returned the salutes of the people on public occasions, following in this respect, we believe, Court precedent in Turkey ...'[15] This appraisal of Abdülaziz was borne out by other sources too.[16] Commenting on the newly enthroned monarch, in a favourable comparison to his uncle, the same journalist added that 'Sultan Murad V acted like a Western monarch'. For example, on his first Friday prayer procession, 'evidently moved and gratified by the extraordinary heartiness of his reception, [he] repeatedly bowed his acknowledgements right and left with gracious and appreciative courtesy'.[17] This obvious difference marked the transition from one *scenario* of power to the next.

There are also other ways to glean a sultan's scenario. In matters of faith, the choice of the imperial mosque for the sultan's first Friday prayer and the flow of the Friday prayer procession itself say much about the new ruler's intentions regarding his own image. Since he chose to visit Aya Sofya (the former church of Hagia Sophia) first, Murad V clearly wished to style himself as a ruler of his father (Abdülmecid)'s type, that is, of Muslims and Christians alike. The public understanding of this act was reflected in the unprecedented acclaim of 20,000 Christians greeting him as he passed by the Galata Bourse on his way back from the mosque.[18] Mainstream Ottoman newspapers also reflected in unusually expressive

Ruler Visibility and Popular Belonging

terms the enthusiasm of the crowds, both Muslim and non-Muslim, for the new sultan. For example, *Ceride-i Havadis* wrote on its cover page: 'The accession of His Majesty which occurred by the wish of the people, was announced with complete delight, and with Muslims and non-Muslims equally conveying their congratulations and felicitations to His Majesty Sultan Murad Khan'.[19] Expressions such as 'according to the wish of the people' and 'readiness to carry out reform',[20] as well as various words for 'joy', permeated the first several columns of this issue.

By contrast, Abdülhamid II chose Eyüp, with its strictly Islamic range of meanings.[21] The choice of Thursday as the day of his sword-girding ceremony (also the day of his accession to the throne) may have additionally reflected legitimacy concerns. In a precarious political situation such as this, with two sultanic depositions over the course of barely three months, it would be all the more important to have the newcomer to the throne sealed as sultan as soon as possible. The Friday noon prayer sermon across the imperial domains, with its mention of Abdülhamid II's name, would certainly accomplish this task. Indeed, Abdülhamid II is the sultan

Figure 4.1 Portrait of Sultan Murad V (1876) by Ivan Ayvazovsky (1817–1900). Ayşe Orbay, *The Sultan's Portrait: Picturing the House of Osman* (Istanbul: Iş Bank, 2000), p. 529.

who took the shortest time (one week) in more than a century to organise his sword-girding ceremony.[22] This time, again, the public was quick to grasp the direction of the reign from its very inception – 'the speciality of the vast assemblage was that it was almost exclusively a Turkish crowd'.[23] Once again, the tone of *Ceride-i Havadis* paralleled that of the *Levant Herald*. The entire description of Abdülhamid II's sword-girding procession made only this mention of local non-Muslims: 'Students from the various Christian and Jewish peoples (*millets*) were lined up in procession and arranged with great pomp'.[24] There is a notable lack of any emotional terms. The expression 'with great pomp (*alay-ı vala*)' is a stock phrase employed on various ceremonial occasions. It therefore reflects the attitude of mainstream observers, rather than that of the participants themselves. Instead, the emphasis clearly falls on the maintenance of proper order.

For his third Friday prayer, Abdülhamid II chose the Fındıklı Mosque, where he proceeded by water, just as Murad V had done for his last Friday prayer as sultan.[25] The distance from the Dolmabahçe Palace is quite short (several hundred metres) so the choice of transport may have been for intended effect on the public witnessing the event. When Abdülhamid II finally did visit Aya Sofya (*Hagia Sophia*), it was only for Ramazan afternoon prayer – an act that carried a very different message. Rather than demonstrate publicly early on a symbolic intention to rule justly over Muslims and Christians or stress the Ottoman dynasty's Byzantine legacy (like his father and older brother before him), Abdülhamid II thus staked an ordinary Muslim claim on the monument. His visit was not widely publicised, did not take place on a Friday and therefore went almost unnoticed by the populace. He visited the shrine not with the pomp of a sultan going to an imperial mosque for his Friday noon prayer, but rather as an ordinary pious Muslim going to mosque during the most significant fast of the Muslim calendar. Apparently, the sultan was accompanied only by his two younger brothers, Reshad and Cemaleddin, and 'a small and unpretending escort'.[26]

What had remained unchanged since the late reign of Mahmud II was the projection of a militarised image of the sultan, both in his first days in power and throughout his reign. As demonstrated earlier, this tendency affected both the sultan's physical appearance and the avenues for staging his visibility. If anything, over time, this ceremonial association with the military only intensified. For example, by the time of Abdülhamid II's sword-girding procession, the unranked blue coat, first donned by Mahmud II, had been replaced with no less than a field marshal's uniform. Significantly, Abdülhamid II, much like Abdülaziz, conveyed an air of simplicity, in stark contrast to his pompous, heavily decorated entourage. Thus, he wore 'a *plain* field marshal's uniform, with the star of the Order of the Osmanie on his breast, but *he did not wear the customary diamond aigrette and plume in front of his fez*'.[27] This pattern of change in the sultan's physical appearance throughout the nineteenth century, away from expressions of Oriental splendour, was at first a sign of embracing modernity, on predominantly (and quite literally) Western terms. By the time of Abdülhamid II, however, it accentuated an austerity and spirituality becoming of a caliph, and made him easily stand out in a procession through bare, unassuming simplicity.

One of the strongest patterns of similarity among late empires, be they Ottoman or Russian, Habsburg or British, was the ever closer integration of religious and military motifs in the composition of the ruler's image, both in first acts and in the long run. For Murad V's first Friday prayer procession, 'the cadets of the Military School at Pancaldi, together with cavalry, infantry and artillery . . . were drawn up in order in the large open square in face of the mosque'. Shortly after the public reading of the şeyhülislam's decision (*fetva*) in favour of his accession to the throne, Abdülhamid II proceeded to the Ministry of War where the troops of the capital's garrison acclaimed him.

When it came to the army, Abdülhamid II initially showed a unique degree of openness and accessibility. Two weeks into his reign, after paying his first mandatory ceremonial visit to the Mantle of the Prophet (*Hırka-yı Şerif*), he once more proceeded to the Ministry of War. There, in the open square, the sultan held a review of garrison troops. Then he dined at the Ministry with his officers, sitting at the same table and eating the same bread, before returning to the Dolmabahçe Palace. The Ministry's building and its tower were illuminated after dusk. Two months later, Abdülhamid II visited a military hospital, remaining 'for some time in the wards speaking words of consolation and encouragement to the men'. Then he announced the payment of 'the whole amount due upon the three ships of war built in England' out of his own savings, accumulated while still a prince or since assuming the throne.[28]

Regular military reviews, initiated by Mahmud II, became more frequent in the reign of Abdülaziz. In the early 1870s, they became increasingly associated with religious occasions, such as Friday prayer processions and Bayram celebrations.[29] It is only with Abdülhamid II, however, that their scheduling became firmly set: they followed Friday prayer processions, which took place every week, almost without fail. These events received increasingly detailed descriptions in the press, serving as a stage for diplomatic exchange as much as public spectacle. Once again, the

The Reign of Abdülhamid II

trend was apparent from the outset of Abdülhamid II's reign. For example, on 13 October 1876, a military parade at the Arsenal (Tophane) followed Friday prayers in the nearby mosque (where the sultan again proceeded by water).[30] Five days later, the end of the Ramazan fast and the beginning of the Bayram celebrations were announced with another military parade near the Sultanahmet Mosque, on the site of the Byzantine Hippodrome.[31]

When he came to power, Abdülhamid II faced a set of dire circumstances remarkably similar to the aftermath of the Janissary disbandment fifty years earlier. In addition to the problems mentioned at the beginning of this section, the Empire was ravaged by an unprecedented financial crisis and several military conflicts, which further threatened the Ottoman dynasty and the sultan's own tenure in power. In his first months on the throne, Abdülhamid II's direct visibility was therefore vital for his survival since it translated into increased legitimacy and made the gradual processes of power consolidation possible and credible. On the one hand, the new sultan had to establish a plane of ceremonial-diplomatic reciprocity with the West; on the other, he had to appease heightened sensitivities and demands at home from an increasingly Muslim body of subjects.[32] He immediately applied himself to each task and eventually accomplished both in novel ways.

For the foreign dignitaries at his sword-girding ceremony, Abdülhamid II provided two more marquees and a tent (compared to the last such event in 1861), commanding a good view and supplied with 'choice and plentiful refreshments'. Yet upon passing by, he did not acknowledge them directly, but through a special messenger. The most one could observe regarding the sultan's visual acknowledgement of anyone in the crowd was that 'his firm, distinctly marked countenance, occasionally lit up with animation as he passed along, the troops presenting arms and crying *Padishah tchok yashah* ("Long live the sultan")'.[33] His acknowledgement of the crowd was so subtle that it may have only existed in the eye of the beholder.

Even more telling was Abdülhamid II's policy regarding the royal image. As described in Chapter 1, Mahmud II had first encouraged the creation and proliferation of such images in public. By the time of Murad V, the public was apparently fully accustomed to them. Thus, on the day of Murad V's accession, the Abdullah brothers had 'the happy thought of exhibiting to public view, at the entrance of their establishment a fine large-sized cabinet photograph of his Majesty set in a gold frame'.[34] This act, repeated over many days, led to an outpouring of requests for portraits of the sultan from Istanbul, the provinces and abroad. Ultimately, it won the Pera[35] brothers a reappointment as 'Court photographers to his Majesty the Sultan and the Imperial Palace'.[36] Naturally, they did not hesitate to demonstrate their loyalty to Abdülhamid II in the same manner immediately after his accession, while also helping their own business. While the Abdullah brothers did indeed gain his favour in the short run, four years later they were sternly reprimanded for 'daring' to reproduce the sultan's image 'without any permission whatsoever'. The circular, issued from the Chancellery of the Imperial Palace (*Yıldız*), went further and ordered that the unlawful images be speedily collected. Most remarkably, it declared that the production thereafter of even a single such image be treated as an 'absolute prohibition (*memnuiyet-i katiye*)'. An infringement of this kind would call for a 'speedy execution of a hefty punishment (*çok cezanın müsaraat icrası*)'.[37] Clearly, this was a matter of key concern to the sultan.[38] We can surmise that by this time his grip on power had consolidated and his policies were shifting in a way acceptable solely to him. It may be hardly a coincidence then that around this time, Abdülhamid II also disposed of his much-hated enemy, the deposer of sultans – Midhat Pasha.[39]

As Deringil points out, Abdülhamid II substituted his portraits with imperial banners, embroidered with the acclaim 'Long Live the Sultan! (*Padişahım Çok Yaşa!*)'.[40] This was certainly true, but with respect to Muslim target audiences only. To date, I have not encountered evidence to suggest that the sultan hampered in any way the propagation of his (respectful) image abroad. On the contrary, from the start, Western perceptions of him were shaped with the aid of a slew of lithographs visualising in elaborate detail the investiture ceremonies in Istanbul. In France alone, journals such as *Le Monde illustré* and *L'Illustration* presented vividly Abdülhamid II's accession, his first Friday prayer procession and the sword girding. They continued to do so in the following years. To the sultan, such portrayals were probably acceptable because they gave him desired publicity. After all, Western rulers received the same type of coverage. In fact, a portrait gallery of the reigning European monarchs, entitled 'Rulers of the World', published in *L'Illustration* in the 1880s, did not fail to include Abdülhamid II's image too.[41]

What also went in line with the images of contemporary Western rulers was the ubiquitous military outlook on photographs and lithographs alike. Much like his predecessors, going back to Mahmud II, Abdülhamid II's image was unfailingly captured with him wearing a uniform (plain or parade) and a sword. The sultan's sword became a fixture of his appearances at Friday prayer processions.[42] However, in the Ottoman context, the sword was much more than a military symbol. Since sword girding was the major investiture ceremony for a sultan, equivalent to coronations in the West, the sword's first and foremost connotation in the short run was legitimacy to rule. Since Murad V never received a sword girding, he was never fully confirmed as a ruler during his brief three-month reign. This made his deposition easier in the eyes of the Ottoman public.[43] By looking more closely at Abdülhamid II's speedy sword girding, mentioned above, we can gain yet another vantage point for analysing the crisis of the dynasty and the sultan's early ceremonial signals in response to it. For example, Abdülhamid II was the only sultan in the last century of the Empire who chose to be girded with not one but two swords. In fact, there were only two other double sword girdings in the entire history of the Ottoman Empire – Murad IV's in 1623 and Mahmud II's in 1808.[44] A closer look at each set of circumstances reveals the probable cause for such a rare ceremonial event. A quick string of depositions preceded each of these sword girdings, bringing about a dynastic 'low' moment in each instance. Thus, it is hardly a coincidence that in the aftermath of each destabilising episode, the new sultan should choose to be girded with two swords. In the case of Mahmud II, as Hakan Karateke points out, this meant one sword of Islamic and one of dynastic significance.[45] Yet the same is true of the other two double sword girdings as well. The Islamic sword – Caliph Umar's – was in fact common to all post-Mahmud II sword girdings.

Here is a hypothesis regarding why Caliph Umar's sword became the sword of choice for Abdülmecid's sword girding in the summer of 1839 and all subsequent sword girdings. As discussed earlier, with the signing of the Rose Chamber Edict in November 1839 Abdülmecid announced a set of profound imperial reforms known as the Tanzimat. One of their main explicitly stated goals was to establish equality between Ottoman Muslims and Christians and guarantee their lawful co-existence. As Butrus Abu-Manneh has convincingly shown, the ideas of this edict were already in circulation even before the new sultan's accession to power.[46] Could it be that the sword of Caliph Umar was selected with the same symbolic significance in mind? After all, Caliph Umar, one of the most venerated caliphs in the Sunni Muslim tradition,[47] was – and is to this day – also remembered for his covenant with the Christians of Jerusalem providing *justice to Muslims and non-Muslims alike*. Girding Abdülmecid with Umar's sword, on the eve of reforms, would send a poignant message. This would also explain why this sword became embedded in the late Ottoman mythology of power.

The latter of Abdülhamid II's swords was announced in the press as the 'sword of the sultanate' (*saltanat kılıçı*). Its actual identity remains unknown to this day. Karateke speculates that it was probably Osman

Gazi's.⁴⁸ If so, with this choice, as with the choice to have two swords girded, Abdülhamid II followed in the steps of his grandfather. More importantly, the decision to name it 'the sword of the sultanate' – a unique and mysterious appellation – was probably intended to bestow in yet another way legitimacy upon the new sultan.

In comparison with his predecessors and successors in the period from 1808 to 1918, Abdülhamid II staged his sword girding in other unique ways too. Whereas all others had visited one or at most two ancestral tombs after their sword girding on the way to the old palace of Topkapı, Abdülhamid II attended at least three. The first was Selim I's – a unique choice in the nineteenth century – declaring in no uncertain terms the new sultan's caliphal claims.⁴⁹ The second tomb was Abdülmecid's. This choice made Abdülhamid II one of only two nineteenth-century sultans who visited the tombs of their fathers (the other one being Abdülaziz, who visited Mahmud II's tomb). In each case, this must have been a legitimation move, within the Ottoman rules of royal succession.⁵⁰ The third tomb was Mehmed II's, common to all sultans, and clearly signifying the conquest of Constantinople for Islam. Interestingly, Abdülhamid II visited the same sacred grounds associated with these three sultans again, barely three weeks later, during Ramazan. This is further proof of their significance to him and the type of visibility he wished to create for himself.⁵¹

As in Russia, beginning with Nicholas I (1825–55), so in the Ottoman Empire, beginning with Abdülmecid (1839–61), the ruler's closest relatives became increasingly involved in his scenario of power and, to some degree, began to share with the ruler the task of presenting the dynasty favourably. At sultanic accessions, accession anniversaries and major religious holidays from the mid-nineteenth century on, a review of the imperial family appeared in the press, both domestically and abroad, with the chief purpose of drawing parallels and locating the new monarch within the line of his ancestors.⁵² For example, Murad V's rise to the throne evoked a comparison with the accomplishments of the previous four Murads, each of whom had 'decorated Ottoman History with great victories, reforms and acts of justice'.⁵³ Abdülhamid II's accession, more than any other, provoked a myriad of comparisons – to his brother, father and even grandfather. Like Murad V, he was 'learned, serene and versed in state government'. Moreover, Abdülhamid II 'exchanged ideas for the saving of the fatherland (*otechestvo*)' with his brother and 'resembled his father in every respect'.⁵⁴ Most surprisingly, Abdülhamid II was immediately juxtaposed with his grandfather, Mahmud II, a parallel that, ironically, escapes most historians of his reign even today – 'of sober habits and energetic disposition, Abdul Hamid possesses many of the sterner virtues of his grandfather'.[55] In 1886, on the occasion of a major religious holiday (Ramazan), Abdülhamid II's accomplishments in his ten-year reign were even compared to Süleyman I's.[56]

The practice of bringing up royal ancestors gradually became internalised and created a novel sense of a temporal continuity between the Ottoman rulers in the public mind. Over time, the family image became more pronounced and its horizon extended ever further back, binding together the living and the dead family members, and strengthening, by way of historicisation, the image and sovereignty of the present ruler. The presentation of a united family front to the outside world at every succession became a tacitly understood public imperative of the first order. This was one of the factors causing a shift in the relations between the living members of the dynasty.

Before the nineteenth century, few princes could evade the rigid constraints of the Cage (*Kafes*). Some exceptions include Mustafa II and Selim III.[57] With the relaxation of the Cage rules in the second quarter of the nineteenth century,[58] Ottoman princes gained an unprecedented freedom of movement, socialisation and knowledge. Abdülaziz gave Murad Efendi[59] further rights – to have his own house outside the palace and to be able to see and correspond with Europeans. Murad even became a Freemason.[60] Abdülhamid Efendi received similarly lenient treatment and much direct visibility in the capital in the 1850s during his father's reign. Both he and Murad accompanied their uncle Abdülaziz on his trip to Europe in 1867.

The tide turned sharply during Abdülhamid II's first days in power and the princes did not even share in the sultan's initial run of extreme direct visibility. Even though, with the exception of Murad Efendi, they remained in close proximity to the ruler, they were rarely exposed to the public gaze. Thus, on the sea journey to Eyüp for Abdülhamid II's sword-girding ceremony, the state boat conveying the princes followed the sultan's boat. Apparently, he met them privately in the Topkapı Palace at the end of the day, but at no point during the land procession itself did they appear in public next to him.[61] Instead, the members of the Imperial Household (both male and female) observed the procession from the building of the Ministry of Finance overlooking the route.[62]

As the princes had previously enjoyed much public attention, and had therefore become more susceptible to foreign and domestic influences, their allegiance to the throne had to be somehow formally renewed. Thus, on the day following Abdülhamid II's accession to power, his cousins, Prince Youssouf Izzedin and Prince Mahmud Celaleddin, sons of Sultan

Abdülaziz, presented their respects to him. Abdülhamid II was said to have 'very cordially' received them.[63] Thereafter, the princes' direct visibility reflected the ruler's own more closely than ever before. When the princes did appear in public, it was usually during Friday prayer processions, overwhelmingly by the side of and in a subordinate manner to the ruler. For example, Abdülhamid II's two younger brothers, Mehmed Reşad Efendi and Ahmed Kemaleddin Efendi, accompanied him on the above-mentioned visit to Aya Sofya early in his reign. By the 1890s, upon Abdülhamid II's return from Friday prayers, male members of the dynasty led the way in the procession *behind* the royal carriage.[64] No one was more affected by this turn of policy than Abdülhamid II's elder brother, Murad Efendi, who was effectively under house arrest in the Çırağan Palace for the remainder of his life.

A discussion of Abdülhamid II's early policies regarding his own visibility would be incomplete without an example of the very real constraints on the new sultan, placed by the highly powerful bureaucrats who brought him to power. Karateke described just such an instance.

For his public oath taking ceremony (*biat*) upon coming to power, Abdülhamid II apparently wished to place the throne in the audience chamber of the old Imperial Palace (Topkapı)'s third court. This would turn the whole event essentially into a private ceremony. According to Karateke, the sultan took this approach 'out of groundless fears (*vehme kapılarak*)'.[65] Security issues notwithstanding, there is an alternative and perhaps more realistic interpretation – this may have been intended as a conscious return to the past, the times when the sultan received ambassadors in the Audience Room of the Third Court. If it had gone through, a staging such as this would have instantly struck a chord with the mainstream Ottoman public. In a slightly different sense, this may be construed as an early attempt to regain a measure of invisibility, and by extension, inviolability for the ruler and the dynasty lost through overexposure in the course of the previous fifty years.

When the powerful Grand Vizier denied the sultan his wish, Abdülhamid II went to the opposite extreme and made this *biat* the most cosmopolitan accession oath ever.[66] He extended the scope of the ceremony, which started in the Topkapı Palace and continued in the Dolmabahçe Palace. For the first time, Abdülhamid II brought in the leaders of the non-Muslim communities, as well as the leading bankers of Istanbul, both Ottoman and foreign. That he chose to do so is, in my view, a testament to the sultan's urgent need to rally support from all quarters and garner sympathies abroad. The new sultan probably grasped that, in the aftermath of Abdülaziz's deposition, openness was the order of the day. Given the circumstances of his coming to power, Abdülhamid II needed to make his mark on the public conscience and do so quickly, if he was to stay in power.

The unusually high number of exceptions to previous and subsequent ceremonial practices in the early days of Sultan Abdülhamid II's reign justify suggestions of deliberate design and strategy. When forced to accept extreme visibility in some respects in the short run, the sultan tried to benefit the most from it. Through some other acts and stagings, however, he was already hinting at his own invisibility preferences. The latter only gained momentum throughout the rest of his long reign.

The Sultan's Mid-reign. Dynastic Pantheon and Ceremonial Ingenuity. Accentuation of the Split in Ruler Visibility

Throughout the 1880s and 1890s, as Abdülhamid II sought to strengthen the Ottoman imperial position abroad, he oversaw two concomitant processes, which were also taking place in other contemporaneous monarchies – the further extension, and complication, of what may be called a *dynastic pantheon* and the ceremonial immersion of foreign dignitaries into this pantheon during state visits. Dynastic pantheon refers to a set of signifiers, ranging from physical objects such as tombs, shrines and flags to abstract concepts such as music, colours, monograms and mottos. Its purpose was to convey a positive image of a monarch and his or her dynasty, stressing their legacy, stability and grandeur. Curiously, a similar term did have a contemporary usage – a book published in Russia in 1850 (permitted by the censor in 1846) was entitled *Pantheon of the Fatherland [Otechestvennyiy Panteon], or the Life of Grand Dukes, Tsars and Emperors*.[67] As the latter part of the title suggests, the pantheon in question was really that of the dynasties ruling Russia over the centuries, beginning with the mythic figure of Ryurik (862–79 CE). At the time of this book's publication, the Ottomans had already embarked on a quest for ceremonial reciprocity with the West. Facilitated greatly by the events of the Crimean War, this goal was largely completed by the late 1860s, with the visit of Abdülaziz to Europe, on the one hand, and the visits of the French Empress Eugenie and the Habsburg emperor Franz Joseph I to Istanbul, on the other. By the 1880s and 1890s, as each empire turned inwards in search of sources of and models for renewal, the interaction of the type mentioned above began to take place. It is interesting to observe in some detail what constituted a dynastic pantheon during these encounters, but even more so to examine the instances of sharing of sacred space and meaning between royal host and royal visitor, especially when they espoused different faiths.

An example from the Russian Empire can best illustrate the inter-imperial nature of this phenomenon and serve as an introduction to the Ottoman equivalent. The object of interest is the Persian Shah's visit to St Petersburg in 1889. Perhaps not coincidentally, it fell on the Russian emperor's coronation anniversary. Naser al-Din Shah Qajar (1848–96) visited Alexander II (1855–81)'s tomb in the Cathedral of Peter and Paul. On his arrival, he took off his shoes at the church's door. Then, at the tomb itself, the shah placed his hands on his chest in prayer and obeisance. This was followed by the placement of 'a gigantic wreath, made from magnificently executed porcelain flowers, decorated with small diamonds' on top of the tomb. As it turned out, this was just one of a whole array of finely crafted and jewel-studded wreaths laid at Alexander II's grave, arranged in the manner of museum exhibits. The shah paused again to pray before the tomb of Empress Maria Aleksandrovna[68] (1855–80) before visiting that of Peter the Great (1682–1725). He was shown the imperial regalia (sceptre, crown and orb), and, allegedly, 'long marvelled at the massive diamonds with which they were decorated'. Then the shah visited the site of Alexander II's assassination where once again he prayed. That same day the shah observed the construction of the Holy Resurrection Church. Earlier, while still in Moscow, the Director of the Moscow State Archive had presented him with an album of watercolour drawings of the coronation of Mikhail Romanov (1613–45).[69]

In short, on his brief visit, Naser al-Din Shah was brought into some form of contact with at least four deceased Romanov rulers – the former royal couple, Peter the Great and Mikhail Romanov, the dynasty's founder. The Shia Muslim shah, head of a sovereign state, prayed for these Orthodox Christian rulers on three occasions and was even present at a church construction site. Other state leaders, visiting St Petersburg in subsequent years, went through the same routine – a mandatory visit to the royal burial complex of St Peter and St Paul, and to the site of Alexander II's assassination on the Ekaterininskiy Canal. The list of visitors included the French president, the Habsburg emperor and even the Siamese king. Even though they exhibited varying degrees of exuberance in their demonstrations of faith and ceremonial cooptation at these sacred sites, all heads of state played the roles seemingly expected of them.[70] It seems that faith, projected onto a dynastic pantheon, was becoming a universalised tool of monarchy, a vital first ceremonial line of defence in the late nineteenth century, and no divide was too wide to be bridged. It goes without saying

The Reign of Abdülhamid II

that such inter-faith ceremonial-diplomatic gestures of inclusion are hard to imagine in the world we live in today.

The Ottomans exhibited signs of the same trend, except much more cautiously and subtly, which probably stemmed from a weaker position of relative power. The most complex instances of such symbolic interaction and the corresponding visibility implications stem from the second visit of the German emperor (Kaiser) Wilhelm II (1888–1918) to the Ottoman Empire in 1898. In order to properly map the changes and get a more nuanced perspective on the overall process, it is worth reviewing the Kaiser's first visit as well.

In 1889, a year after his ascent to power, on his way back to Germany after attending his sister's wedding in Greece, the Kaiser passed through Istanbul. The visit lasted only four days and was restricted to the capital. During this visit, the emperor lavished his attention on sites related to the German colony and the Byzantine landmarks. Thus, he visited the German school, the embassy, the Protestant church and the Moltke monument, then under construction. He also inspected the ancient walls of Constantinople, from Yedikule[71] to Eyüp. Neither the former nor the latter, however, seems to have received any attention at all, despite the fact that both were important Ottoman dynastic markers. The only site of key Ottoman significance the Kaiser visited was the Topkapı Palace, but there he only saw the Treasury, which could be easily construed as a simple museum visit, deprived of any spiritual dynastic meaning.[72]

The second visit was much longer, and included not only Istanbul, but also Jerusalem and Syria. As he had done before, the Kaiser visited the ancient walls, among other Byzantine landmarks. This time, however, he proceeded in a traditional Ottoman state boat with fourteen rowers directly to the quay of Eyüp, which had been specially renovated.[73] As in 1889, commemorative medals were issued, with the Ottoman coat of arms (*arma-ı osmani*) and the Muslim calendar date (Cemaziülahir 1, 1316) on one side, and the German eagle and inscription on the other.[74] In addition, silver vases were cast and decorated once again with the German eagle and the Ottoman coat of arms. They were presented to the emperor by the town Payables Office 'in the name of the people of Istanbul (*Istanbul ahalisi namına*)'.[75] The German imperial standard appeared on the cover page of *Servet-i Fünun* (Treasure of the Arts), an Ottoman illustrated journal, in black and red. The fact that colour (moreover, red, the colour of the Sultanate and Ottoman flags) was used in the domestic press, with reference to a royalty other than the sultan in a flag of another state, may be a subtle indication of the extraordinary welcome extended to the Kaiser.[76] On the cover of the next issue, the black German eagle was

Ruler Visibility and Popular Belonging

displayed gently embracing the Ottoman imperial standard with its right wing.[77] During the royal couple's visit to the imperial factory at Hareke, three girls presented them with bouquets. Their names must have been a factor in their selection – Ümme (*community of the faithful*), Münevver (*enlightened*, also a popular epithet for Medina) and Binaz(ir) (*matchless, unequalled*). Once again, a fourteen-oared state boat conveyed the Kaiser to his ship upon departure.[78] In the meantime, the local Ottoman press was framing the Kaiser's visit in sacred, unusually embracing terms too. According to the newspaper *Sabah* (Morning), 'the devout prayer of the Ottoman nation is that it may please Providence long to preserve the Emperor'. . . *Ikdam* [Advance] spoke of 'the consecration of the friendship' between the two peoples.[79] The intimate terms of contact between the two monarchs, dynasties and states reveal a novel symbolic strategy of inter-imperial legitimation, unprecedented both in its creativity and in its level of abstraction.

The most interesting part of the Kaiser's visit to the Ottoman Empire was yet to come – his trip to Jerusalem and Syria, under the pretext of inaugurating a new Protestant church there. For the Kaiser's comfort, a gorgeous tent was 'purposely (*mahsusan*)' sent to Jerusalem by the 'Holy Personage (*Taraf-ı Eşref*)' of the sultan. Equipped with latticed windows and topped by an Ottoman sun, the tent conveyed a sense of Oriental splendour becoming of an Ottoman sultan from bygone times.[80] For the Kaiser's entry to Jerusalem, a triumphal arch stood in his honour near the Yafe Gate (*Bab-ı Halil*). This in itself was not unusual. During his previous visit, the Kaiser had passed through several such structures in Istanbul, beginning with the one at the quay of Scutari (Üsküdar) placed precisely at the spot where he would first step on Asian soil. The design of the latest triumphal arch in Jerusalem, however, was highly syncretic and painstakingly elaborate. Its two rectangular bases resembled minarets, equipped with galleries and topped by domes bearing a striking resemblance to the Hohenzollern crown.[81] The minaret walls had painted black motifs resembling keyholes. It seemed as if the city was offering its symbolic keys to the Kaiser.[82]

In Jerusalem, the Kaiser visited 'the Mussulman cemetery and historic tombs, the mosque of Umar'.[83] He entered *Harem-üş şerif* (lit. 'the Sacred Noble Sanctuary', also known as the Temple Mount) through the famous Golden Gate. The latter had two vaulted halls which led to the 'Door of Mercy' (*Bab ül-Rahme*) and the 'Door of Repentance' (*Bab ül-Tevbe*). Even though to the emperor, the importance of entering through the Golden Gate must have been paramount, the photograph which appeared in *Servet-i Fünun* only showed him emerging on the other side. The accompanying text identified the passage as the 'Door of Repentance'. Apparently, there were limits even to the very generous terms of the Kaiser's incorporation into Ottoman Muslim symbology and some lines simply could not be crossed. A photograph in the Ottoman press of the Kaiser's entry through the Golden Gate could be easily construed as an act of Christian conquest, offensive to many. The need to accommodate both the august visitor and the domestic public required such subtle manoeuvres, and even led to bizarre extremes. For example, a specially made breach in the city walls next to the famous *Bab-ı Halil* allowed the Kaiser to enter Jerusalem on horseback, but apparently did not disturb Ottoman Muslim opinion. Had he entered on horseback through the gate itself, things might have stood very differently. Still, the emperor and empress did enter not only the Temple Mount, as another photograph clearly showed, but also the 'Dome of the Rock' (*Sahret-i Allah*) itself. A third photograph in the same issue captured their exit through the mosque's southern door, oriented towards Mecca.[84]

In Damascus, some of the most intriguing episodes of sharing of sacred space and prayer between the German and the Ottoman monarch took place. A picture of the Kaiser and his wife visiting the Umayyad Grand Mosque shows two German imperial standards hanging over them. One resembles the emperor's, and the other may possibly be the crown prince's. At least three court ladies in the empress's escort were allowed to enter the sacred grounds of the mosque too.[85] Much like the Persian shah in St Petersburg nine years earlier, the Kaiser visited a royal tomb and laid a wreath on the greatest Ayyubid ruler's grave. He praised Saladin (1174–93) as the exemplary knight and even donated a marble sarcophagus for him.[86] Then, in a speech, the Kaiser even uttered a prayer for the sultan – 'It is my earnest hope that the respect and veneration of his subjects and of the 300 million Muslims existing on earth may always centre upon his Majesty Sultan Abdul-Hamid II . . . May Almighty God grant long life and health to the sultan'.[87]

Finally, the drive for dynastic memorialisation, which the two monarchs shared, found one more expression. On the way back to Beirut, at the site of the ancient Heliopolis ruins near Baalbek, a plate commemorating the Kaiser's visit was inaugurated with a special ceremony in his presence.[88] A photograph of it in *Servet-i Fünun* featured the German eagle next to the sultan's monogram (*tuğra*), above inscriptions in German and Ottoman, respectively. The intended message was conveyed by various sources with only minor differences – a 'souvenir (*yadıgar olmak üzere*)', a 'striking token of the solid friendship between the two empires' and '[a symbol of] the reciprocal and unalterable friendship'.[89]

Ruler Visibility and Popular Belonging

The Kaiser's two visits, related in minute detail on the pages of the *Levant Herald*, also provide a vivid illustration of the split in the terms of Abdülhamid II's ceremonial engagement with his royal peers on the one hand and with his domestic public on the other. To the former the sultan remained accessible, but their association was usually not directly visible in public; to the latter, the sultan was both less accessible and less visible. Before reviewing the evidence for this claim, it would be useful to examine briefly some key elements of protocol from the two earlier state visits to Istanbul already mentioned.

In 1869, when the French empress Eugenie (1853–71) visited the Ottoman capital on her way to the opening of the Suez Canal, Sultan Abdülaziz proceeded by state barge to her ship in order to welcome her. Then they disembarked, in plain view, walking arm in arm. According to Hristo Stambolski, a long-term Bulgar resident of Istanbul, such proximity and intimate terms of contact between the two monarchs had a mixed effect upon the public, provoking curiosity as well as resentment. The latter was couched in orthodox Muslim terms. Both men and women found that the sultan, a married Muslim, should not mix so freely with another woman, even if it was an empress. By doing so, he was setting an inappropriate model of family life for the young. The latter, especially young women, were curious and open to the innovation.[90] Mary Patrick, a long-term American resident of Istanbul, however, viewed the event entirely from a Western perspective. To her, the sultan 'played the part of royal host with great distinction'.[91] When Emperor Franz Joseph I, also en route to Egypt, visited Istanbul two weeks later, Abdülaziz was once again so courteous as to pay him a similar visit, this time in the Palace of Beylerbeyi.[92]

Abdülhamid II avoided any such controversy altogether. Even though he was just as civil and polite to his guests, he staged their encounter in a way that few were able to observe with their own eyes. Contrary to Abdülaziz's practices, each time the Kaiser's ship approached the shores of Istanbul, it was high Ottoman dignitaries who actually went aboard to welcome him. The sultan remained at the Dolmabahçe Palace. On both visits, the sultan gave an arm to the empress on many occasions, helping her ashore, as well as in and out of carriages. All of this, however, occurred away from the public, at Dolmabahçe's private quay, where they could be witnessed only from the sea, or in the secluded palatial complex of Yıldız. The fact that the sultan did not accompany the German royal couple on *any* of their many day trips around Istanbul is one of the strongest indications of his agenda with respect to his own subjects. He clearly did not wish to be seen. Instead, the Kaiser would telegraph the sultan on more than one occasion, even from a distance of only a few kilometres.[93]

The Reign of Abdülhamid II

Such conduct was in unison with Abdülhamid II's long-standing and remarkably consistent policy of making himself unavailable to the public eye. It enhanced his mystic status in the eyes of the Ottoman (especially Muslim) public.

In public, Abdülhamid II preferred to communicate to his royal peers by way of messengers, as mentioned earlier in the context of his sword-girding procession. The following procedure was kept during Friday prayer processions throughout his reign – a messenger conveyed greetings to the foreign dignitaries on the sultan's way out of the Hamidiye Mosque, followed by an audience only later, invariably behind closed doors. I have come across only one exception to this rule, at a Friday prayer procession during the Kaiser's second visit – 'in passing in front of the pavilion [erected for the Kaiser] the sultan saluted his imperial guests who stood at one of the windows'.[94] This seems to be a singular gesture of good will towards the Kaiser.

It was the spectacle of the Friday prayer procession that brought foreigners, natives and the monarch together, and at this regularised

Figure 4.2 Hamidiye Mosque during *Selamlık* (Friday prayer) by uncredited photographer. Vlas Doroshevich, *Vostok i Voina* (Moscow: I. D. Sytin, 1905), p. 221 (Wikimedia Commons).

juncture, the contrast between the two types of ruler visibility seems most jarring. For example, the sultan would be equally at ease providing money for Hajj pilgrims from Central Asia as ordering champagne for foreign tourists from the *Lusitania*.[95] Distinguished foreigners would be invited to special kiosks for privileged viewing while local bystanders would be hard pressed to catch a single glimpse of the caliph whose passage was routinely obscured by a double line of soldiers on each side.[96]

The process of Ottoman inclusion into the Western system of signs and symbols, initiated daringly by Mahmud II, had by Abdülaziz's time inspired attempts to do the exact opposite – bring the Westerners back into the Ottoman fold, in large part by feeding their fantasies of the Orient. Abdülhamid II's reign witnessed a full-scale turn towards indigenous authenticity due to a number of factors. One of them was the same desire to be accepted as an indelible part of the international order which had prompted the imitation of the West in the first place. By the late nineteenth century, however, this cultural turn relied on the understanding that a well-articulated difference based on alleged indigenous roots was a new and strong legitimating factor. This new direction in the field of ceremonial stemmed from harder realities and fashions of the day, from imperial thinking and state making as much as from a growing sense of the value of self-determination. This is why the Ottomans were sometimes happy to play the Oriental card – at World Fairs or during foreign royal visits to Istanbul – along with the Western one, as long as they could control the symbolic message of each. After all, an Orient that could be civilised without losing its dignity was worthy of existence.

This 'auto-Orientalist' mode of thought, which permeated the dynastic pantheon discussed above, was most frequently visible at Friday prayer processions. For example, for his Friday prayer attendance on 1 September 1888, the Duke of Edinburgh was accommodated with 'a spacious tent, specially provided and richly ornamented with Oriental carpets and tapestry'.[97] An equally effective way for ceremonial incorporation of Westerners involved the review of elite military units in their splendid exotic uniforms.

Abdülhamid II maintained the traditional imperial guard of halberdiers (*baltacı*) in their archaic scarlet uniforms, and he brought back other elite regiments, founded by his predecessors, under Western influence. These included the Lancers (*Mızraklı*), a concept Mahmud II borrowed from the British, and the Zouave[98] (*Zühaf*), a French (North African) invention, first observed by Abdülmecid during the Crimean War and eventually introduced domestically by Abdülaziz. At the same time, Abdülhamid II invented his own section of the Imperial Guard, which ultimately formed its core – the Ertuğrul regiment. Its ranks consisted of tall, handsome Turks from Söğüt, the Anatolian birthplace of the dynasty.[99] The point was to demonstrate the extent of the Empire and the various, increasingly ethnic pillars of monarchic support. An American eyewitness of Friday prayer processions perceptively observed: 'today a regiment from the Soudan, tomorrow a battalion from Albania . . . Every part of the dominion is represented by the troops'.[100] This was also a conscious return to Oriental splendour, on a scale unknown since the end of the Janissaries. After all, what had been, from a Western perspective, a marker of Oriental indulgence at the beginning of the nineteenth century had become an acceptable marker of otherness by its end. Reined in by the Western format of the military review, the Oriental content fulfilled contemporary validating functions.

With the approach of a foreign dignitary's visit to Istanbul, military reviews grew exponentially in size. For example, on 11 October 1889, two regiments (the Ertuğrul and infantry of the line), with their respective bands playing, marched past after Friday prayer. A week later, more than six units (troops of the line, a battalion of marines, some regiments of artillery, the Ertuğrul, Zühaf and Mızraklı regiments) participated. The following week a review of more than fifteen battalions of infantry and four regiments of cavalry took place, with four bands playing in turn. Finally, on 3 November 1889, a Saturday, Kaiser Wilhelm II and the sultan witnessed from the specially erected pavilion a march past of eighteen battalions of infantry, including the troops of the line and the Zühaf, four regiments of cavalry and four batteries of artillery. As Western practice dictated, Ottoman honorary aides-de-camp[101] were assigned to the Kaiser. The review lasted more than an hour.[102]

All of these units projected a conservative Muslim image of a ruler steeped in both ancient and recent dynastic traditions (or rather, their credible fabrications). In this, as in everything else, Abdülhamid II came through as a complete antithesis of his elder brother Murad, whose brief reign witnessed the unprecedented introduction of squadrons of various Christian volunteers (*muhtelif gönüllü Hıristiyan taburu*).[103] To date, this very brief but fascinating page of Ottoman military history has not received the scholarly attention it deserves.[104] Perhaps the most striking aspect of this troop was its flag – a red banner, with a crescent and cross of equal size and (pale green) colour.[105] In my view, it best captures the syncretic, and with hindsight, hard-to-believe nature of the late imperial project.

In non-military matters, however, Abdülhamid II could be quite accommodating to the Empire's Christians. When it came to the celebration of the sultan's accession anniversary in 1888 in Izmir (Smyrna), a town with a large non-Muslim (especially Greek-speaking) population and a very important Western consular presence, the use of royal portraits was once again unabashed: 'Everywhere the portrait of His Majesty, surrounded by flowers or surmounted by a crescent of gas jets was conspicuous'.[106] It seems that the sultan's portrait also took centre stage at the top of one of the most ornate triumphal arches ever designed in honour of Abdülhamid II. The structure was erected on the sultan's accession anniversary in Hanya (Chania in present-day Greece), administrative capital of the island of Crete, in 1894.[107] In both cases, the use of royal portraits was probably condoned because the sultan was in direct competition for subject loyalty with the sovereign of Greece, who certainly had no qualms about exhibiting his likeness in public. Thus, in 1889, the same Greek-speaking population in Izmir celebrated the wedding of the Greek crown prince in the following manner: 'the shops looked quite unusually brilliant, decorated with flags, Chinese lanterns, illuminated portraits of the Prince and his fiancée'. The *Levant Herald* correspondent felt obliged to add that 'the Smyrna Greeks are very loyal, and would not let the marriage of their Prince pass without some demonstration'.[108]

Despite the sultan's openness to foreign dignitaries, and the flurry of his images in the foreign press, he did not endorse the production and dissemination of memorabilia bearing his likeness, even for restricted private consumption. Thus, he discontinued both the policy, dating back to Selim III, of exchanging royal memento portraits (*tasvir-i hümayun*) with foreign heads of state, and its later adaptation – distributing these special tokens of royal favour at home. To the best of my knowledge, the last such act domestically took place in 1872 when Abdülaziz awarded his portrait to the outgoing Grand Vizier, Mahmud Nedim Paşa.[109]

Clearly, Abdülhamid II could not respond in kind to the profusion of image-based souvenirs[110] the Kaiser distributed all around him on his second visit. These gifts ranged from cigarette holders and snuffboxes with portraits engraved on them to framed, diamond-studded portraits, to the marble busts of the Kaiser and Kaiserin, reserved for the sultan himself. Instead, Abdülhamid II opted for the following replacements of his own visage on the lid and case of a snuffbox for the Kaiser – 'a Turkish warrior, holding a rifle with bayonet, to the point of which is attached a crescent in brilliants' and the sultan's monogram, respectively.[111] This is not to say that the sultan did not appreciate photography. In fact, such a statement could not be further from the truth. For each of the Kaiser's two visits,

Abdülhamid II had photographers assigned. They recorded events from beginning to end, that is, from the Kaiser's meeting with the Ottoman fleet in the Dardanelles in 1889 to the Kaiser's departure from the Holy Lands in 1898.[112] Moreover, the sultan sent large and elaborately detailed photographic albums containing a carefully staged and highly presentable version of the life and accomplishments of the Empire to the United States and Britain in the early 1890s.[113] Allegedly, at least on one occasion, namely the twenty-fifth accession anniversary, he used full-length photographs in deciding which prisoners would benefit from a royal amnesty. Finally, upon the sultan's deposition in 1909 even a small photographic atelier belonging to him was discovered on the grounds of the Yıldız Palace.[114]

Interestingly, during the Kaiser's second visit, members of the Ottoman dynasty were allowed an unprecedented degree of ceremonial involvement and direct visibility. In some cases, this occurred 'at the request of the emperor and empress';[115] in others, it was probably by domestic design, in accordance with perceived standards for contemporary royal houses. Thus, Abdülhamid II's sons, sons-in-law and brothers-in-law could often be seen by the sultan's side in a carriage or in command of their respective squadrons during military reviews. Even a six-year-old daughter, Refiye Sultan, had a role to play – she was sent to the guest residence in Yıldız to deliver a bouquet to the empress on her birthday. These innovations may have at least in part stemmed from Abdülhamid II's need to counteract accusations of Oriental despotism, which were by this time mounting in the Western press. Still, all interactions between the Ottoman princes and the German guests took place behind closed doors.

The Sultan's Late Reign. Cult of Personality

This section will explore the topic of the ruler's increasingly sacred aura in the late period by recourse to several themes – acts of charity and generosity, trends in period monumental architecture, the myth of naming and the concept of cross-dating.[116] In reality, these themes were closely interwoven and will appear accordingly in this section. In the process, special attention will be paid to the ways in which the language of official documents and newspapers deliberately projected a specific, carefully designed image of the monarch onto the canvas of public consciousness. The main difference from the past was in the degree of monarchic usurpation of ceremonial space, with more celebrations being tied back to the ruler than ever before, resulting in a full-blown cult of personality.

In the Ottoman Empire's late period, *mercy* seems to have been the chief prerogative of the male ruler, predictable in its cyclicality and widening both in its impact across the domains and in its press coverage. Reasserted norms of faith-based moral propriety, after a period of relatively more relaxed social rules in the middle decades of the nineteenth century, demanded yet again that female members of the dynasty be kept largely outside the public eye. Rules of succession and the troubling events of 1876 translated into a long shadow cast over the ruler's male relatives. Therefore, on his accession anniversaries, the sultan was the prime object of attention. There was one major obstacle, however. Abdülhamid II's self-imposed withdrawal from society meant that, unlike his Western counterparts, he had many fewer opportunities to preside over the process of his own image making in public. Therefore, the acts of mercy had to speak louder. The posting of commemorative plaques on buildings certainly helped in this respect, as did the widespread publication of their photographs in the press, along with the flowery formulaic language glorifying the monarch.

Among the institutions Abdülhamid II founded, which attested to his piety, hospitals were a prominent group. Judging by announcements in the periodical press, within this group the lion's share went to institutions targeting the poor, children (especially orphans), refugees and strangers, social outcasts and, increasingly, religious minorities.[117] Thus, hospitals for the poor (*gureba hastahanesi*) opened in all corners of the Ottoman Empire, from Yanya in the Balkans through Çankırı in Anatolia to Sana'a[118] in the Yemen. The target patients included ever more narrowly defined and often socially marginalised segments of the population, not because the monarch so desperately needed their loyalty, but because he rather wished to present himself as an all-encompassing, all-merciful figure, both at home and abroad. Thus, a 'Special Hospital for Poor Men and Women' opened in Konya, as well as a poorhouse in Istanbul with separate quarters for Muslims and Christians.[119]

The overwhelming majority of these inaugurations took place on or around the sultan's accession anniversary or his birthday, and, just as importantly, usually carried the name of their august patron – Hamidiye.[120] Across the Empire, roadhouses for travellers (*misafirhane*) opened, such as in Dedeağaç (Alexandroupoli in present-day Greece) on the sultan's birthday.[121] Houses for Muslim refugees (*muhacirin-i islamiye*) were also erected, such as in the Haşine[122] and Hamdani[123] villages in Syria, again on the sultan's birthday.

Sometimes local residents would take up the sultan's cues themselves, as occurred in the town of Karahisar-ı Sahib (Afyonkarahisar in present-day Turkey) where 'an official ceremony of laying the foundation of houses, a school and a holy mosque expressly for the settlement of

Muslim refugees, *as it was agreed upon*', took place on accession day.¹²⁴ Moreover, completely new settlements, alternatively called Hamidiye or Osmaniye, would thus be founded. Such was the case with Al-Hamidiyah (Hamidiye) in Syria, established for Cretan immigrants after the war of 1897, and with a certain Osmaniye in the Aydın province (*vilayet*), near Efes, established for recent immigrants in 1906.¹²⁵

Many of the Hamidian establishments would then add ceremonial input of their own to official celebrations, thus causing *ripple effects* of the original foundational act over time. For example, the management of the Poor Asylum in the Şişli district of Istanbul issued an illustrated pamphlet in 1906, in connection to accession day, about the twenty-four-year history of the institution.¹²⁶ The pamphlet contained some curious statistics on the religious background of the asylum's students – 595 Muslim, 116 Greek, 53 Armenian, 5 Armenian-Catholic and 26 Jewish.¹²⁷ This list reveals a clear discrepancy between, on the one hand, the high sensitivity in cataloguing minorities, including awareness of the presence of Armenian Catholics, and, on the other, the indiscriminate manner whereby all Muslims were lumped together in the same category. The intended message of this data manipulation may not be so complex after all – a tolerance and care for non-Muslims and an unquestioned, undivided authority over co-religionists. Both were traits of a good caliph. Not surprisingly, this spiritual title, in various derivative forms and combinations, flourished in the late Ottoman Empire. In fact, it accompanied most of Abdülhamid II's charitable acts. For example, the picture of a new hospital, published in *Malumat* (Information), an illustrated contemporary Ottoman journal, carried the following title: 'The sublime Hamidiye Children's Hospital – a testament to His Majesty the Caliph's scattered acts of mercy'.¹²⁸

I have identified more than a dozen formulaic ways to introduce ceremonies of laying the foundation or building inaugurations (of the type 'under the ... auspices of His Majesty'). Three are of explicitly religious nature. In addition, 'His Majesty the Caliph' served as a pointer to some particularly pious acts. Over time, both the ingenuity behind some of these terms and their intensity only grew. Thus, on the twenty-seventh royal accession anniversary, the text accompanying the inauguration photograph of a hospital for the poor in Kavala (in present-day Greece) contained the following phrase – a synonym for the festive day – *ruz-u feyz-i efruzende*, that is, 'the day of bright spiritual enlightenment [emanating from the person of the ruler]'.¹²⁹

Another uplifting quality of the sultan, which radiated out towards the domains and was emphasised repeatedly, was his extraordinary ability to 'make happy'. To be sure, this was no novelty for the Ottomans – felicity

Ruler Visibility and Popular Belonging

(*saadet*) had been emanating from the ruler and, by extension, his proxies, such as the Third Gate of the Topkapı Palace (*Babüssaadet*, the Gate of Felicity) or Istanbul itself (*Dersaadet*, the Abode of Felicity) for centuries. However, in the late period the same glow issued forth from new, recently introduced and essentially secular holidays, such as the sultan's birthday. In 1901, the teachers and students of the senior secondary school in Lefkoşa (Nicosia), Cyprus posed for a photograph in front of the 'Zaman' (Time) printing press 'on the superior birthday of felicity, the prosperous and felicitous day of His Majesty the Sultan'.[130] The same merrymaking capacity belonged to the Russian royals, except it was shared by their extended family as well.[131]

The patriotic motif and the story of its weaving, at first almost imperceptibly, but over time ever more visibly, into the fabric of Ottoman society provides one of the most fruitful ways of exploring and explaining the late Empire. It is all the more pertinent to the subject of this section because of its varied avenues of association with mercy and religiosity in this period.

Fig. 4.3 provides a snapshot of the foundations of loyalty to the sultan – a picture of the students of the Hamidiye School for the Deaf and Mute, founded by Abdülhamid II in the 1880s,[132] which was published on accession day in 1893. In the picture, the students (all male) congratulated the sultan, with the older ones each signing a letter of the 'Long Live the Sultan (*Padişahım Çok Yaşa*)' slogan, while the youngsters held their hands out in a prayer position.[133] As the text underneath indicated, this prayer for the sultan's health was '[a duty] one was obliged to discharge (*dua-yı*

Figure 4.3 Students of the Hamidiye School for the Deaf and Mute. *Servet-i Fünun*, no. 129, 19 August 1309 (31 August 1893), p. 388. Courtesy of the Turkish National Library, Ankara.

The Reign of Abdülhamid II

vacibüleda)'. In the background, overlooking the whole group, was the framed, glass-covered royal monogram, brought out and set up especially for the occasion of this outdoor photo session. The accompanying article called these students *etfal-ı vatan* – 'children of the fatherland'.[134]

The sultan's example of patriotic mercy must have proved contagious to the general population of co-religionists. Eight years later, on the cover page of the same journal, there is evidence of a broader charitable-cum-patriotic zeal in yet another school picture. It portrayed students (both male and female) in a recently founded Muslim school in Vidin, Bulgaria (Fig. 4.4). The heading underneath clarified a key point, namely that these were 'children of the poor dressed by patriotic people (*ahali-yi hamiyetmendan tarafından elbas edilmiş fukara etfalı)*'.[135]

Since Bulgaria was already a separate, albeit still dependent entity at that time, the *patria* in question must have been faith-based, that is, geographically unbounded. The photograph's publication date was once again significant – 1 March 1317 (in the Rumi (Muslim solar) calendar) – the first day of the New Year. What better way for an Ottoman journal to start the New Year than with a cover-page picture of Muslim students, all in neat uniforms (each girl wearing a headscarf, each boy a fez), sitting

Figure 4.4 Students of the Muslim school in Vidin. *Servet-i Fünun*, no. 522, 1 March 1317 (14 March 1901). Courtesy of the Turkish National Library, Ankara.

Ruler Visibility and Popular Belonging

around a tablet with the Muslim calendar date propped up against a model of the globe?

Many such images would appear in the press on the sultan's accession anniversary and birthday. The regions depicted in them would range from previously held and still, at least ceremonially, contested territories, such as the Crimea and the Caucasus, to Muslim areas where no Ottoman political sovereignty had ever existed, such as India and Singapore. In a powerful display of religious allegiance transcending any viable political claims, the sons of notables from faraway Dutch-held Batavya (Jakarta in present-day Indonesia) were admitted to the Tribal School (*aşiret mektebi*) in Istanbul – a prestigious school for the sons of Ottoman provincial notables. Not surprisingly, they too were included in the ceremonial show of support for Abdülhamid II: a photograph depicted them in prayer for the sultan on accession day in 1899 (Fig. 4.5). Apparently, distance did not matter much so long as they were 'Muslim people (*ahali-yi islamiye*)'.[136]

Abdülhamid II's twenty-fifth anniversary on the throne at the turn of the twentieth century was remarkable for the scale of provincial celebratory activity it provoked. It is even more impressive considering the fact that, as Deringil pointed out, there was no religious importance to the number

Figure 4.5 Tribal School students from Batavya (Jakarta). *Malumat*, no. 168, 7 January 1314 (19 January 1899), p. 969. Courtesy of the Turkish National Library, Ankara.

twenty-five, nor an Ottoman precedent. Judging by the enormous number of reports the Ottomans kept on various foreign twenty-fifth anniversary celebrations, from their embassies all over the world, they must have borrowed this number from the West in an attempt to present the Ottoman monarch as equal to all the rest.[137] Among the various types of buildings dedicated to the sultan on this day, the most numerous and perhaps least explored are the public fountains.[138] In terms of tracing a ruler's mythology of power visually, fountains may be the closest Ottoman equivalent to Western royal statues. Both their structural variety and their stylistic diversity are staggering.

As with contemporary church architecture in Russia, Abdülhamidian fountains combined a vast and often overly ornate array of motifs, both domestic and foreign, from a number of different historical periods. Moreover, as the Sultan's reign progressed, the sources of architectural inspiration were sought further back in time. For example, in 1893, less than a month before the accession anniversary, a free-standing fountain pavilion (*çeşme*) was inaugurated at Kağıthane (Istanbul) (Fig. 4.6).[139] Both the cartouche and the shell-shaped voussoirs displayed a strong Rococo influence. The same picture of the Kağıthane fountain would appear seven years later on the pages of the same journal in connection to the sultan's

Figure 4.6 The Kağıthane Fountain in Istanbul. *Servet-i Fünun*, no. 122, 22 July 1309 (3 August 1893). Courtesy of the Turkish National Library, Ankara.

twenty-fifth accession anniversary.¹⁴⁰ Apparently, the readers had to be reminded that this was one 'from among the multitude of the caliph's pious deeds (*cümle-yi hayrat-ı Hazret-i Hilafetpenahiden olarak*)', as the heading of the first picture had said. This phrase, in reference to a fountain, seems to be a throwback to elements of seventeenth-century epigraphic rhetoric – 'the pious deed' and 'benevolent act' (*hayr ü hasenat*; *ihsan*) of a fountain's patron (*sahib-ül hayrat*) in those times.¹⁴¹

Two years later, on the twenty-seventh royal accession anniversary, the newly inaugurated Tophane fountain in Istanbul displayed a mixture of Rococo (cartouche) and Baroque (undulating eaves) motifs (Fig. 4.7).¹⁴²

It thus harkened back to the second quarter of the eighteenth century – the reigns of Ahmet III and Mahmud I. Moreover, the new fountain was located near one of its models – Mahmud I's Tophane Fountain (1732) (Fig. 4.8).¹⁴³ In addition, two wall fountains (Figs 4.9 and 4.10) were inaugurated in the Taksim and Nişantaşı quarters of Istanbul. The press proudly announced that all three drew their waters from Kağıthane.¹⁴⁴ Such association placed the sultan in line with many of his ancestors since Kağıthane had been for many generations a preferred locale for elite promenades and outdoor entertainment.

Yet the vast majority of fountains in honour of Abdülhamid II were erected in the provinces.¹⁴⁵ Contrary to the early eighteenth century

Figure 4.7 Abdülhamid II's Tophane Fountain in Istanbul. *Malumat*, no. 352, 29 August 1318 (11 September 1902), p. 1981. Courtesy of the Turkish National Library, Ankara.

Figure 4.8 Fountain of Mahmud I at Tophane in Istanbul (1732). Drawing by Antoine-Ignace Melling. Reproduced from Melling, *Voyage pittoresque de Constantinople et des rives du Bosphore* (Istanbul: Yapı ve Kredi Bankası, 1969).

Figure 4.9 The Taksim Fountain in Istanbul. *Malumat*, no. 352, 29 August 1318 (11 September 1902), p. 1985. Courtesy of the Turkish National Library, Ankara.

Figure 4.10 The Nişantaşı Fountain in Istanbul. *Malumat*, no. 352, 29 August 1318 (11 September 1902), p. 1988. Courtesy of the Turkish National Library, Ankara.

when the passion for fountains focused mainly on the capital,[146] the late nineteenth and early twentieth centuries witnessed a wave of fountain construction throughout the provinces. This wave penetrated the imperial domains in all directions in a credible effort to make the sultan's symbolic imprint felt even on the outmost periphery. While it is hard to estimate the exact number of fountains erected throughout the empire and the degree of the sultan's personal involvement in the process, it is clear that the vast majority of them were inaugurated on one of the sultanic anniversaries. In this way, at least, they marked a symbolic connection to the centre. If the fountains constructed in the capital can serve as a measure to go by, then the rate of construction seems to have more than doubled in the last decade of Abdülhamid II's reign compared to the previous two decades.[147] In 1900 alone, sketches were drawn, and foundation or inauguration ceremonies held in places ranging from Sakız (Chios) to Adana and Diyarbakır, from Kastamonu and Yozgat to Beirut and Quds (Jerusalem).[148] Most of the fountains were named 'Hamidiye'. Some common structural elements of curious provenance incorporated in them included the obelisk and the Choragic monument of Lysicrates.

The Reign of Abdülhamid II

Examples of the obelisk range from 1892 – the Hamidiye fountain in Selanik[149] (Fig. 4.11)[150] – to at least 1900 – the Kastamonu fountain (Fig. 4.12).[151] Not surprisingly, an image of the Selanik fountain reappeared in the press on the twenty-fifth anniversary in 1900, yet another memento of the reign's accomplishments.[152] In the meantime, Istanbul's obelisks had featured prominently in the photographic albums, sent by Abdülhamid II as gifts to London and Washington, DC in the 1890s, displaying the Ottoman Empire's historical legacy and lively present state. The Ottoman Pavilion of the Chicago World Exhibition in 1893 also included an obelisk, adjacent to a mosque (Fig. 4.13).[153]

Figure 4.11 The Hamidiye Fountain in Selanik. *Servet-i Fünun*, no. 65, 28 May 1308 (9 June 1892). Courtesy of the Turkish National Library, Ankara.

Ruler Visibility and Popular Belonging

Figure 4.12 The Kastamonu Fountain. *Servet-i Fünun*, no. 501, 5 October 1316 (18 October 1900), p. 104. Courtesy of the Turkish National Library, Ankara.

Figure 4.13 The 1893 Chicago Fair Obelisk. *Servet-i Fünun*, no. 136, 7 October 1309 (19 October 1893). Courtesy of the Turkish National Library, Ankara.

The Reign of Abdülhamid II

Figure 4.14 Telegraph monument in Damascus. Raimondo d'Aronco. Unrealised project in the form of an obelisk. Drawing from Manfredi Nicoletti, 'D'Aronco e la Turchia', in *D'Aronco Architetto* (Milan: Electa, 1982), Fig. 55.

As Kreiser points out, Raimondo D'Aronco (1857–1932), Abdülhamid II's palace architect, sketched a bold design for a monumental fountain, the Telegraph Monument in Damascus (Fig. 4.14) whose top in the shape of an obelisk sat on a Baroque (*meydan* fountain) base. Unfortunately, the project was not realised.[154]

Finally, one of the multiple gifts the sultan received for his twenty-fifth anniversary was an artistic model of a monument in his honour from the Muslims of Bulgaria (Fig. 4.15). The monument resembled a massive pavilion (not unlike a mausoleum), which had a square base with four staircases leading up to the respective entrances, protected from the elements by four broad semi-circular eaves. Its equally massive onion-shaped dome, befitting a mosque, had a base reminiscent, once again, of Mahmud I's Tophane fountain, mentioned above. The most curious component of the model, however, was a group of four obelisks, placed at the corners of the base and rising up as minarets would – an impression made all the stronger by the long, pointed tip, protruding from each end, parallel to that of the dome itself.[155]

Figure 4.15 A gift to Abdülhamid II from Bulgarian Muslims. *Malumat*, no. 252, 24 August 1316 (6 September 1900), p. 242. Courtesy of the Turkish National Library, Ankara.

Was the sudden widespread use of obelisks in this period an Ottoman way of sharing in the contemporary international passion for them or was it an authentic claim to ancient roots by way of the Byzantine and Egyptian past? Perhaps it was a bit of both.

Even more startling was the use of architectural motifs clearly borrowed from the Choragic monument of Lysicrates. It dated back to the fourth century BCE and became an icon of the Greek Revival architectural movement in the second quarter of the nineteenth century. Restored between 1876 and 1887, under the auspices of the French government, the monument was widely influential in Europe and the United States at the turn of the century. A prominent contemporary example of it can be seen in the masonry counterweights of the Alexander III Bridge in Paris, completed in 1900. That same year, in honour of Abdülhamid II's twenty-fifth anniversary, a marble column fountain was inaugurated in Beirut (Fig. 4.17). Its top alluded, in miniature, to the Choragic monument, with several columns closely spaced, supporting an oval entablature.[156]

Figure 4.16 The Lysicrates Monument from the north-west, c. 1853–4, by James Robertson (1813–88) (Wikimedia Commons).

Barely a few months later, the picture of another fountain, inaugurated on the same occasion in Sakız (Chios in present-day Greece), appeared in the press (Fig. 4.18).[157] Its lower portion was in the shape of a cross, with four taps and water basins, nestled inside each right angle. Its upper portion, however, represented a full-blown version of the Choragic monument – four engaged fluted columns, with Corinthian capitals, supporting an oval entablature. As in the Beirut fountain, the topmost section was typically Ottoman – a stylised sun vs crescent, respectively, each resting on a turnip-shaped cupola.

Figure 4.17 The Beirut Fountain. *Malumat*, no. 254, 7 September 1316 (20 September 1900), p. 273. Courtesy of the Turkish National Library, Ankara.

Figure 4.18 The Sakız Fountain. *Servet-i Fünun*, no. 514, 4 January 1316 (17 January 1901). Courtesy of the Turkish National Library, Ankara.

The Reign of Abdülhamid II

The choice of the Choragic monument may have been justified by more than contemporary international fashions, of which the late Ottomans were doubtless fully aware and all too eager to partake. Since Beirut did have a substantial Greek population and Sakız – a Greek majority at the time – it might not be so far-fetched to interpret the use of such a potent Greek symbol as an accommodationist strategy, a device to strike a chord with the locals on a conscious or subconscious level.[158] Finally, and perhaps most importantly, it could be a thinly veiled statement of imperialist domination since each fountain ultimately celebrated the Ottoman sultan and stood for the Ottoman state.[159] In fact, the Sakız fountain was partially executed in red marble, a rare and expensive material, whose colour also happened to be that of Ottoman imperial flags, a colour generally signifying the Ottoman sultanate. St Laurent and Riedlmayer have pointed to a similarly symbolic contemporary Ottoman use of materials – the construction of a clock tower in Jerusalem (near the Jaffa Gate) in 1907 from white stone, which came from a cave important to the city's Jewish architectural tradition.[160]

A localising architectural approach of a slightly different kind can be seen in one of the two Kuds (Jerusalem) fountains, inaugurated on the occasion of the twenty-fifth anniversary in 1900 (Fig. 4.19). It adjoined

Figure 4.19 The Kuds (Jerusalem) Fountain. *Servet-i Fünun*, no. 498, 14 September 1316 (27 September 1900), p. 52. Courtesy of the Turkish National Library, Ankara.

the ancient city walls in the same area of *Bab-ı Halil* (Jaffa Gate), and, in an attempt to blend in, it also closely imitated the pattern of their masonry (golden Jerusalem stone), both in the execution of the fountain's cylindrical body and in its spherical dome.[161]

Such 'non-intrusive' architecture appeared at the same time with the same connection to the monarch in Sana'a (Yemen) where a hospital for the poor was built in the local, highly distinctive style of public buildings (as were the government building and the imperial barracks, for example).[162] Far from being solely attuned to priorities of the immediate political moment, this approach was reflective of a long-standing Ottoman state-making philosophy and practice. This was certainly not true of the state-making mission of Russian religious architecture in the late period. As Wortman has shown, it rudely imposed itself on the local landscape, with Orthodox shrines physically dominating and aesthetically disturbing Catholic environments in Poland or Protestant ones in some Baltic regions.

Figure 4.20 The Adana Fountain. *Servet-i Fünun*, no. 504, 26 October 1316 (8 November 1900). Courtesy of the Turkish National Library, Ankara.

The Reign of Abdülhamid II

Even in the capital, Alexander III did not hesitate to erect the seventeenth-century Russian-style church of 'Christ on the Blood' commemorating Alexander II's assassination, much to the aesthetic detriment of its surrounding eighteenth-century West-inspired (Baroque and Neoclassical) architecture.[163]

Other fountains dedicated to the sultan toyed with the design of clock towers, such as the onion-domed *meydan* fountain in Adana (Fig. 4.20),[164] or actually fulfilled the role, such as the structure adjoining the Hamidiye School of Arts and Crafts in Diyarbakır (Figs 4.21 and 4.22). The latter also had a full-blown imperial coat of arms (*arma-ı osmani*) on prominent display, topped by the ubiquitous crescent and star.[165]

By the end of Abdülhamid II's reign, there were few limits to what could be done, as long as it spoke well of the monarch, as the Giresun fountain (Fig. 4.23) illustrates. Built deep in the provinces, in a small town on the Anatolian Black Sea coast, the structure nonetheless resembled an Empire-style triumphal arch, supported by two Corinthian columns, with a fountain on each side.[166]

Figure 4.21 The Diyarbakır Fountain I. *Malumat*, no. 259, 12 October 1316 (25 October 1900), p. 385. Courtesy of the Turkish National Library, Ankara.

Figure 4.22 The Diyarbakır Fountain II. *Servet-i Fünun*, no. 502, 12 October 1316 (25 October 1900). Courtesy of the Turkish National Library, Ankara.

Figure 4.23 The Giresun Fountain. *Malumat*, no. 354, 12 September 1318 (25 September 1902). Courtesy of the Turkish National Library, Ankara.

The Reign of Abdülhamid II

Such was the passion for fountains at the time that even the German Kaiser's second visit to the Ottoman Empire in 1898 was commemorated with a special gazebo fountain – the prominent *Alman Çeşmesi* (the German Fountain) standing to this day on the site of the Byzantine Hippodrome in the heart of Istanbul. Curiously, it was the Kaiser's own idea and he even provided the initial sketch for it during the visit.[167] While the model and its inscriptions first appeared in the Ottoman press in the summer of 1900 (Fig. 4.24),[168] the fountain's inauguration was planned to coincide with the sultan's twenty-fifth anniversary. In yet another example of cross-dating, it ultimately took place on the Kaiser's birthday early the following year.[169] Rendered in the neo-Byzantine style, the fountain had an octagonal dome, supported by eight marble columns, and four staircases leading up to the four respective entries.

By chance, in the Turkish prime minister's Ottoman Archives in Istanbul, I came across sketches for a strikingly similar gazebo fountain, dated less than six months after the inauguration of the German fountain (Figs 4.25 and 4.26). Apparently, the intention was to erect it in London, also in honour of the sultan's twenty-fifth anniversary.[170]

Figure 4.24 The Kaiser's Fountain. *Malumat*, no. 241, 8 June 1316 (21 June 1900). Courtesy of the Turkish National Library, Ankara.

Figure 4.25 Soul-Nourishing Fountain (Çeşme-yi Dilara) I. Y.PRK.BŞK. 66/53. Courtesy of the Turkish Prime Ministry's Ottoman Archives.

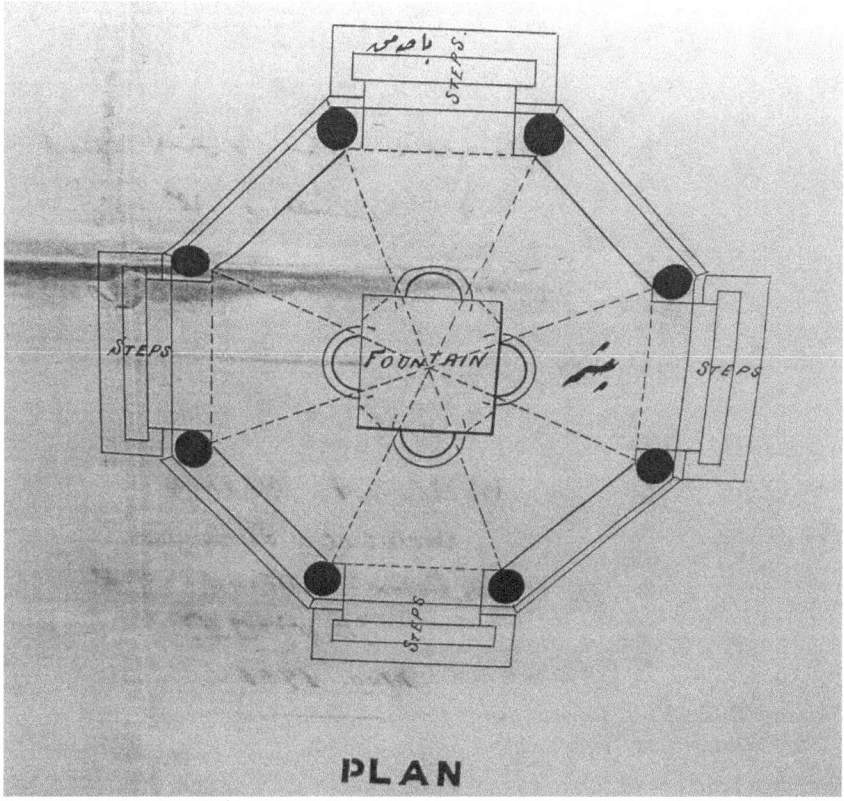

Figure 4.26 Soul-Nourishing Fountain (Çeşme-yi Dilara) II. Y.PRK.BŞK. 66/53. Courtesy of the Turkish Prime Ministry's Ottoman Archives.

The Ottoman inscription regarding the fountain's purpose – 'as a token of remembrance (*tezkir zımnında*)' – is very similar in phrasing to the actual German inscription on *Alman Çeşmesi* – 'in grateful remembrance (*in Dankbarer Erinnerung*)'. Perhaps emboldened by the Kaiser's visit and gesture, Abdülhamid II finally intended to take the 'memory' message of fountains, centred on himself, beyond his imperial domains in an attempt to achieve a measure of dynastic acceptance and reciprocity abroad.[171]

Even if the 'Soul-Nourishing Fountain'[172] did not materialise in the end, a similar fountain did. On 18 October of that same remarkable year of 1900, the cover of *Servet-i Fünun* featured a hexagonal gazebo fountain erected next to the Mosul branch of the 'Department of Imperial Lands (*Emlak-ı Hümayun Dairesi*)' in honour of the sultan's twenty-fifth anniversary on the throne (Fig. 4.27).[173] This appears to be the only

Figure 4.27 The Mosul Fountain. *Servet-i Fünun*, no. 501, 5 October 1316 (18 October 1900). Courtesy of the Turkish National Library, Ankara.

gazebo fountain actually built and dedicated to the sultan. Its shape aside, the fountain's design seems to be strongly influenced by those discussed above. For these reasons, it would be interesting to find out more about this structure's pre-history, inauguration circumstances and subsequent fate.[174]

The theme, struck by the Kaiser's favourite phrase – 'in grateful remembrance' – echoed in the Istanbul press far beyond his visit.[175] An exact Ottoman rendition – *hatıra-yı şükrgüzarisi olmak üzere* – was used in reference to another monument, dedicated to the sultan's twenty-fifth anniversary. This was 'a pillar of solid marble, with the height of *ten farmers*, built in grateful remembrance of the wharf, erected by the Bandırma Municipality on the occasion of the twenty-fifth anniversary . . .'[176] One can only marvel at the ripple effects of munificence and the degree of abstract ceremonial imagination the sultan's anniversary had inspired by this time throughout the domains. Situated at the port of Bandırma on the Marmara coast of Anatolia, the marble column left no doubt about the imperial constituency it represented – both the side of the column and its top were graced by crescents. Not to be outdone, in honour

The Reign of Abdülhamid II

of the same jubilee, the residents of the district capital of Balıkesir erected a Hamidiye clock tower, which was twenty-five metres tall.[177]

At least in one respect, late-nineteenth-century fountains resembled their seventeenth-century counterparts. They both sought to focus the attention of the beholder not so much on themselves as on their virtuous patron. Unlike his seventeenth-century ancestors, however, Abdülhamid II outdistanced all competition for fountain patronage in the late nineteenth century while the rhetoric accompanying it became progressively more intense, laced with richer and ever more inventive religious references.

Certainly, some older expressions survived. Thus, the sketch of a yet another Hicaz Railway fountain was introduced to the public with the words that it was 'an increment to the pious deeds and good works of His Majesty the Caliph (*zamime-yi hayrat ve meberrat-ı Hazret-i Hilafetpenahi*)'. The sketch displayed a very imaginative design of a namazgah fountain with a meydan fountain base and a clock-tower top (Fig. 4.28).[178]

Over time, direct references to Abdülhamid II's holiness (*kudsiyet*) became more frequent and vivid, with the rhetoric spilling over to other,

Figure 4.28 The Namazgah Fountain. *Malumat*, no. 246, 13 July 1316 (26 July 1900). Courtesy of the Turkish National Library, Ankara.

less numerous types of public monuments too. In the inscription of the 'Soul-Nourishing Fountain', it was merely the twenty-fifth anniversary that was 'holy'.[179] The realised Telegraph Monument in Damascus was 'decreed as a gift and an act of grace by the Holiest Personage of His Majesty the Caliph (*taraf-ı eşref-i Cenab-ı Hilafetpenahiden inayet ve ihsan buyurulup)*'.[180] The sketches for the completed Beirut clock tower in commemoration of the twenty-fifth anniversary reveal an inscription of an unusually intense kind: 'in reverence and remembrance of the revered twenty-fifth anniversary of His Majesty the Caliph . . . the matchless Caliph Sultan Abdülhamid Khan . . .'[181] Here, the words 'caliph' (2), 'revered' (2), 'matchless' (1) and 'remembrance' (1) appeared in only three lines of text.[182] Until the very end of Abdülhamid II's reign, fountains dedicated to him served as 'an eternal material mark of devotion to God with faith and obedience'.[183]

The New (Modern) Realm of Negative Symbolic Encounters

The personality cult of the ruler, successful as it was, also invited a broad range of symbolic challenges on both the individual and the group levels. The purpose of this section is twofold – first, to illustrate, based on archival evidence, the broad range of negative symbolic encounters, and second, to shed light, whenever possible, on their circumstances and the implications for the various parties involved, as well as the public space/sphere as a whole. Naturally, the sultanic celebrations themselves became some of the most common sites of symbolic contestation. The most obvious possibilities included malevolent words about or actions against the sultan, whether at home or abroad. For example, a partially ciphered telegram to the province (*vilayet*) of Aydın, on a last-minute signal by the Ottoman embassy in London, instructed the local authorities not to allow entry to 'harmful materials (*evrak-ı muzırre*)' printed in Egypt and sent by mail in order to be distributed on accession day in Istanbul. The telegram is dated 27 August 1901 (N.S.), that is, barely five days before the target date of 1 September 1901 (N.S.).[184] Three years later, another report reflected the fact that among the phrases of prayer the official journal of the provincial subdivision (*sancak*) of Mt Lebanon published on the occasion of accession day were words 'causing doubt/ exciting suspicion (*ihamlı*)'. Its conclusion was that 'the time has come not to have such things written (*bu gibi şeyler yazılmaması için vakit olunmuş)*'.[185]

The most extreme actions against the sultan were attempts at armed provocations on accession day. In late August 1903, in the midst of a major Bulgar revolt in Ottoman Macedonia,[186] a letter from the chief imperial secretary to the commander of the Third Imperial Army's Ninth Division, Marshal Ibrahim Pasha, warned him that 'Bulgar disturbers of the peace (*Bulgar müfsidleri*)' would 'try to cause an agitation (*bir karışıklık çıkarmağa çalışacakları*)' in Siroz (Serres), Razlık (Razlog),[187] Selanik (Thessaloniki) and other places.[188] The letter advised the commander to adopt timely measures for counteracting such 'men of sedition (*erbab-ı fesad*)'.[189] A day before the eve of the anniversary, another letter, this time from the Grand Vizier himself (Mehmed Ferid Paşa), on a tip from a coded telegram of the Rumelian Inspectorate (*Rumeli Müfettişliği*), discussed potentially serious trouble brewing in Manastır (Bitola in present-day Macedonia). According to this letter, on the day and night of the accession anniversary, rebels (*komita*) would attempt 'to stir up an insurrection with the detonation of a bomb (*bomba endahtıyla ika' iğtişaş etmek üzere*)'.[190] The letter went on to recommend that the state take measures 'against impropriety (*uygunsuzluğa karşı*)'.[191]

These examples illustrate the authorities' legitimate concern in extreme cases, which left little doubt about the perpetrators' motives. In reality, however, motives were far from always as clear; instead, there was a wide grey area within which most negative symbolic incidents fell or were thought to have fallen. The sometimes wide disparity between central objectives and provincial vigilance, and the murky nature of the symbolic terrain itself created much room for mistakes and second-guessing. At times, even eulogies could get one into trouble. For example, the celebrations of the sultan's twenty-fifth accession anniversary[192] in the Orthodox church on the Aegean island of Kalimnoz (Kalymnos) which included 'speeches containing the sacred qualities belonging to his imperial majesty ... and a reciprocal speech by the head district official (*kaymakam*) who repeatedly invoked benediction prayers for his Majesty'[193] caused a local uproar. According to a certain Hasa Ağa, a captain of the local militia, and someone identified as 'the clerk of the Chios Officer Battalion', the papers containing these speeches should be 'counted as harmful papers (*evrak-ı muzırre addederek*)', treated as insults (*tahkirat*) and subject to seizure (*zabt*). After the incident reached the centre, however, an opposite statement was issued. It treated such eulogies as expressions of 'perfect loyalty and devotion (*kemal-ı sadakat ve ubudiyet*)', and reprimanded, undoubtedly to the local enforcers' dismay, their 'ignorant opinions (*efkar-ı cahilaneleri*)'.[194]

It is quite likely that the militia captain and the battalion clerk were propelled into action by religious motives. To have the caliph's sacred qualities listed and prayers for his health read in a Christian church must have seemed a blasphemy to them. Perhaps, then, this ironic incident demonstrates how the syncretism, which should have worked from the central perspective, was beginning to fail locally, a failure driven, among other things, by a zealous over-subscription to a new, fewer-dimensional image of the sultan in consequence of a quarter-century of relentless caliphal propaganda. One way or another, by the turn of the twentieth century, such a purist attitude would not have been unique to these particular characters. For a number of reasons, starting with the sheer imperial demographics in the aftermath of a series of Russo-Ottoman wars leading to Balkan state formations, the tsarist title was quickly receding into the background.

The exponential metaphoric growth, centralisation and proliferation of the sultanic image during the reign of Abdülhamid II led to a state of unprecedented symbolic saturation of the public space/sphere, which validated and perpetuated the sultan's authoritarian regime. Paradoxically, as the image supremacy became more pronounced, potential challenges to it stood to gain more by attempting to disrupt and subvert it in the eyes of an ever more interconnected and informed public. This was due to a number of factors. One is the perception that the weight of monarchic-dynastic legitimacy and sovereignty increasingly rested on ethereal rather than material grounds. Another is the nature of symbolic power itself, which requires that it be complete (undented) in order to properly fulfil its function. As a result, Ottoman central authorities became less and less tolerant of celebrations of the sultan, which were other than perfect in their execution. In this regard, they developed an acute sensitivity towards potential sources of malevolent intention, be they foreign or domestic. The fact that the reign of Abdülhamid II abounded with accounts and investigations of ceremonial contestations attests as much to the accelerating imperial trend towards a new, modern, total sense of sovereignty and legitimacy as to the sultan's alleged paranoia *per se*.

One of the rare early accounts of symbolic offence taken, outside the realm of maritime ceremonial cannon salvos, a topic worth its own study,[195] comes from the same report about Abdülaziz's 1863 accession festivities in Halep, analysed above. This report also included an observation to the effect that the French consul in Halep had stood alone in neither attending festivities nor sending a representative, and in neither sending a letter nor congratulating in any other way the Ottoman sovereign on his official day.[196] Foreign diplomatic affronts to Ottoman self-esteem were not always so obvious, yet by the turn of the century, the Ottoman authorities were even more keen on detecting them. For example, a report from a certain Celal Bey, dated on the day after accession day, made note of the fact that the French consul, alone among the consuls of friendly states, had not lit lanterns in honour of the sultan in Kal'a-yi Sultaniye (Çanakkale).[197] Similarly, when the Russian consul in Cidde (Jedda in present-day Saudi Arabia) did not receive the provincial and district governors on the sultan's accession day and birthday in 1905, the Ottomans saw his excuse of being sick as a mere pretext.[198]

This hyper-sensitivity towards foreign recognition of Ottoman sovereignty on Ottoman soil carried over to areas that were still at least nominally Ottoman (such as Egypt) or that had only recently been lost to the Empire (such as Bosnia and Herzegovina).[199] In this 'near' or 'new' abroad, the sultanic festivities served as a platform for rallying support for the Ottoman sultan among a local Muslim population, which could easily be swayed against its new Christian imperial masters – the British Empire and Austria-Hungary, respectively. Thus, in 1897, the celebration of accession day in Egypt led to major disturbances, including cases of throwing stones at the British in the name of the sultan. The incidents prompted the authorities to dispatch a cavalry squadron from Cairo (Kahire) and Alexandria (Iskenderiyye) to Tanta and Al-Mansura (Mensure), resulting in a number of arrests.[200] Similarly, when a letter appeared on the pages of a Budapest newspaper stating that the Muslim population of Bosnia (Bosna) and Herzegovina (Hersek) was prevented from participating in the illuminations for the sultan's twenty-fifth accession anniversary in Travnik and Sarajevo (Saraybosna), the Ottoman authorities had to react. The incident drew the attention of the embassy in Vienna, the Foreign Ministry and even the Grand Vizier, prompting a detailed inquiry.[201]

If the top echelon of Ottoman government followed sultanic celebrations abroad so closely then the concealment of transgressions at their domestic equivalents would be practically impossible. Even the outmost periphery of the Empire was not beyond reach for Istanbul's watchful eye, as the following incident shows.

In 1905, a certain Şakir Pasha duly reported to the centre that the celebrations of accession day, 'the holy and revered day (*yevm-i mukaddes ve mübeccel*)', at Hüdeyde (Al-Hudaydah) in Ottoman Yemen had included a performance of the Egyptian Khedive's March (*Hıdiviye Marşı*). Şakir Pasha also observed that the deputy governor (*vali muavini*) had come late to the official reception. With the insertion of a communication (*ihbar*) that 'this behaviour resulted from a service of the treacherous thought of Arab union (*şu halın ittihad-ı araban-ı fikr-i hainanesine hizmetten münbais bulunduğu*)', the Pasha called for a meticulous investigation of all aspects of the incident. In the meantime, the notated sheets of music were seized so that neither the Khedive's March nor any other Egyptian tune whatsoever could be played. According to preliminary findings,

Ahmed Pasha, Commander of the Fourteenth Division, was responsible for the Khedive's March rendition; 'however, there was no evidence [lit. "foundation"] for such a bad thought and intention (*maamafih bunun bir sev-i fikir ve maksada mebna olmadığı)*'. Finally, the letter recorded the fact that the fourteen pages of played music had been torn out of the notebook and enclosed, adding that, upon arrival in Istanbul, they would be presented to the Minister of War (*serasker*).[202]

There are a number of ways to read this letter, which are not mutually exclusive. One is to interpret it as an insinuating account of one disgruntled official, seeking to ingratiate himself with the centre at the expense of another. This may have indeed been the case here.[203] If so, it could have been quickly dismissed. However, it was not. It was taken very seriously. Ahmed Pasha was arrested, sent to Istanbul and tried. In the meantime, a certain Bahtiyar Pasha, probably his replacement, prohibited performances of the Egyptian march. In the end, more than seven months after the incident, Ahmed Pasha was acquitted and restored to his previous rank.[204]

The fact that Şakir Pasha's report had repercussions on such a scale attests to the enormous importance of cyclical ceremonies and their constituent symbology by the turn of the century. Even music had by this time become a site conducive to the clash of conflicting allegiances, and a medium for drawing new boundaries where none or few had existed before.[205] The cyclical ceremonies had thus come to increasingly and credibly define the parameters of state belonging and state loyalty, not only in the eyes of the monarch, but also of his proxies, and on to ever wider circles of subjects, Christian and Muslim alike. Among the ceremonies, centred on the sultan-caliph, none cut more directly to the core of his legitimacy and sovereignty, nor occurred more frequently than the Friday noon prayer culminating in a sermon in the ruler's name (*hutbe*). Therefore, it should come as little surprise that this recurring religious practice too provided a platform for individual protest, on the one hand, and constant vigilance, on the other.

In 1888, multiple allegations of preacher misdemeanour were brought to the attention of the deputy judge of canon law (*naib-i şer'iye*) in Erzurum. The allegations stated that prayers for the health of the ruler at the end of the Friday sermon had been deliberately read too slowly or in a lower, unintelligible voice. Though unsubstantiated, they were treated seriously and corresponding recommendations were issued locally. News of the incidents reached the office of the Şeyhulislam.[206]

Reports of violations and inquiries regarding *hutbe* kept coming in throughout the rest of Abdülhamid II's reign. The gamut ran from general issues of a purely theological nature, such as the propriety of 'the congregation's voicing of its agreement during prayer (*dua ettiği vakitte cemaatın cehren amin demeleri*)'[207] to concrete, eyebrow-raising incidents such as 'the special expressions (*cümel-i mahsuse*)' a certain Hafız[208] Kemal delivered in Arabic during the sermon itself.[209]

Some cases in this category were handled with astonishing speed. A question about the Friday sermon (of undisclosed exact content), asked by a student at the Imperial School of Civil Service (*mekteb-i mülkiye-yi şahane*), reached the sultan's ear almost immediately. The sultan wrote to the Minister of Education (*Maarif Nazırı*), who assured him in writing that 'an investigation has at once commenced today (*tahkikat hemen bugün ibtidar olunduğu*)'. All of this took place on the same day – 27 January 1892, a Wednesday. In the same letter, the Education Minister notified the sultan that the results would be brought in person and presented to the Imperial Chambers (*mabeyn-i hümayun*) by the school's deputy head, along with all teachers, on Saturday morning.[210] The incident's point of origin and its proximity to the centre of power surely helped turn it into such a matter of top priority.

Most reports sought to assist central authorities by exposing a suspected subversive activity whether out of genuine concern, a desire for individual gain, or both. When the official preacher (*hatib*) of the principal mosque in Biga (Anatolia) mentioned the name of the previous sultan, Murad V, in the midst of reading the Friday noon sermon from a piece of paper, 'possessed by an evil spirit (*cinniden* [sic] *çıkardığı*)', as the report said, the ensuing investigation uncovered a mini-conspiracy. A search of the preacher's home yielded the sermon's draft, torn to pieces, yet still legible upon realignment, which clearly showed a text prepared in the name of the previous sultan. Therefore, both the preacher and his accomplice, who handed him the piece of paper, one Plevneli Nalband Ahmed, were arrested.[211]

Far from all cases were so swiftly and decisively resolved. Some ended in a draw. In 1898, the former regional governor of Divaniye (Al-Diwaniyah in present-day Iraq), Ibrahim Hakkı, reported that in the sermon read by the preacher from the pulpit following the morning 'Feast of the Sacrifice (*Kurban Bayram*)' prayer at the local government mosque, the holy name of the caliph was not mentioned. Nor was the obligatory prayer for him performed. He added that in the presence of the governor of Bağdad, Ataullah Pasha, everyone 'remained silent (*sükut ettikleri*)'. To Ibrahim Hakkı, this was a demonstration of trickery (*müstefenn*).[212]

The governor's response to Istanbul in the form of a coded telegram is an exercise in rhetorical evasion. First, he denied that anything of this sort had taken place at the government mosque service on that religious holiday. According to him, 'the holiest imperial name was mentioned with the customary proper and excellent honours and reverence, and the obligatory prayers for His Majesty the Caliph were chanted aloud'.[213] Moreover, he assured the centre that 'a perfect degree of serious attention and care is given to the incumbent duty (*zimmet*) of devotion and loyalty to this holy sacred duty (*feriza*) in all public holy mosques of the province's interior'.[214] This stylistic circle of symbolic submission was followed by the governor's admission that an incident did indeed take place in his presence only at the mosque across the street from the government building. With reference to the prayer and mention of the caliph's name, Ataullah Pasha noted the official preacher's 'leaving of such a holy sacred duty undone'.[215] Taking for granted the impossibility (*farz-ı muhal olarak*) that he might have done so out of forgetfulness (*zühul*), something 'inconceivable and impossible (*tasavvur ve imkan haricinde*)', the governor did not immediately see to the necessary measures. Instead, Ataullah Pasha would opt for a face-to-face encounter with the preacher, according to 'his finding [this sacred duty] to be an article of faith (*mu'takad bulunduğumu*)'. Therefore, the governor concluded, 'the denunciations were a mere lie (*ihbaratın kizb-i mahz olduğunu*)'.[216]

Clearly, the governor of Bagdad had to go out of his way to allay any doubts the centre might have. He did so by resorting to loops of repetitive, effusive language. Judging by word choice alone, he certainly outdid his accuser. Whereas Ibrahim Hakkı had called the sultan's name 'holy (*mukaddes*)', Ataullah Pasha called it 'holiest (*akdes*)'; whereas the former explicitly referred to 'duty' only once, the latter brought it up four times.[217] In the end, it seems that the governor's eloquence paid off. Instead of being summarily dismissed, Mehmed Ataullah Ibrahim Pasha retained his office for another eight months following the date of his telegram to Istanbul (4 June 1898). He served a total of two and a half years as governor of Bagdad, quick turnover being a long-standing Ottoman administrative norm.[218]

A final example of the hyper-sensitivity with which the late Ottoman authorities guarded the Ottoman monopoly of sovereignty on Ottoman soil concerns the Maronite (*Maruni*) Christians of Mount Lebanon (*Cebel-i Lübnan*).[219] In 1897, the governor of Beirut, Reşid Bey, stated in a letter to Istanbul that in most districts of his province fires had been lit for an illumination the previous Sunday. The alleged purpose was the expression of gratitude for the bestowal of 'sublime decorative orders (*nişan-ı aliye*)' to the Maronite Patriarch and bishops. However, he astutely observed that this illumination took place fifteen days after the event itself and that it also happened to fall on the Russian emperor's 'special day (*yevm-i mahsus*)'.²²⁰ Therefore, Reşid Bey thought that this coincidence should 'in any case be viewed with appropriate attention (*her halde şayan dikkat görünmekle*)'.²²¹ The centre's reaction remains unknown. Nonetheless, the governor's vigilance must have played a part in his long tenure in office.²²²

Conclusion

This chapter has attempted to chart chronologically Sultan Abdülhamid II's multi-layered and constantly evolving policies regarding his own image. This has been accomplished through the analysis of a broad spectrum of evidence and the use of key concepts, some employed earlier, others newly introduced, such as *ruler visibility, target audiences, dynastic pantheon, auto-Orientalism, cross-dating, personality cult* and *negative symbolic encounters*.

Far from being an anomaly, this sultan's long reign exhibited trends which had long been under way. In a manner reminiscent of his grandfather, Mahmud II, half a century earlier, Abdulhamid II responded to a severe geopolitical crisis with strong authoritarian tendencies, combined with, among other measures, intense ceremonial innovation aimed at shoring up loyalties at home and abroad. One legitimating strategy involved a symbolic play on the past, more commonly known as *invented traditions*. Whether one looks at Mahmud II's Islamic references, the artificial ageing of the sultanic ceremonies during Abdülmecid's reign or the pronounced shift towards dynastic history and monuments under Abdülaziz, *time* remained a key dimension of sultanic image-making policies not only over the period leading up to Abdülhamid II's reign but also throughout it. Another common legitimating strategy was the tendency towards increased simplicity of the sultanic dress and demeanour, away from Oriental splendour, coupled with a more pronounced militarisation thereof – whether by the carrying of (and being portrayed with) a sword or the regular partaking of military reviews.

What was indeed new and amply demonstrated throughout this chapter was Abdülhamid II's shift towards Muslim target audiences in unison not only with the changed demographic realities at home, but also with the perceived significance of contemporary pan-movements (especially, in this case, pan-Islam) abroad. Thus, this chapter traced various ceremonial steps in his early reign, ranging from Friday mosque and ancestor tomb visits to sword-girding choices and timing, most of which marked a sharp contrast with the conduct of his immediate predecessors. As soon as he was able to consolidate his grip on power, Abdülhamid II prohibited the domestic circulation of his portraits and substituted them with imperial banners, embroidered with the acclaim 'Long Live the Sultan!'. Thus, in a systematic effort to present himself as a rightful caliph, Abdülhamid II caused a reversal, along faith-based lines, of Mahmud II's long-standing mythology of royal power.

Far from being a close-minded Oriental despot, Abdülhamid II was acutely aware of and skilfully exploited contemporary international shifts in the discourse of royal power in order to strengthen his personal regime. In the process, the sultan acted very much like a contemporary imperial-cum-national monarch, both in terms of the mixed, re-constituted sources of his legitimacy and sovereignty, and in terms of the direct bonds of subject loyalty he sought to create. By examining closely the Kaiser's two visits, this chapter has provided a vivid illustration of the split in the terms of Abdülhamid II's ceremonial engagement with his royal peers, on the one hand, and with his domestic (especially Muslim) public, on the other. To the former the sultan remained accessible, but their association was carefully staged and usually not directly visible in public; to the latter, the sultan was both less accessible and less visible. The intimate terms of contact between the two monarchs, dynasties and states revealed a novel symbolic strategy of inter-imperial legitimation, unprecedented both in its creativity and in its level of abstraction.

The process of Ottoman inclusion into the Western system of signs and symbols, initiated daringly by Mahmud II, had by Abdülaziz's time inspired attempts to do the exact opposite – bring the Westerners back into the Ottoman fold, in large part by feeding their fantasies of the Orient. Abdülhamid II's reign witnessed a full-scale turn towards indigenous authenticity due to a number of factors. One of them was the same desire to be accepted as an indelible part of the international order which had prompted imitation of the West in the first place. By the late nineteenth century, however, this cultural turn relied on the understanding that a well-articulated difference based on alleged indigenous roots was a new and strong legitimating factor. This new direction in the field of ceremonial stemmed from harder realities and fashions of the day, from imperial thinking and state making as much as from a growing sense of the value of self-determination. This 'auto-Orientalist' mode of thought, which permeated the dynastic pantheon, was most frequently displayed at Friday prayer processions. From splendid imperial tents to parading elite regiments in exotic uniforms, dazzling Western dignitaries became the order of the day, turning Oriental splendour from a liability into an asset for the sultan-caliph.

The Reign of Abdülhamid II

This chapter has traced the ruler's increasingly sacred aura in the late period by recourse to several themes – acts of charity and generosity, trends in period monumental architecture, the myth of naming and the concept of cross-dating. Among the institutions Abdülhamid II founded which attested to his piety, hospitals were a prominent group. Curiously, the smaller their demographic share in the Empire, the greater attention minorities received from the sultan. The target patients included ever more narrowly defined and often socially marginalised segments of the population, not because the monarch so desperately needed their loyalty, but because he rather wished to present himself as an all-encompassing, all-merciful figure, both at home and abroad. Many of the Hamidian establishments would then add ceremonial input of their own to official celebrations, thus causing ripple effects of the original foundational acts over time.

The personality cult of the ruler, successful as it was, also invited a broad range of symbolic challenges, on both the individual and the group levels. In their totality, the negative symbolic encounters illustrate well the interventionist nature of the modern state, whose instrumentarium for symbolic control was all but installed by the end of Abdülhamid II's reign. They delineate an imperial public space/sphere, quite removed from its immediate antecedents, and strongly resembling the one still in place today. Some of its modern dimensions include the tight-fitted marriage of territory and sovereignty, the intended and increasingly enforceable standardisation and totalisation of loyalty, and the rising number and inflexible nature of demands levied on the individual as a prerequisite for an abstract form of belonging. This imperial public space/sphere witnessed the first bouts of modern symbolic warfare, which raised the value of symbolic action and counter-action, of information and disinformation. Much has been written about Abdülhamid II's regime of surveillance and censorship. More often than not, it has been traced to the sultan's personal idiosyncrasies. When seen against the back foil of long-term modernising processes, however, an alternative explanation emerges, which is of a systemic rather than personal nature. Therefore, it may be more accurate and useful to speak of the inception of a (modern) culture of surveillance in the turn-of-the-century Ottoman Empire. What the negative symbolic encounters also point to, in a cause-and-effect fashion, are the beginnings of a shift from top-down censorship and symbolic policing to individual auto-censorship (self-policing), another thoroughly modern phenomenon very much active to this day. With all of these considerations in mind, the next step, to the symbolic dictatorship of the nation-state and its attendant mythology, may be much smaller than currently thought.

Ruler Visibility and Popular Belonging

The Young Turk Revolution of 1908 brought an end to Abdülhamid II's authoritarian regime.[223] Even though he did not abdicate until a year later, in the aftermath of a failed counter-revolution, his effective power had been much curtailed and his monopoly on public space/sphere had been instantly removed. Moreover, the sultanic celebrations were swiftly downgraded to a bare minimum of popular recognition. So, in a very palpable way, even before Abdülhamid II's exit from the political scene, his own 'sacred aura', as well as the public image of the monarch's office in general, had been irreparably damaged.[224] Neither of his two younger brothers – Mehmed Reşad and Vahideddin – who successively rose to the throne before the Empire finally crumbled, held a personal sway over their subjects that even remotely approximated Abdülhamid II's.

To judge the success of this sultan's endeavour by his eventual deposition and the Empire's ultimate demise is to write history backwards. Instead, as this chapter has demonstrated, there are a number of alternative indicators that can serve as benchmarks for late imperial rulership. By delving deeper into matters of protocol and cyclical celebration, which until recently have been dismissed as trivial or irrelevant, it is possible to, first, reconstruct power projections in the proper context of their times and, second, evaluate the nature and degree of their impact on the popular mind.

Notes

1. The list of key events in this respect includes the Russo-Ottoman War of 1877–8 and the disturbances leading up to it, on the one hand, and Italy's invasion of Libya, the Balkan Wars and World War I, on the other.
2. See Akarli, 'The Tangled Ends', *Comparative Studies of South Asia, Africa and the Middle East*, 353–66.
3. See Fortna, *Learning to Read*; Evered, *Empire and Education*; Boyar, 'The Press and the Palace', *Bulletin of the School of Oriental and African Studies*, 417–32; Karpat, *The Politicisation of Islam*; Worringer, 'Sick Man of Europe', *International Journal of Middle East Studies*, 207–30; Schull, *Prisons in the Late Ottoman Empire*; Maksudyan, *Orphans and Destitute Children*; Akcasu, 'Migrants to Citizens', *Die Welt des Islams*, 388–414, among others.
4. Deringil, *The Well-Protected Domains*. See also Georgeon, *Abdülhamid II*.
5. As I will demonstrate shortly, what made Abdülhamid II a national monarch was not the putative ethnic homogeneity of his subjects, but rather the new principles informing the shaping of his public persona and, by extension, the new terms of symbolic interaction with his subjects. For a fascinating recent global survey on this subject from a different perspective, see Miller

The Reign of Abdülhamid II

and Berger, *Nationalizing Empires* and Eissenstat, 'Modernisation, Imperial Nationalism, and the Ethnicisation of Confessional Identity in the Late Ottoman Empire', in particular.
6. Mahmud II set up permanent embassies, which held celebrations of him, in the same influential foreign capitals where Selim III had opened legations before – Paris, London, Berlin and Vienna.
7. Abdülmecid toured the imperial domains following his father's example. In 1867, Abdülaziz became the only sultan to ever visit Europe. On his way back, he passed through some of the same Ottoman lands (present-day north-eastern Bulgaria), which Mahmud II and Abdülmecid had visited before him.
8. Among other things, he was the only Ottoman sultan who ever attended a Christian wedding. In December 1852, Abdülmecid attended the wedding of Fotiadi Bey and Maria, daughter of Stefan Bogoridi (1775–1859), the most prominent Bulgar ever to rise in the ranks of Ottoman statesmen, in Arnavutköy, Istanbul. For a detailed description, see Balabanov, *Gavril Krustevich*, pp. 78–91.
9. Some studies still erroneously point to the beginnings of Abdülmecid's or Abdülaziz's reigns as the starting points for annual royal birthday and accession-day celebrations in the Ottoman Empire, instead of the year 1836 in Mahmud II's reign. See Zandi-Sayek, 'Ambiguities of Sovereignty', in *Imperial Geographies*, p. 147; Çelik, *Empire, Architecture, and the City*, p. 217; and Demirel, 'A Modern Performance', in *Celebration*, p. 261.
10. See Ersoy, *Architecture*.
11. Banerjee, Backerra and Sarti continue the list of relevant (real or legendary) monarchs with 'King Arthur in Britain, Frederick Barbarossa in Germany, Shivaji in India, Amir Timur in Uzbekistan, and Emperor Jimmu in Japan'. See their chapter 'The Royal Nation in Global Perspective', in *Transnational Histories*, p. 5.
12. After becoming sultan, Abdülhamid II never left the capital in his thirty-three-year reign.
13. As mentioned earlier, this term includes both a physical public appearance and a public display/dissemination of royal portraits.
14. See the eponymous chapter in Davison, *Reform*.
15. *Levant Herald*, 5 July 1876.
16. See de Amicis, *Constantinople*, pp. 198–9.
17. *Levant Herald*, 5 July 1876.
18. Ibid.
19. '*Müşarileyh Hazretlerinin Cülus-u Hümayunları milletin arzusundan bulunmakla kemal-ı memnuniyetle ilan olunmuştur müslim ve gayrimüslim Sultan Murad Khan Hazretlerini alettesavi bir mahzuziyetle tebrik ve tehniyet eylediler*'. See *Ceride-i Havadis*, 31 May 1876.
20. '*islahatın icrasına hazır bulunduğu*'.
21. Eyüp al-Ansari, a Companion of Muhammad who participated in one of the earliest Arab sieges of Constantinople, was allegedly buried outside the city

walls. After the fall of Constantinople, the site where his remains had been laid to rest became a major funerary complex and one of the holiest Muslim sites in all of the Ottoman Empire.
22. See the table in Karateke, *Padişahım Çok Yaşa!*, p. 224.
23. *Levant Herald*, 8 September 1876.
24. '*milel-i muhtelife-yi iseviye ve museviye şakirdanı dizilerek alay-ı vala bu suretle tertib olunmuştur*'. *Ceride-i Havadis*, 28 August 1876.
25. *Levant Herald*, 26 August 1876 and 16 September 1876.
26. Ibid., 22 September 1876.
27. Ibid., 8 September 1876. The italics are my own. The main reason I am drawing so much on this English-language daily Ottoman newspaper is that the mainstream Ottoman newspapers contain little if anything in the way of visual information about the sultan. For example, the above-mentioned *Ceride-i Havadis* article about Abdülhamid II's sword girding contains no information about the sultan's appearance whatsoever. See *Ceride-i Havadis*, 28 August 1876.
28. *Levant Herald*, 5 July 1876, 31 August 1876, 15 September 1876, 11 November 1876 and 16 December 1876.
29. Ibid., 8 February 1873.
30. Ibid., 14 October 1876.
31. Ibid., 19 October 1876.
32. The most vociferous and quite sizeable group consisted of recent refugees and immigrants from imperial borderlands and recently lost territories in the Balkans and the Caucasus.
33. *Levant Herald*, 8 September 1876.
34. Ibid., 6 July 1876.
35. This is the historic European quarter of Istanbul.
36. *Levant Herald*, 6 July 1876.
37. Y.PRK.BŞK. 4/33. The document was dated 24 December 1880. According to Eldem, who draws on Öztuncay, this stern reaction may have had to do with the fact that the studio had just a year earlier lost the imperial warrant of 'appointment to the sultan'. See Eldem, 'Powerful Images', in *Camera Ottomana*, p. 151, footnote 18. See also Öztuncay, *The Photographers of Constantinople*, p. 222.
38. For Abdülhamid II's court painter's statement, corroborating this, see Özendes and Makzume, *Ottoman Court Painter Fausto Zonaro*, pp. 78–82. See also Ersoy, 'Ottomans and the Kodak Galaxy', *History of Photography*, 356.
39. Midhat Pasha was a key figure among the deposers of both Abdülaziz and Murad V. According to contemporaries, he had strong autocratic tendencies and was even at one point greeted with 'Long Live Midhat Pasha!' (see Davison, *Reform*, p. 337 and p. 340 with reference to *Stamboul*, 30 May and 1 June 1876). Midhat Pasha's trial for treason took place in 1881. His death sentence was commuted to life imprisonment, but he was eventually

The Reign of Abdülhamid II

    murdered in prison in 1884. See Berkes, *The Development of Secularism in Turkey*, p. 250.
40. Deringil, *Well-Protected Domains*, p. 22. Eldem adds the sultan's monogram and the Ottoman coat of arms, which he himself devised in 1883, to the list of his symbolic proxies. See Eldem, 'Powerful Images', pp. 119–120.
41. See Kabacalı, *Tanzimat'tan II*, p. 68.
42. Ibid, p. 68. In this book alone, there are two portraits of Abdülmecid with a sword (p. 12 and p. 20), one of Abdülaziz (p. 21) and seven of Abdülhamid II (pp. 42, 43, 117, 119, 129, 145 and 223).
43. According to both Alderson and Davison, Murad V's unstable mental condition ultimately prevented the sword girding from taking place. See Table VIII in Alderson, *The Structure of the Ottoman Dynasty*, p. 343. The extensive yet ultimately fruitless preparations for Murad V's sword girding must have contributed in more ways than sheer logistics on the ground to the speed with which Abdülhamid II's own sword girding became a fact.
44. See Karateke, *Padişahım Çok Yaşa!*, p. 54 and the table on p. 224.
45. Ibid., p. 54.
46. See Abu-Manneh, 173–203.
47. See Lapidus, *A History of Islamic Societies*, p. 58, and Kennedy, *The Prophet*, p. 57, respectively. Lapidus notes Caliph Umar's 'closeness to Muhammad and great religious integrity' whereas Kennedy calls him 'the epitome of the stern, uncompromising, incorruptible ruler'.
48. Karateke, *Padişahım Çok Yaşa!*, p. 54.
49. An additional piece of evidence which may be relevant in this respect is that, according to a popular story which first appeared in the late eighteenth century, the last Abbasid Caliph allegedly girded Selim I with Caliph Umar's sword at Aya Sofya (Hagia Sophia) after his conquest of Egypt and the Holy Cities (see Karateke, *Padişahım Çok Yaşa!*, pp. 54–5). It remains an open question whether this story had anything to do with the reassertion of Ottoman caliphal claims in the late eighteenth century after the Treaty of Küçük Kaynarca. The two are, however, suspiciously close in time and symbolic content.
50. When Abdülaziz became sultan, he assumed the reins of power from his older brother Abdülmecid, thus pre-empting the claims of his sons, Murad and Abdülhamid, and establishing his own line. When first Murad and then Abdülhamid became sultans, the opposite power shift occurred.
51. *Levant Herald*, 30 September 1876.
52. Here I refer to provincial (*Tuna/Dunav*) and Istanbul (*Tsarigradski Vestnik*) Bulgar newspapers as well as both domestic (*Levant Herald*) and foreign (*The Times*) English-language publications.
53. See *Tuna/Dunav*, 19 May 1876.
54. Ibid., 25 August 1876.
55. *Levant Herald*, 31 August 1876.

56. Ibid., 3 July 1886.
57. For Mustafa II, see Abou El Hajj, 'The Narcissism of Mustafa II', *Studia Islamica*, 125–7. For Selim III, see Davison, *Reform*, p. 24.
58. Unfortunately, the history of the Cage institution in the late Ottoman Empire remains to date largely unknown. What follows here is a set of preliminary observations and suggestions.
59. This title was attached to the name of every Ottoman crown prince.
60. Davison, *Reform*, p. 339.
61. *Levant Herald*, 8 September 1876.
62. Karateke, *Padişahım Çok Yaşa!*, p. 63.
63. *Levant Herald*, 2 September 1876.
64. Deringil, *Well-Protected Domains*, p. 23, referring to Esenbel, *Istanbul'da Bir Japon*, 40.
65. Karateke, *Padişahım Çok Yaşa!*, p. 33.
66. Ibid., pp. 33, 36.
67. *Otechestvennyiy Panteon*, part 1. I wish to thank the staff of the Library of Congress for making this rare book available to me.
68. Alexander II's wife and Alexander III's mother.
69. *Novoe Vremia*, 13 May 1889 and 15 May 1889.
70. For his part, the Catholic Habsburg emperor did pray very attentively at Alexander II's tomb.
71. Yedikule (lit. 'The Seven Towers') is the point at which the walls of Constantinople reach the Sea of Marmara. The towers were for centuries a prison for high-profile Ottoman and foreign prisoners, very much like the Tower of London.
72. The account of events during this visit is based on *Levant Herald*, 3–7 November 1889.
73. *Levant Herald*, 10 October 1898, 19 October 1898 and 20 October 1898.
74. Ibid., 17 October 1898.
75. *Servet-i Fünun*, 29 October 1314 (10 November 1898).
76. Ibid., 8 October 1314 (20 October 1898). Normally, the use of colour (usually green or gold) was reserved for the sultan's accession anniversary and birthday dates only.
77. Ibid., 15 October 1314 (27 October 1898).
78. *Levant Herald*, 24 October 1898.
79. Ibid., 18 October 1898.
80. For images of the tent's interior and exterior, see *Servet-i Fünun*, no. 402, 12 Teşrin-i Sani 1314 (24 November 1898).
81. This speculation may not be so far-fetched in light of a curious crown which appeared on the cover of an Abdülhamidian album (see Karateke, *Padişahım Çok Yaşa!*, p. 47). Its design seems to borrow from the Western concept the overall shape and pearl bridges, but with Ottoman/Muslim touches, such as the little stars and crescents around the base, and, most importantly, the large crescent and star in place of the cross sitting on top.

82. *Servet-i Fünun*, no. 403, 19 Teşrin-i Sani 1314 (1 December 1898). See also Çelik, p. 225.
83. *Levant Herald*, 4 November 1898.
84. *Servet-i Fünun*, no. 402, 12 Teşrin-i Sani 1314 (24 November 1898).
85. Ibid., 19 Teşrin-i Sani 1314 (1 December 1898).
86. Naltchayan, 'Kaiser Wilhelm II's Visits', *Armenian Review*, 53, with reference to *Annual Register*.
87. *Levant Herald*, 10 November 1898.
88. See Scheffler, 'The Kaiser in Baalbek', in *Baalbek*.
89. *Servet-i Fünun*, no. 403, 19 Teşrin-i Sani 1314 (1 December 1898); *Levant Herald*, 12 November 1898; Naltchayan, 53, with reference to *Annual Register*.
90. See Stambolski, *Avtobiografiya*, pp. 373–4.
91. See Patrick, *Under Five Sultans*, p. 80.
92. Stambolski, *Avtobiografiya*, p. 378.
93. This was the Kaiser's customary way of apprising the sultan of the progress of the day trip and expressing his gratitude for the warm welcome he received everywhere.
94. *Levant Herald*, 22 October 1898. The capitalisation is in accordance with the original.
95. Ibid., 8 October 1898.
96. See Halid, *The Diary of a Turk*. See also Murphey, *Exploring Ottoman Sovereignty*, pp. 11–12, with reference to Bowman Dodd, *In the Palaces of the Sultan*, pp. 49–50.
97. *Levant Herald*, 1 September 1888. See Dimmig, 'Fabricating a New Image', *International Journal of Islamic Architecture*, 341–72.
98. This section of the Imperial Guard was notably split into two squadrons, based on headgear – a fez (Fesli) or a turban (Sarıklı). Their photographs appeared frequently on the pages of Ottoman journals, such as *Servet-i Fünun*, as well as on contemporary postcards. Even though their formal names did not indicate it, the squadrons also differed according to area of recruitment – the Albanian and Arab lands respectively. Over time descent intensified the rivalry between the two units and occasionally even led to open brawls, which were extremely embarrassing to the authorities.
99. Deringil, *Well-Protected Domains*, p. 25, with reference to Konyalı, *Söğütte Ertuğrul Gazi Türbesi ve Ihtifalı*.
100. Cox, *Diversions of a Diplomat*, pp. 35, 28, respectively.
101. An aide-de-camp is a subordinate military or naval officer acting as a confidential assistant to a superior.
102. *Levant Herald*, 12 October 1889, 19 October 1889, 26 October 1889, 3 November 1889 and 1 November 1889.
103. See Stambolski, *Avtobiografiya*, pp. 655–7. He witnessed the arrival of these units in the town of Nish (in present-day Serbia) in the summer of 1876 during the Ottoman war with Serbia.

104. On the topic of Jewish volunteers, see Cohen, *Becoming Ottomans*, pp. 30–4 ('Defending the Empire, Defending the Nation').
105. See the weekly newspaper *Zornitsa*, 2 July 1876 and 9 July 1876 as well as Stambolski, *Avtobiografiya*, pp. 655–7. *Zornitsa* was an organ of the American Evangelical Society published in Bulgar in Istanbul from 1876 to 1878.
106. *Levant Herald*, 4 September 1888.
107. *Servet-i Fünun*, 29 September 1310 (11 October 1894). The portrait is unrecognisable in the photograph. It is so small and placed so high in the actual decorative structure that it probably would not have been visible from the ground.
108. *Levant Herald*, 7 November 1889.
109. Stambolski, *Avtobiografiya*, pp. 466–7. According to Eldem, we can view the sultan's bestowal of the same decoration to his own son and preferred successor, Prince Yusuf Izzeddin, as 'an exceptional move of public relations'. See Eldem, *Pride and Privilege*, p. 229.
110. The German monarchy seems to have developed a particularly strong consumerist dimension quite early on. See Giloi, *Monarchy*.
111. *Levant Herald*, 19 October 1898, 22 October 1898 and 24 October 1898.
112. Ibid., 24 October 1889. See also Unruh, 'Imaging an Empire'.
113. See Gavin and the Harvard Semitic Museum, 'Imperial Self-Portrait', *Journal of Turkish Studies*.
114. See Özendes, *Photography in the Ottoman Empire*.
115. *Levant Herald*, 24 October 1898.
116. As already mentioned, cross-dating refers to the act of combining one ceremonial occasion (such as the inauguration of a building) with another (such as the royal accession anniversary) on the same day for a cumulative effect on the public mind. This was a major strategy for autocratic legitimation in many late empires.
117. Curiously, the smaller their demographic share in the empire, the greater attention minorities received from the Sultan.
118. *Servet-i Fünun*, 19 August 1316 (1 September 1900); 1 August 1312 (13 August 1896).
119. Ibid. 27 July 1316 (9 August 1900) and 19 August 1316 (1 September 1900); 15 July 1309 (27 July 1893).
120. See Georgeon, 'Le sultan caché', *Turcica*, 116–17 and Murphey, *Exploring Ottoman Sovereignty*, pp. 12-13.
121. *Servet-i Fünun*, 17 December 1314 (29 December 1898).
122. *Malumat*, 16 January 1318 (29 January 1903).
123. These refugees came from Dağıstan. *Malumat*, 23 January 1318 (5 February 1903).
124. '*iskanlari kararlaştırılan muhacirin-i islamiye'ye mahsus cami-yi şerif, mekteb ve hanelerin vaz esas resmi*', *Servet-i Fünun*, 19 August 1315 (31 August 1899). Italics in the text are my own.

125. *Levant Herald*, 19 September 1906.
126. In other words, the asylum was set up in 1882, six years into the reign of Abdülhamid II.
127. *Levant Herald*, 10 September 1906.
128. '*asar-ı merahimnisar-ı cenab-ı hilafetpenahiden hamidiye etfal hastahane-yi alisi*', *Malumat*, 24 August 1316 (6 September 1900).
129. *Malumat*, 3 October 1318 (16 October 1902).
130. '*veladet-i bahir as-saadet-i hazret-i padişahi yevm-i mes'udunda . . .*', *Malumat*, 16 March 1316 (29 March 1900).
131. See *Novoe Vremia*, 12 May 1893.
132. See *Levant Herald*, 9 October 1889. The school was already in existence by this time. The article made a point of the fact that both Muslim and Christian children attended it.
133. I wish to thank Edhem Eldem for pointing out that this slogan was in the Ottoman sign language and that the children spelled the text from their right to left, resulting in a photograph that spelled the words backwards to a reader of the Arabic script. According to him, this suggests that nobody really expected viewers to be able to read the text. See Eldem, 'The Search for an Ottoman Vernacular Photography', p. 54, footnote 16, in *The Indigenous Lens*.
134. *Servet-i Fünun*, 19 August 1309 (31 August 1893), p. 388. See a more detailed discussion of this image in Eldem, 'Powerful Images', pp. 135–6, based on this photograph's reappearance in the same journal in connection to the twenty-fifth anniversary of the sultan's accession, in 1900. [*Servet-i Fünun*, 19 August 1316 (1 September 1900)], p. 418.
135. Ibid., 1 March 1317 (14 March 1901).
136. *Malumat*, 2 September 1315 (14 September 1899).
137. Examples include the Austro-Hungarian emperor's twenty-fifth wedding anniversary (HR. SYS. 161/10, 22 May 1879), the twenty-fifth anniversary of the Greek king's accession (Y.A.HUS. 218/51, 19 October 1888), the twenty-fifth anniversary of the German emperor's office (HR. SYS. 37/3, 15 May 1896) and so on.
138. For a brief section on fountains erected on this anniversary, see Celik, *Empire, Architecture, and the City*, pp. 137–40.
139. *Servet-i Fünun*, 22 July 1309 (3 August 1893).
140. Ibid., 19 August 1316 (1 September 1900).
141. For a very insightful discussion of seventeenth- and eighteenth-century Ottoman fountains, see Hamadeh, 'Splash and Spectacle', *Muqarnas*, 123–48.
142. *Malumat*, 19 August 1318 (1 September 1902).
143. Hamadeh, 'Splash and Spectacle', 139.
144. *Malumat*, 19 August 1318 (1 September 1902).
145. The emphasis seems to have fallen on Anatolia, which was by this time turning from an imperial backwater into the heartland of the Empire in the

public mind (after the mounting losses of European territory). For more information on this gradual process, see Kushner, *The Rise of Turkish Nationalism*.

146. According to Hamadeh, this trend marked a symbolic effort to reclaim the capital after the Sultan had resided in Edirne, the old capital, for a number of years and 'the image of imperial sovereignty ... had fallen to an all-time low in the last decades of the seventeenth century'. See Hamadeh, 'Splash and Spectacle', 143.
147. According to Pilehvarian, Urfalıoğlu and Yazıcıoğlu, in the period from 1877 to 1899, nineteen fountains were constructed in Istanbul, three of them by the sultan. By contrast, in the period from 1900 to 1908, sixteen fountains were constructed, four of them by the sultan. See Pilehvarian et al., *Fountains*, pp. 142–4 and 198–9.
148. In Jerusalem alone, at least two fountains were built.
149. Thessaloniki in present-day Greece. The fountain still exists.
150. For an unrealised 1840 sketch of an obelisk-shaped Hatt-i Şerif monument in Istanbul by Gaspare Fossati, see Kreiser, 'Public Monuments', *Muqarnas*, 103.
151. *Servet-i Fünun*, 5 October 1316 (18 October 1900).
152. Ibid., 19 August 1316 (1 September 1900).
153. Ibid., 7 October 1309 (19 October 1893).
154. Kreiser, 'Public Monuments', p. 111.
155. *Malumat*, 24 August 1316 (6 September 1900).
156. Ibid., 7 September 1316 (20 September 1900). For a more detailed description of this fountain, in its urban context, see Çelik, *Empire, Architecture, and the City*, p. 137.
157. *Servet-i Fünun*, 4 January 1316 (17 January 1901).
158. Çelik also speaks of a 'repertoire of elements derived from an area's heritage' and points to Greco-Roman antiquity in particular. See Çelik, *Empire, Architecture, and the City*, p. 140.
159. As with many other images of fountains (see Figs 4.6, 4.7 and 4.12, to name but a few), a guard on duty is clearly visible in the background of the Sakız fountain perhaps to prevent attempts at defacing it.
160. St. Laurent and Riedlmayer, 'Restorations of Jerusalem', *Muqarnas*, p. 82.
161. *Servet-i Fünun*, no. 498, 14 September 1316 (27 September 1900), p. 52, and *Malumat*, no. 259, 12 October 1316 (25 October 1900). For a detailed description, see Çelik, *Empire, Architecture, and the City*, p. 137. According to St. Laurent and Riedlmayer, the fountain was destroyed by the British in 1918, with the cooperation of the Supreme Muslim Council of Jerusalem.
162. *Servet-i Fünun*, 19 August 1316 (1 September 1900). See Kühn, 'Ordering Urban Space', in *The Empire in the City*.
163. See Wortman's *Scenarios of Power* ('The Resurrection of Muscovy').
164. *Malumat*, no. 258, 5 October 1316 (18 October 1900) and *Servet-i Fünun*, no. 504, 26 October 1316 (8 November 1900).

165. Both *Servet-i Fünun* and *Malumat* published photographs of this fountain on the same day – 12 October 1316 (25 October 1900).
166. *Malumat*, 12 September 1318 (25 September 1902).
167. *Levant Herald*, 24 October 1898. The notice points out that the site of the fountain is 'to be designated by the sultan'.
168. *Malumat*, 8 June 1316 (21 June 1900).
169. Deleon, *Anıtsal İstanbul*, p. 197.
170. Y.PRK.BŞK. 66/53. The actual date is 17 July 1901. The plans and sketches bear the signature of the Ottoman Ambassador to London. The document's brief description in the archival catalogue refers to plans for an identical fountain in Berlin. Unfortunately, I was not able to find any further information about it.
171. Notably, the albums sent to Britain and the United States in the early 1890s depicted no fountains personally dedicated to Abdülhamid II.
172. I wish to thank Ahmet Ersoy for suggesting this translation and for his critical comments.
173. *Servet-i Fünun*, 5 October 1316 (18 October 1900).
174. Drawing on another photograph from the same year and journal, Çelik calls it 'a different kind of fountain, light and playful with open arches and delicate details in an elcletic "Islamic" style', Çelik, *Empire, Architecture, and the City*, p.137.
175. See *Levant Herald*, 31 October 1898, for a more elaborate version – 12 November 1898 – and, in a slightly different wording, 8 November 1898.
176. 'yirmi beşinci sene-yi devriye-yi cülus-i meymenet-i menus-i hümayun-u şerifine Bandırma daire-yi belediyesi tarafından yapılan rıhtımın hatıra-yı şükrgüzarisi olmak üzere on zerra irtifanda som mermerden inşa olunan sütun', *Malumat*, 31 August 1316 (13 September 1900).
177. Ibid. Photographs of the two monuments appeared on the same page.
178. *Malumat*, 13 July 1316 (26 July 1900). As their name implies, namazgah fountains were located in the open air at a place suitable for prayer. Due to its scale, architectural character and level of detail, Çelik speculates that this fountain-cum-clocktower was most likely intended for Istanbul, signifying its connection to the Hijaz and, by extension, the importance of the Arab provinces. Çelik, *Empire, Architecture, and the City*, pp. 148–50.
179. '*devr-i senevi-yi kudsi*'.
180. *Servet-i Fünun*, 13 July 1316 (26 July 1900).
181. '*halife-yi bimüdani Sultan Abdülhamid Han . . . hazret-i hilafetpenahi'nin yirmi beşinci sene-yi devriye-yi mübeccelesini tezkaren ve ta'zimen . . .*' It should come as no surprise that the tower was also 25 metres tall.
182. Y.MTV. 206/127 – 25 July 1316 (7 August 1900).
183. '*ila al-abd mücessem bir nişane-yi ubudiyetgarane olmak*'. *Malumat*, 28 September 1316 (11 October 1900). The expression refers to the Yozgat Fountain, whose foundation was also laid on the twenty-fifth anniversary.
184. See Y.EE.KP. 14/1310.

185. See Y.PRK.UM. 72/15 (27 October 1904).
186. The Ilinden-Preobrazhenie Uprising erupted at different locales over a large swathe of Ottoman European territory from early to mid-August 1903. Prepared and carried out by the Internal Macedonian Revolutionary Organisation (IMRO), the revolt was suppressed by the Ottoman authorities within a month.
187. Serres is in present-day Greece and Razlog in present-day Bulgaria.
188. The signal came from the Ottoman Commissariat in Bulgaria.
189. See Y.PRK.BŞK. 70/75. The letter was dated 25 August 1903, that is, a week before accession day.
190. Two years later, Armenian rebels would choose the sultan's Friday prayer procession as the site for detonating a bomb (see Deringil, *Well-Protected Domains*, p. 22). The sultan survived and his courageous conduct during the incident only served to boost his popularity.
191. See Y.A.HUS. 455/133 (30 August 1903).
192. Notably, it was celebrated at the start rather than the completion of that jubilee year, that is, on 1 September 1900. This choice itself may have been an act of cross-dating since the year 1900 initiated, in the minds of an increasing number of Ottomans, not to mention all Westerners, the twentieth century. Moreover, this choice would also guarantee an extended period of time for all regions of the Empire, no matter how distant or backward, to get involved in ongoing ceremonial activities centred on the sultan.
193. '*evsaf-ı kudsiyatittisaf-ı cenab-ı mulukane-yi mutazzamın nutuklar . . . ve kaymakam canibinden dahi mukabele nutuk iradıyla ediye-yi hayriye-yi hazret-i şahinşahi tekrar ve yad edildiği*'.
194. DH.MKT. 2428/33 (14 November 1900).
195. For one such attempt, see Stephanov, 'Cannon Salvos for the Monarch', an unpublished paper.
196. A.MKT.UM.573/88.
197. Y.PRK.ASK.174/7 (2 September 1901). Adding insult to injury, the French consuls in the towns of Sofia (Sofya) and Plovdiv (Filibe), both in the dependent Principality of Bulgaria, did not take part in celebratory activities at all, in sharp contrast to the rest of the diplomatic community, the local Muslim population and the Ottoman subjects. See Y.A.HUS. 419/99 (12 September 1901).
198. Y.PRK.UM.77/85. The lunar Muslim calendar dates of the two events were only four days apart.
199. By a decision of the Congress of Berlin, which concluded the 1877–8 Russo-Ottoman War, Austria-Hungary occupied Bosnia and Herzegovina on 13 July 1878 and took over its administration. The Habsburgs officially annexed the region on 7 October 1908, holding onto it until the end of World War I.
200. See Y.E.E. 129/81 – the Ottoman Extraordinary Commissary (*fevkalade komiseri*) Ahmed Muhtar Paşa's report, dated 3 September 1897. See also Y.A.HUS.377/7 and Y.PRK.MK.7/88.

201. See Y.A.HUS.411/107 (29 October 1900).
202. See Y.PRK.ASK.232.107 (19 September 1905).
203. I have not yet been able to verify with complete certainty the identity of the author of this letter. There is evidence to suggest that this may be the same Şakir Paşa who had been recently (April 1905) dismissed from his post as governor of the Province of Kosovo (see Kuneralp, *Son Dönem Osmanlı Erkân ve Ricali*, p. 122). Perhaps he found himself exiled to Yemen. If so, his rank of marshal (müşir), which the letter indeed stated, would account for the considerable power he apparently wielded in Yemen. He would also have a motive to embarrass the newly installed (as of August 1905) governor of Yemen (Ahmed Fevzi Paşa) by including the remark about his deputy's conduct. On this governor's identity and tenure in office, see Kuneralp, *Son Dönem Osmanlı Erkân ve Ricali*, p. 43.
204. For the account of his trial, see Y.MTV.285/177 (21 April 1906).
205. See Erol 'Surveillance', *Urban History*.
206. See Y.MTV.31/88 (10 April 1888) and Y.MTV.32/5 (1 March 1888).
207. This question was raised by the deputy judge of canon law (*naib*) of the Anatolian town of Eğin (Kemaliye) Halid Ferid in 1894. See Y.E.E. 14/210 (18 October 1894).
208. '*Hafız*' refers to someone who knows the whole Qur'an by heart.
209. This is what the deputy preacher at the Orhan Ghazi Mosque in Bursa apparently did in 1902. See Y.PRK.DH.12/12 (16 September 1902).
210. See Y.PRK.MF.2/28. Specifically, '*mabeyn-i humayun*' signified the private apartments of the palace (in this case, Yıldız) where the sultan received visitors on ordinary occasions, and in which the male officers of the household were on duty.
211. See Y.PRK.DH.5/64 (23 October 1892).
212. See Y.PRK.UM.42/18 (1) (1 May 1898).
213. '*mu'tad olan ta'zimat ve tekrimat-ı layıka ve faika ile nam-ı akdes-i hümayun yad ve de'vat-ı mefruze-yi cenab-ı hilafetpenahiyi tilavet eyledi*'.
214. '*dahil vilayetteki umum cevami-yi şerifede bu feriza-yı mukaddese'ye mütahattım zimmet-i ubudiyet ve sadakat olduğu üzere kemal-ı mertebe-yi dikkat ve itina edilmekte*'.
215. '*hatibin öyle bir feriza-yı mukaddese'yi terk etmesi*'.
216. See Y.PRK.UM.42/18 (2) (4 June 1898).
217. A similar comparison can be drawn in terms of the relative use of the notion of 'necessity' in the two reports – not at all in the first one versus three times in the second.
218. On Ataullah Pasha's tenure in office, see Kuneralp, *Son Dönem Osmanlı Erkân ve Ricali*, p. 27.
219. The Maronite Christians belong to an Eastern Catholic Church in full communion with the Holy See of Rome.
220. The day in question is the Orthodox Christian feast of St Nicholas (6/19 December), which was also Emperor Nicholas II's 'name day'

(*den' tezoimenitstva*). Thus, although the letter was dated 22 December 1897 (a Wednesday), it referred to the previous Sunday, 6/19 December.
221. Y.PRK.UM.40/88 (22 December 1897).
222. Reşid Mümtaz Bey was governor of Beirut for a period of over six years (see Kuneralp, *Son Dönem Osmanlı Erkân ve Ricali*, p. 28).
223. See Levy and Georgeon, *The Young Turk Revolution*.
224. By all accounts, a similar fate befell Nicholas II of Russia in the aftermath of the 1905 Revolution, even though he would reign for another twelve years.

Conclusion

This book has analysed the complex interconnected transformations of ruler visibility and popular belonging over the course of a century – from the accession of Sultan Mahmud II in 1808 to the Young Turk Revolution in 1908.

In the aftermath of the Greek Revolution of 1821–9 and the abolition of the Janissary corps in its midst (1826), Mahmud II was able to press on with some of his most sweeping military, bureaucratic-administrative, socioeconomic, legal and, as this book has focused on above all, sociocultural reforms. The sultan thus engineered the first shift in modern ruler visibility, with a view to (1) establishing a plane of diplomatic reciprocity with and acceptance by the increasingly powerful West and (2) cultivating and cementing the loyalty of his Ottoman (especially non-Muslim) subjects. Breaking away from century-long Ottoman thinking and protocol, Mahmud II began dressing and carrying himself as a Western ruler before revolutionising public dress codes accordingly. The sultan made himself available to the public gaze (and vice versa) by going on ever longer and more extensive tours of the Ottoman countryside. He even ordered the unprecedented production, dissemination and embedding of his own portraits into innovative public rituals of popular allegiance. While Mahmud II would not live long enough to reap the fruit of his labours, by initiating the annual royal (birthday and accession day) celebrations in the Ottoman capital, the provinces and the newly opened permanent embassies abroad, in 1836, he did indeed set in motion powerful and long-lived processes of internal social reconfiguration and greater cultural homogenisation.

Until recently, the overall Ottoman reform process of the mid-nineteenth century, collectively known as the Tanzimat, was uniformly and rather indiscriminately referred to as 'Westernisation', with its inevitable corollary of 'secularisation' in most standard narratives of the period. Moreover, its start was fixed to the date of the Gülhane Rescript (3 November 1839), that is, the beginning of Sultan Abdülmecid's reign.

This book instead has added further weight to the growing scholarly opinion that the Tanzimat had been effectively under way well before 1839. Moreover, its central engine was not a Western (especially British) agent, but the sultan himself, who, with the help of his advisers, designed new annual pan-imperial public ruler celebrations with a view, yet again, of centralisation, in line with his other reforms, only this time of subject loyalties. Finally, regardless of long-term implications, the immediate contemporary context of the ruler's reformed image was secular only if viewed from abroad. At home, Mahmud II strove to present himself in strictly Muslim terms to Muslims, and universal kingly terms to non-Muslims. In doing so, he initiated two momentous long-term trends, which have been underappreciated by period Ottoman scholars, but which are indispensable to a realistic understanding of the history of communal ethos in the late Ottoman Empire. The first is the direct active engagement with non-Muslims and the monarch-initiated split in the manner of relation of the ruler to his Muslim and non-Muslim subjects, which accordingly conditioned reverse attitudes and modes of attachment. The second is the creation and fostering of an integrative, universalist conception of faith as a binding factor between the Muslim ruler and his non-Muslim subjects, which, in tandem with the influential 'father-children' metaphor of society and the related trope of love by and for the ruler, gave Ottomanism, the doctrine of all-Ottoman belonging, its most substantive content in the mid-nineteenth century.

The reigns of Mahmud II's sons – Abdülmecid (1839–61) and Abdülaziz (1861–76) – constitute the most formative period for the above-mentioned transformations. Both of these rulers enjoyed high levels of visibility and accessibility vis-à-vis their subjects from the late 1830s to at least the late 1860s, a time when autocracy still had no viable alternative as an anchor of popular allegiances. Therefore, they share many of the same parameters of the symbolic ruler-ruled interaction. At the same time, there are also some differences between the two sultans, based on areas of individual preference and accentuation in their policies of image management on the one hand (for example, education vs the military), and adaptive popular expectations in the escalating give-and-take of popular ceremonial involvement on the other.

From the outset of his reign, Abdülmecid adhered closely to a number of Mahmud II's image-making policies. First, he perpetuated the ruler's high direct visibility, making it palatable to foreign and domestic audiences alike. This is not to say that he did not encounter substantial resistance from conservative domestic circles, which resulted in the inconsistent timing of sultanic celebrations (away from the annual cycle and the Western solar calendar Mahmud II had prescribed) and unequal enthusiasm about them

Conclusion

(away from the secular-sourced accession anniversary) during his reign. However, even if such developments did slow somewhat the spread and growth of ruler celebrations, they did not reverse the overall turn towards modern ruler visibility. Second, Abdülmecid regularised the distribution of medals and orders as visible markings of royal favour, especially on sultanic occasions (an early instance of cross-dating), which fostered a vigorous competition for these status symbols cutting across socioeconomic, sociocultural and even state boundaries. Consequently, the system of targeted royal munificence played an important role in reshaping individual aspirations and reinforcing (elite and other) attachments to the monarch, both at home and abroad, thus helping perpetuate the imperial order. Third, the sultan firmly established the trope of love for the ruler, broached by his father, as the mainstay of his own scenario of power. In part, he did so through sultanic tours of the type Mahmud II had first embarked on in the nineteenth century. Evidence from one of them, the 1846 tour of Rumelia, perhaps the largest yet still under-researched, demonstrates the avenues for the creation of a lasting image of the ruler in the minds of multitudes of ordinary people, where, in most cases, none had existed before. Among them, the songs of praise and prayer, frequently tied to the discourse of Tanzimat reform, occupied a central place. With their effusive, increasingly complex metaphoric ornamentation, and standardised, repetitive, incantatory performances, the songs were converted into a powerful, large-scale medium for letting a heretofore distant ruler into the hearts and minds of his subjects across the imperial domains. Although launched, in the Bulgar case at least, in the aftermath of a unique direct encounter with the sultan, these songs quickly infiltrated a host of cyclical communal events, such as the school examination ceremonies, as well as entirely new communal festivities under the aegis of the ruler, such as the newly invented St Cyril and St Methodius celebrations. With the publication of the first major communal newspapers (such as the Bulgar *Tsarigradski Vestnik*, 1848–62) in the Ottoman Empire, a major new medium compounded the sporadic decentralised influence of songbooks. By bringing to its readers all across the far-flung imperial domains events and high personages from the capital on a weekly basis, the paper enhanced their awareness of an Ottoman centre, personalised by the sultan, his family and government ministers. One could therefore approach *modernity as mindset* from this angle as the process of extension of long-standing localised *micro* forms of belonging and linkage to the centre for a *macro* form of belonging. In this vein, it is important to keep in mind that the groundbreaking term '*millet*' (a community of co-religionists), employed in the Gülhane Rescript with reference to Ottoman faith-based (including non-Muslim) communities, was not a term the designated people or putative groups had earlier used with reference to themselves. If anything, it was an Ottoman diplomatic concession, as was the rescript itself, and an innovation in internal bureaucratic parlance. Thus, to speak of an entire *millet* system before the mid-nineteenth century is in the view of this author misleading. However, once it became obvious that this appellation was not only acceptable to the Ottoman authorities, but seen as a lasting measure, a mode to be encouraged, beginning in the early 1840s, groups in the making far and wide across the Empire started embracing it. Within a decade or so, an increasingly influential public discourse and mode of self-identification arose, which I have called '*millet*-ism' elsewhere.[1] The cultivation of a new and correspondingly abstract territorial attachment further aided the process of enhancement of communal belonging. The most obvious harbinger of this shift was a change in the dominant image of the land itself. Until the mid-nineteenth century, one's relationship to the land was overwhelmingly construed from a local, microregional vantage point. This construction stemmed from lived realities whereby property was accumulated and perpetuated through the male line. So one's place of birth and the land nearby were overwhelmingly viewed through the prism of 'patrimony'. Hence, the term 'fatherland', signifying above all one's place of birth, a sense which the 1845 *ferman*, analysed earlier, skilfully attempted to extend to the macro level of the entire imperial domains on the basis of the fatherly metaphor of the sultan. By the 1850s, however, the earlier versions of 'fatherland' began to yield ground to an alternative (abstract, macro-) concept – 'the land of the Bulgars, Bulgaria'. This gradual and subtle transformation, the by-product of a deliberate project of mental and spiritual centralisation around the figure of the sultan, signalled a paradigm shift. Whereas Chapter 2 revealed its opening phase, the following one – on the reign of Sultan Abdülaziz – completed the task.

The accession of Abdülaziz in 1861 was celebrated more widely throughout the Empire and with more pomp and circumstance than ever before. A closer look at some of these celebrations – in Anatolia, Rumelia and the capital – by different congregations of Muslim and non-Muslim subjects – shows a remarkable degree of continuity from the previous reign, in the rhetoric of power and the acts of popular appeal for divine intercession in its name. In particular, the consistent, long-term strategy of presenting the sultan as a rightful ruler to various non-Muslim communities along lines and with symbols familiar to them carried on. If Abdülmecid had become 'tsar' to the Bulgars in the mid-1840s, gradually acquiring proper Christian (imaginary, not necessarily real) regalia, as explained earlier, the rise of Abdülaziz to power led to the further

Conclusion

elaboration of the sultanic portrait in the minds of his Bulgar subjects. In consequence, the Bulgar press presented the new accession as an act of 'becoming tsar' and the Ottoman Muslim investiture ceremony of sword girding as its universal Christian counterpart, a coronation. This is but one example of the increasingly complex, multifocal and syncretic apparatus of ruler glorification and subject loyalty creation.

Several months into the new sultan's reign, the decision to celebrate the royal accession day and royal birthday on a regular (annual) basis as public holidays was announced. Domestic resistance to the Western (solar) calendar must have been strong, since even in 1861, with the lasting regularisation of these holidays, the shift was not complete – it affected the accession, but not the royal birthday, which continued to be celebrated in the Muslim (lunar) calendar. Nonetheless, further analysis of local sultanic celebrations in this chapter revealed not only traces of two-way strategies of accommodation but a still higher degree of cultural penetration and indoctrination of provincial populations, and their corresponding activation along lines acceptable to the centre. At the same time, such ceremonies created a host of novel opportunities for intra- and inter-communal interaction, (re-)drawing boundaries and clarifying the nature and essence of group belonging in the process. Collective notions of Bulgar 'feeling' and 'brotherhood' continued to evolve, tending towards a new conceptual stage. The ever more frequent transplantation of terms, such as 'kin' and 'people', from their native local/regional settings onto an imaginary macro canvas of Bulgar-ness signalled the rise of a putative blood connection as the basis for an abstract macro belonging.

This chapter demonstrated the intricate interweaving of motifs of sultanic and Bulgar communal (self-)celebration as well as the gradual intersection of the more established duties to the ruler with the newly arising duties to the group. This relationship, for a while mutually reinforcing, was illustrated via a cross-section of celebrations of 11 May, the Day of St Cyril and St Methodius. The concept of group memory, the discourse of communal rights and their sanctification, not to mention the more visible and commanding presence of a reified 'Bulgaria', were clear indications of a novel, macro-communal consciousness. Gradually, the stream of popular excitement for the ruler was diverted towards communal causes, at first slightly and subtly, then more substantially and assertively. The centrality of the ruler even in core ruler celebrations was at first dulled, then altogether displaced.

Here is a complete list of the key constituent elements and openended processes of the modern worldview, derived from the case of the Bulgar(ian)s of Rumelia and open to testing in other (Ottoman or not) contemporary communal cases. It began as a popular cult of the emperor, set in motion by the above-mentioned ceremonies and their attendant cultural production, before converting into the nation-centred mindset still alive today:

1. new practices of naming oneself and a rising value of the blood connection
2. new practices of naming 'the other'; transition from 'enemies of the ruler' to 'enemies of the community' to 'enemies of the nation'
3. evolving notions of a social pact and social (organic and familial) metaphors
4. innovative notion of a temporal continuum backward and forward, timelessness of the 'us'-group
5. extension of the *micro* fatherland into a *macro* fatherland; conversion into motherland
6. personification, victimisation and sanctification of the motherland
7. veneration of an abstract, faraway, imaginary centre (first 'ruler', then 'father-/motherland', then 'nation')
8. faith-based notions of community; transition from loose local forms of religious belonging to integrative practices of universalised faith and on to religious particularism and exceptionalism of the 'us'-group
9. increased tendency towards mental geographic mappings of the father-/motherland
10. innovative concepts of necessity, duty and sacrifice (first for the ruler, then for the 'us'-group)
11. rising importance of group unity and loyalty
12. accelerating processes of group mobilisation and totalisation
13. intensification of images of and justifications for militarism and violence

A quick point to take away from this flood of particles of modern ethnonationalism is that they all began somewhere else, orbiting around the figure of the monarch. Thus, this framework allows the composition of a continuous account linking the late imperial and the early ethnonational eras. Although the Bulgars remained nominally within the Empire until 1908, the creation of the principality of Bulgaria in 1878 gave an institutional foundation as well as a Christian monarch[2] to their increasingly ethnonational project. Therefore, even though the dynamics of the symbolic connection to the Ottoman sultan, which did not cease after the Russo-Ottoman War of 1877–8, are certainly worth exploring, they lie beyond the scope of this book. Instead, the last chapter studied the second

Conclusion

shift in modern ruler visibility, along faith-based lines, during the reign of Abdülmecid's son, Abdülhamid II (1876–1909).

Chapter 4 demonstrated the multiple pathways whereby the sultan-caliph strove to present himself as a pious Muslim to Muslims at home and abroad, and as a Western ruler to non-Muslims at home and abroad. Therefore, the sultan tended to deprive the former of his direct visibility (public appearances and public display of royal portraits), while at the same time channelling that visibility and staging it selectively towards the latter. Split chronologically into early-, middle- and late-reign sections, this chapter placed a special emphasis on the overall shift from direct to indirect sultanic visibility over time by way of resorting to material objects and abstract metaphors as ruler proxies. It traced the escalation of celebration in the second half of Abdülhamid II's reign in an attempt to capture the deliberate personality cult, centred on the sultan. This personality cult set a regional precedent for the use of techniques for mass appeal (now known as PR), which have since been repeatedly employed and are largely still with us today. As the sultanic ceremonies came to affect and involve ever-larger segments of the Ottoman population, the range of symbolic possibilities shrank and came under ever stricter control whereas the emotional intensity and abstraction from reality of the reference terms increased. This trend mirrored contemporary European and global processes of redefinition of monarchic sovereignty. Taken a step further, the analysis in this chapter also leads to some tentative but highly suggestive links between the personality cult of the late Ottoman sultan and the personality cults of later twentieth-century (national authoritarian/totalitarian) regimes, including the effects of *symbolic over-extension*.[3]

Finally, this chapter also analysed a range of alleged provocations and attempts at subversion (ceremonial or otherwise) of symbolic central power in order to shed new light on the later channels for group activation and increasingly ethnic group realisation. In other words, the sultanic ceremonies also played a role in conditioning various groups, increasingly perceiving themselves in ethnic terms, to a type of monarchic national mindset and society, which some of them replicated immediately after gaining independence from the Ottoman Empire. Therefore, analysis of this type is also indispensable to a comprehensive understanding of the history of national consciousness in Ottoman successor states,[4] a connection that has been completely ignored or denied by the respective national historiographies. The ultimate demise of the imperial system and its supplanting with the nation-state led to powerful processes of national rewriting of history and nationalisation of public memory, which still underwrite prevailing conceptions of (individual and group) identity today. It is against such narratives that this book takes a stand, arguing against the need for pendulum-like paradigm shifts in the social sciences, a frequent occurrence in the past several decades.

Notes

1. See Stephanov, 'Ruler Visibility', in *Living in the Ottoman Realm*, pp. 266–9.
2. First, Prince Alexander I Battenberg (1879–86) and then, after the coup and unification with Eastern Rumelia in 1885, Prince Ferdinand I (1887–1918).
3. By 'symbolic over-extension', I mean the process whereby ever-escalating terms of glorification of the monarch (or state/party leader) made him appear superhuman, an intended consequence, but also, by extension, made his image much vaguer and not so emotionally binding on ordinary people, clearly an unintended consequence. For a similar phenomenon in the case of Franz Joseph I, see Hamann, 'Der Wiener Hof', in *Hof und Hofgesellschaft*, p. 66 and Unowsky, *The Pomp and Politics of Patriotism*, p. 112.
4. See Ellis, 'King Me'; Podeh, *The Politics of National Celebrations* and Mestyan, *Arab Patriotism*, especially the conclusion.

Epilogue

The cycles of ruler visibility and popular belonging analysed in this book are not unique to the Ottoman Empire. In fact, as the Auspicious Event was unfolding in mid-June 1826 in Istanbul, the neighbouring Russian Empire, which had just had its own traumatic, game-changing event in the Decembrist Revolt six months earlier, was eagerly awaiting the elaborate coronation ceremonies of its new sovereign, Emperor Nicholas I (1825–55), in the old capital of Moscow.[1] Whereas Mahmud II faced an acute security crisis in the absence of the Janissary forces, which was to plague most of the rest of his reign, his counterpart in Russia rose to the throne amidst an acute legitimacy deficit. Thus, Nicholas I embarked even more quickly on reforms in all spheres of public life, beginning with the public image and popular symbolic functions of the sovereign. At the core of this new policy of modern ruler visibility lay the systematic pan-imperial public ruler celebrations of a larger number of holidays (not only the royal birthday and accession day, but also the coronation day, patron saint (namesake)'s day, etc.), which the emperor introduced a full decade before Mahmud II, and which had a similarly broad and long-lasting impact (at least until the Russian Revolution of 1905). Much like its Ottoman equivalent, this expanding ceremonial intervention into the lives of Romanov subjects from all social strata has not been studied to date.

Comparing the evolution of symbolic interaction between the ruler and the ruled in these two empires has interested me since the inception of the present book, all the more so since the trajectories of the two empires in the nineteenth century were closely intertwined in a number of ways. It suffices to call to mind the series of wars they fought (1806–12, 1828–9, 1853–6, 1877–8) as well as the largely contemporaneous programmes of economic, legal, fiscal, administrative and infrastructural modernisation they implemented in the nineteenth century. A serendipitous recent discovery at the National Library of Finland, once a depository library[2] of the Russian Empire, gave my evolving research an additional boost and new directions, opening up a range of inter- and trans-imperial lines

Ruler Visibility and Popular Belonging

Figure E.1 Portrait of Emperor Nicholas I (1856) by Vladimir Sverchkov (1821–88) (Wikimedia Commons).

of inquiry. It turned out that during the above-mentioned crucial decade between 1826 and 1836, Emperor Nicholas I had not one, but two direct, extensive opportunities to set an example for Mahmud II to follow in the composition and implementation of his own innovative visibility policies.

Epilogue

The first of them came up in the course of the 1828–9 Russo-Ottoman War in Europe and Asia. As their troops advanced on the Balkan and the Caucasian fronts, the Russian authorities celebrated lavishly a large number of their recently standardised royal festivities, centred not only on the reigning monarch, but also on members of the royal family, both living and deceased (in the case of Nicholas I's predecessor, Alexander I (r. 1801–25)). These were unprecedented acts for a foreign royalty on Ottoman (provincial) soil, with no equivalent even for Ottoman royalty itself. Moreover, rather than being isolated, small-scale ceremonial events, they engaged and impressed local populations of all creeds to the extent of drawing them en masse into feasts of genuine mixed merrymaking.[3]

The second opportunity was even more spectacular, not to mention far closer to home. It presented itself during the four-month stay of Russian troops on the upper Bosphorus in early 1833, per Mahmud II's express invitation to provide security against the advancing troops of Ibrahim Pasha, son of the rebellious governor of Egypt, Mehmed Ali, following the Ottoman defeat at Konya.[4] In this stretch of time, the Russians staged dazzling festivities on land and sea, and enjoyed unprecedented access to the sultan, who himself visited them on numerous occasions and took part in joint military reviews as well as elaborate ceremonial exchanges. Even if one ignores entirely the provincial wartime ceremonies, the 1833 events on the Bosphorus take the argument of inter-imperial influence, entanglement and transfer to a new level.[5] In consequence, these two episodes of undoubtedly profound, yet thoroughly uncharted significance shed an entirely new light both on the initiation of annual sultanic ceremonies in 1836 and on Mahmud II's tour of Rumelia in 1837, which took place as soon as the occupying Russian troops had withdrawn.

All of these related events, processes and linkages will be the object of further research, drawing attention to the closed loop between elitist projection and popular reception, especially among those of the tsar's and sultan's respective subjects who belonged to a different faith or denomination. In my view, the thirteen-point model of modern belonging, derived from the Ottoman Bulgar(ian) case, can serve as the point of departure for fruitful explorations of the celebratory experiences and changing self-conceptions of a number of religious communities in the Russian Empire, including Armenians, Muslims and Jews. For my part, I intend to focus on the communal trajectory of the non-Orthodox Christian (Lutheran) Finns from the Grand Duchy of Finland, a territory wrested from Sweden and held by the Russian Empire from 1809 to 1917. My choice is inspired by another fortuitous discovery in 2005 of a cache of ceremonial texts at the imperial archive in Moscow (GARF) on the occasion of Alexander II

Ruler Visibility and Popular Belonging

(1855–81)'s twenty-fifth accession anniversary held at the Imperial Alexander University (the future University of Helsinki) in 1880. Upon a close reading, these materials, couched in a rhetoric of subject loyalty, under the guise of the ruler occasion, reveal the contours of a more or less fully-fledged ethnonational project. Further research confirmed my hypothesis that, as in the case of the Bulgars, the field of education served as the backdrop, first, for the nurturing of vertical ties of loyalty to monarch and dynasty and, then, for their subtle transformation into horizontal (macro) communal-cum-ethnonational belonging. Since education also provided a legitimate setting and a host of occasions conducive to repeated improvisations on the father-children metaphor of society and the trope of love for and by the ruler (point 3 of the model), it may be useful as an illustrative line of entry into the subject of comparative analysis.

Unlike the Bulgars, the Finns had a century-old and venerable institution of higher education in the Royal Academy of Åbo, which was renamed the 'Imperial Alexander University' and moved to the newly established capital of Helsingfors (Helsinki) in 1829. Thereafter, it served as the urban fulcrum of imperial ceremonies, be they personal royal visits or royal anniversaries. In addition, its own annual graduation ceremonies (much like the Bulgar school examination ceremonies) and monumental 200th anniversary celebrations in 1840 (much like the Bulgar St Cyril and St Methodius festivities) provided ample platform for demonstrations of subject loyalty and popular enthusiasm for monarch and empire. In fact, the university was connected to the ruling Romanov house by more than its name, since its royally appointed chancellor, beginning on 30 December 1825[6] with Grand Duke Alexander Nikolaevitch (the future Alexander II), was none other than the heir apparent.[7]

Here is the text of a song composed by a university professor of oratory, Johan G. Linsen (1785–1848), on the occasion of Nicholas I's name day in 1833 and sung by the invited guests at a grand ball in Helsingfors:

> Glory to Nicholas glory.
> To the great, happy, prosperous
> Father of [his] subjects, glory!
> Wherever your power reaches
> You meet the good will of the peoples
> For you every heart beats
> In the palaces and the huts.
> You are our hope, our comfort,
> For you in our faithful hearts
> We harbour love;

Epilogue

> You will become our shield, our might,
> You are the guard of our huts,
> You – memory of our forgotten region.
> Hope and joy are dawning,
> Want and darkness are vanishing
> At a single glance of yours,
> Under the protection of your sceptre
> Stand peace and social manners
> Guarding our country,
> Law and order.
> All your people seeing,
> In you their bliss,
> Pray for you now . . .[8]

The extant detailed descriptions of the 1833 name day festivities in Helsingfors allow us to place this song of praise and prayer in its proper context and shed light on other trends already under way. To begin with, in an act of cross-dating, the inauguration of the newly constructed Society House in Helsingfors was purposely made to coincide with the royal name day.[9] In fact, the building served as the venue for the holiday's pivotal celebration in town – the evening ball. Furthermore, Linsen's poem was not the only poignant expression of subject loyalty that evening. Equally, if not more impressive, was a rendition of the brand new 'God Save the Tsar',[10] performed to Swedish verses especially written for the occasion.[11] The lyrics were printed on 400 pamphlets and sung by the elite of local society with 'tears of tender emotion (*umilenie*) and a slight quiver of the choir'.[12] Last but not least, a novel ceremony took place, most probably inspired by Nicholas I's second visit to the city only six months earlier. Here is its description in context, worth quoting at length:

> In the large hall [of the Society House], a bust of the beloved Monarch could be seen [lit. 'presented itself to the eye'], on a stage covered in red cloth. Above it, an image of the monogram of His Majesty's name, circled by laurel and oak leaves in shining splendour [*osiyannoe slavoyu*]. On top hovered the Russian [*Rossiyskiy*][13] double-headed eagle with the coat of arms of Finland in its shield. The coats of arms of the Grand Duchy's eight Governorates were displayed on four pillars on both sides of the bust. With the blinding light of four magnificent chandeliers and marvellous lights, placed before the bust, all these had a majestic appearance. And when at the appearance of General Teslev,[14] who stood still, along with the persons accompanying him, before the bust, thundered the sound of trumpets from the choirs, then the common feeling of awe filled those present, as though they were seeing the most beloved Father of the Fatherland with His firmness and serenity.[15]

Centred as it was on a bust, i.e. a proxy of the monarch, this fascinating stylised homage *in absentia*, which would have been unthinkable only a few years earlier, provides an early indication of the rising importance of modern ruler visibility in reaching out to the hearts and minds of imperial subjects near and far. Clearly, it opens the door to a personality cult, which did indeed form and grow successfully for many decades thereafter. In fact, one can already observe here the careful and complex interweaving and staging of various motifs, be they of heraldic nature, colour/light or sound, tying in the ruler and the people, Russia and Finland, and forging, both symbolically and physically, a shared public space for them.

Institutional and other structural differences notwithstanding, examples such as these reveal the striking similarity of ceremonial channels and functional patterns whereby the cycles of ruler visibility and popular belonging unfolded in the Russian and the Ottoman Empires. Similar processes of *mental centralisation*, which paralleled other ongoing forms of centralisation – fiscal, administrative, infrastructural and so on, went on in many other state formations across the globe in the course of the nineteenth century. My future research will provide a more advanced blueprint for mapping the complex syncretic modernities of late imperial regimes and a template for designing further comparative imperial studies across the nineteenth-century world and beyond. These empires engaged in fascinating acts of ceremonial experimentation, but also exhibited many ominous sides of the looming modern state, with its unparalleled abilities to censor, discipline, control, expel and even annihilate.

By looking afresh at the symbolic ways through which the (imperial) centre came into cyclical contact with the individual, and repeatedly attempted to cajole, coerce and coopt him or her, one can study some of the first abstract lessons in modernity that were taught and learned by each side. As a result, one can better understand the emergence of the end product, both across space and over time.

Notes

1. On the reign of Emperor Nicholas I, see Wortman, *Scenarios of Power*, vol. 1, part 4: 'The Dynastic Scenario', pp. 247–418; Riasanovsky, *Nicholas I and Official Nationality in Russia, 1825–1855*; Lincoln, *Nicholas I: Emperor and Autocrat of All the Russias*, among others.
2. A depository library was entitled to receive a copy of every major periodical which was published in the Empire.
3. Detailed reports appeared in the contemporary Russian periodical press.
4. On the 1828–9 Russo-Ottoman war, the Russian troops' presence on the

Epilogue

Bosphorus in 1833 and the Russo-Ottoman treaty signed, see Aksan, *Ottoman Wars*, pp. 343–76; Shaw and Shaw, *History of the Ottoman Empire and Modern Turkey*, vol. 2, pp. 31–4. See also Finkel, *Osman's Dream*, pp. 444–5 and Kutluoğlu, *The Egyptian Question, 1831–1841*, pp. 93–94, 101–7.

5. See the accounts in the contemporary Russian periodical press.
6. Barely two weeks after the Decembrist Revolt.
7. I borrow the following examples from my article 'Public Celebrations of Emperor Nicholas I', in *400th Anniversary of the Romanov Dynasty*, pp. 89–103.
8. Borodkin, *Istoria Finlyandii*, pp. 491–2, 702 (footnote 793). Punctuation is in accordance with the original.
9. Here is another example of cross-dating. In 1835, the 'Empress' Stone' – the monument commemorating the spot where Nicholas I's royal consort, Alexandra Feodorovna, first set foot in Helsingfors in 1833, thereby becoming the first empress to ever visit the city, was inaugurated. The ceremony took place on the emperor's name day. See Schoolfield, *Helsinki of the Czars*, p. 33.
10. In what appears an act of astonishing coordination, the Helsingfors performance took place on the same day as the Moscow premiere of the anthem.
11. One of the poets – Johan L. Runeberg (1804–77) – would thirteen years later pen the poem which would eventually become the Finnish national anthem. The other author was Bengt O. Lille (1807–75), a theologian.
12. *Russkiy Invalid ili Voennyiia Vedomosti*, 21 December 1833.
13. The Russian words '*russkii*' and '*rossiiskii*' are invariably translated as 'Russian' in English, although they have quite different meanings in the original language. In my view, the former is best rendered as 'Russian popular (later and nowadays "Russian ethnic")' and the latter 'Russian imperial'.
14. Alexander P. Teslev (1778–1847) served at the time as Assistant (Civil) Governor-General and vice chancellor of the Imperial Alexander University.
15. *Russkiy Invalid ili Voennyiia Vedomosti*, 21 December 1833. Underlining is my own.

Bibliography

Primary Sources

ARCHIVAL SOURCES

Başbakanlık Osmanlı Arşivi (BOA), Istanbul, Turkey.
   A.DVN. Sadaret Divan Kalemi Evrakı
   A.MKT. Sadaret Mektubî Kalemi Belgeleri
   A.MKT.MHM. Sadaret Mühimme Kalemi Evrakı
   A.MKT.UM. Sadaret Umum Vilayat Evrakı
   C.SM. Cevdet Saray
   DH.MKT. Dahiliye Mektubi Kalemi
   HAT Hatt-ı Hümayûn Tasnifi
   HR.SFR.3. Hariciye Nezareti Londra Sefareti
   I.DH *Iradeler Dahiliye*
   I.HR *Iradeler Hariciye*
   Y.A.HUS. *Yıldız Hususi Maruzat*
   YEE *Yıldız Esas Evrakı*
   Y.EE.KP. *Yıldız Esas ve Sadrazam Kamil Paşa Evrakı*
   Y.MTV. *Yıldız Mütenevvi Maruzat*
   Y.PRK.ASK. *Yıldız Askeri Maruzat*
   Y.PRK.BŞK. *Yıldız Başkitabet Dairesi Maruzatı*
   Y.PRK.DH. *Yıldız Dahiliye Nezareti Maruzatı*
   Y.PRK.MF. *Yıldız Maarif Nezaleti Maruzatı*
   Y.PRK.MK. *Yıldız Müfettişlikler ve Komiserlikler Tahriratı*
   Y.PRK.UM. *Yıldız Umum Vilayetler Tahriratı*

NEWSPAPERS

Blugarski Knizhitsi
Bulgaria
Ceride-i Havadis
Dunavski Lebed
Levant Herald

Bibliography

Lyuboslovie
Malumat
Napreduk
Novoe Vremia
Russkiy Invalid ili Voennyiia Vedomosti
Servet-i Fünun
Stamboul
Suvetnik
Takvim-i Vekayi
The Times
Tsarigradski Vestnik
Tuna/Dunav
Vestnik Evropyi
Vremya
Zornitsa

OTHER PRIMARY SOURCES

Annual Register: a Review of Public Events at Home and Abroad, for Year 1898 (Unknown: Longmans, Green and Co., 1898).

Auldjo, John, *Journal of a Visit to Constantinople, and Some of the Greek Islands, in the Spring and Summer of 1833* (London: Longman, Rees, Orme, Brown, Green & Longman, 1835).

Balabanov, Marko, *Bulgarska Kolonia v Edin Ostrov* [A Bulgarian Colony on an Island] (Sofia: Durzhavna Pechatnitsa, 1910).

Belchev, Nikola Gerov, *Pesnopoyche* [Songbook] (Istanbul: Tadeya Divitchiyan, 1860).

Brewer, Josiah, *A Residence at Constantinople in the Year 1827: with Notes to the Present Time* (New Haven, CT: Durrie & Peck, 1830).

de Busbecq, Ogier Ghiselin, *The Life and Letters of Ogier Ghiselin de Busbecq*, vol. I (London: C. Kegan Paul and Co., 1881).

Burmov, Todor, *Spomenite Mi: Dnevnik, Avtobiografia* (Sofia: Izdat. Ljubomădrie, 1994).

Cevdet, Ahmet Pasha, *Ma'ruzat* (Istanbul: Cagri Yayinlari, 1980).

Cox, Samuel, *Diversions of a Diplomat in Turkey* (New York: C. L. Webster & Co., 1893).

Dodd, Ann Bowman, *In the Palaces of the Sultan* (New York: Dodd, Mead & Co., 1903).

Çelebi, Evliya, *Evliya Çelebi Seyahatname* (Ankara: Turizm ve Tanıtma Bakanlığı, 1980).

Fresne-Canaye, Philippe de, *Le Voyage du Levant (1573)* (Paris: E. Leroux, 1897).

Gyurova, Svetla (ed.), *Vuzrozhdenski Putepisi* (Sofia, 1969).

Halid, Halil, *The Diary of a Turk* (London: A. & C. Black, 1903).

Hobhouse, John, *A Journey through Albania and Other Provinces of Turkey in*

Europe and Asia, to Constantinople, during the Years 1809 and 1810 (London: J. Cawthorn, 1813).

Ikonomov, Todor, *Memoari* (Sofia: Bŭlgarski Pisatel, 1973).

Iliev, Atanas, *Spomeni* (Sofia: Gluškov, 1926).

Kelly, Laurence (ed.), *Istanbul: A Traveller's Companion* (London: Constable, 1987).

Kisimov, Pandeli, *Moite Spomeni*, part 2 (Sofia: Pechatnitsa na P.M.Buzaytov, 1900).

Lütfi, *Tarih-i Lütfi*, vols 4 and 5 (Chicago, IL: Middle East Documentation Center for Middle Eastern Studies, 1993).

MacFarlane, Charles, *Constantinople in 1828* (London: Saunders & Otley, 1829).

Melling, Antoine-Ignace, *Voyage pittoresque de Constantinople et des rives du Bosphore* (Istanbul: Yapı ve Kredi Bankası, 1969).

Moltke, Helmuth von, *Lettres sur l'Orient* (Paris, 1872).

Moltke, Helmuth von, *Briefe über Zustände und Begebenheiten in der Türkei aus den Jahren 1835–1839* (Berlin: Posen, 1841).

Otechestvennyiy Panteon, ili Zhizn' Velikih Kniazey, Tsarey i Imperatorov, s 64 portretov, part 1 (Moskva: Tipografii Avgusta Semena, 1850).

Pardoe, Julia, *The City of the Sultans and Domestic Manners of the Turks in 1836* (London: H. G. Clarke, 1845).

Patrick, Mary, *Under Five Sultans* (New York: Century Co., 1929).

Popruzhenko, M.G. (ed.), *Arkhiv na Nayden Gerov*, vols 1 and 2 (Sofia: Bulgarska Akademia na Naukite, 1931–2).

Prokesch-Osten, Anton von, *Geschichte des Abfalls der Griechen vom türkischen Reiche in Jahre 1821 und der Gründung des hellenischen Königreiches. Aus diplomatischen Standpunkte* (Vienna: Gerold in Komm, 1867).

Rilsky, Neofit, *Hristomatia Slavenskago Iazika* (Istanbul, 1852).

Selaniki, Mustafa Efendi, *Tarih* (Istanbul: İstanbul Üniversitesi, 1989).

Slade, Adolphus, *Records of Travels in Turkey, Greece, and of a Cruise in the Black Sea* (London: Saunders and Otley, 1833).

Stambolski, Hristo, *Avtobiografiya, Dnevnitsi, Spomeni 1852–1879* (Sofia: Dŭrjavna Pechatnitsa, 1972).

Turski Dokumenti za Makedonskata Istorija, vol. 5 (Skopije: Institut za nacionalna istorija, 1951–8).

Vazov, Ivan, *Subrani Suchinenia, tom 19 (Biografichni Materiali)*, (Sofia: Bulgarski Pisatel, 1957).

White, Charles, *Three Years in Constantinople, or Domestic Manners of the Turks in 1844* (London: H. Colburn, 1845).

Yoannovich, Hadzhi Nayden, *Almanac or Calendar for the Year 1847* (Bucharest: I. Copaynig, 1846).

Yoannovich, Hadzhi Nayden, *Novi Bulgarski Pesni s Tsarski i Drugi Novi Pesni ili Pohvali* (Belgrade, 1851).

Zafirov, Spas and Tsani Zhelev, *Blugarska Gusla* (Istanbul, 1857).

Bibliography

Secondary Sources

Abou El Hajj, Rifat, 'The Narcissism of Mustafa II (1695–1703): A Psychohistorical Study', *Studia Islamica*, 1974, 40, 115–31.

Abu-Manneh, Butrus, 'The Islamic Roots of the Gülhane Rescript', *Die Welt des Islams*, 1994, 34(2), 173–203.

Acun, H., *Anadolu Saat Kuleleri* (Ankara: Atatürk Kültür Merkezi, 1994).

Akarli, Engin, 'The Tangled Ends of an Empire: Ottoman Encounters with the West and Problems of Westernisation – An Overview', *Comparative Studies of South Asia, Africa and the Middle East*, 2006, 26(3), 353–66.

Akcasu, A. Ebru, 'Migrants to Citizens: An Evaluation of the Expansionist Features of Hamidian Ottomanism, 1876–1909', *Die Welt des Islams*, 2016, 56(3–4), 388–414.

Akiba, Jun, 'Preliminaries to a Comparative History of the Russian and Ottoman Empires: Perspectives from Ottoman Studies', in Kimitaka Matsuzato (ed.), *Imperiology: From Empirical Knowledge to Discussing the Russian Empire* (Sapporo: Hokkaido University Press, 2007), pp. 33–47.

Aksan, Virginia, *Ottoman Wars, 1700–1870: An Empire Besieged* (Harlow: Pearson Education, 2007).

Aksan, Virginia, 'What's Up in Ottoman Studies?', *Journal of the Ottoman and Turkish Studies Association*, 2014, 1(1–2), 3–21.

Aksan, Virginia and Daniel Goffman (eds), *The Early Modern Ottomans* (Cambridge: Cambridge University Press, 2007).

Alderson, Anthony, *The Structure of the Ottoman Dynasty* (Oxford: Clarendon Press, 1956).

Al-Sayyad, Nezar (ed.), *Hybrid Urbanism: On the Identity Discourse and the Built Environment* (Westport, CT: Praeger, 2001).

Amanat, Abbas, *Pivot of the Universe: Nasir al-Din Shah Qajar and the Iranian Monarchy* (London: I. B. Tauris, 2008).

de Amicis, Edmondo, *Constantinople* (New York: G. P. Putnam, 1888).

Anagnostopoulou, Sia, 'The "Nation" of the Rum Sings of Its Sultan: The Many Faces of Ottomanism', in L. Baruh and V. Kechriotis (eds), *Economy and Society on Both Shores of the Aegean* (Athens: Alpha Bank, 2010), pp. 79–105.

Anagnostopoulou, Sia and Matthias Kappler, 'Bin Yaşa Padişahımız: the Millet-i Rum Singing the Praises of the Sultan in the Framework of Helleno-Ottomanism', *Archivum Ottomanicum*, 23 (2005–6), 47–78.

Anderson, Benedict, *Imagined Communities: Reflections on the Origin and Spread of Nationalism* (London: Verso, 1983).

Anderson, M. S., *The Eastern Question, 1774–1923* (New York: St. Martin's Press, 1966).

Anscombe, Frederick, *State, Faith, and Nation in Ottoman and Post-Ottoman Lands* (Cambridge: Cambridge University Press, 2014).

Artan, Tülay, 'Architecture as a Theatre of Life: Profile of the Eighteenth-Century Bosphorus' (PhD dissertation: Massachusetts Institute of Technology, 1989).

Aymes, Marc, 'Reform Talks: Applying the Tanzimat to Cyprus', in Michalis Michael (ed.), *Ottoman Cyprus: A Collection of Studies on History and Culture* (Wiesbaden: Harrassowitz, 2009).

Bacque-Grammont, Jean-Louis and Aksel Tibet (eds), *Cimetières et traditions funéraires dans le monde islamique* (Ankara: Türk Tarih Kurumu Basımevi, 1996).

Balabanov, Marko, *Gavril Krustevich (Naroden Deets, Knizhovnik, Sudia, Upravitel)* (Sofia: Pechatnitsa Den, 1914).

Banerjee, Milinda, 'Ocular Sovereignty, Acclamatory Rulership and Political Communication: Visits of Princes of Wales to Bengal', in Frank L. Mueller and Heidi Mehrkens (eds), *Royal Heirs and the Uses of Soft Power in Nineteenth-Century Europe* (London: Palgrave Macmillan, 2016).

Banerjee, Milinda, *The Mortal God: Imagining the Sovereign in Colonial India* (Delhi: Cambridge University Press, 2019).

Baramova, Maria et al. (eds), *Power and Influence in South-Eastern Europe, 16th–19th Century* (Berlin: LIT Verlag, 2014).

Barkey, Karen, *Empire of Difference: The Ottomans in Comparative Perspective* (Cambridge: Cambridge University Press, 2009).

Barkey, Karen and George Gavrilis, 'The Ottoman Millet System: Non-Territorial Autonomy and its Contemporary Legacy', *Ethnopolitics*, 2016, 15(1), 24–42.

Bartov, Omer and Eric Weitz, *Shatterzone of Empires: Coexistence and Violence in the German, Habsburg, Russian, and Ottoman Borderlands* (Bloomington, IN: Indiana University Press, 2013).

Bayerle, Gustav, *Pashas, Begs and Effendis: A Historical Dictionary of Titles and Terms in the Ottoman Empire* (Istanbul: Isis Press, 1997).

Baykara, Tuncer, *Osmanlılarda Medeniyet Kavramı ve Ondokuzuncu Yüzyıla dair Araştırmalar* (Izmir: Akademi Kitabevi, 1992).

Berkes, Niyazi, *The Development of Secularism in Turkey* (Montreal: McGill University Press, 1964).

Bhabha, Homi, *The Location of Culture* (New York: Routledge & Kegan Paul, 1994).

Bierman, John, *Napoleon III and His Carnival Empire* (New York: St. Martin's Press, 1988).

Blumi, Isa, *Rethinking the Late Ottoman Empire: A Comparative Social and Political History of Albania and Yemen, 1878–1918* (Istanbul: Isis Press, 2010).

Blumi, Isa, *Reinstating the Ottomans: Alternative Balkan Modernities, 1800–1912* (New York: Palgrave, 2011).

Blumi, Isa, *Foundations of Modernity. Human Agency and the Imperial State* (London: Routledge, 2012).

Borodkin, Mikhail, *Istoria Finlyandii Vremya Imperatora Nikolaya I* (St Petersburg: Gosudarstvennaya Tipografia, 1915).

Bouquet, Olivier, 'Is It Time to Stop Speaking about Ottoman Modernisation?', in Marc Aymes, Benjamin Gourisse and Elise Massicard (eds), *Order and*

Compromise: Government Practices in Turkey from the Late Ottoman Empire to the Early 21st Century (Leiden: Brill, 2015).

Boyar, Ebru, 'The Press and the Palace: The Two-Way Relationship between Abdülhamid II and the Press, 1876–1913', *Bulletin of the School of Oriental and African Studies*, 2006, 69(3), 417–32.

Braude, Benjamin and Bernard Lewis (eds), *Christians and Jews in the Ottoman Empire. The Functioning of a Plural Society* (New York: Holmes & Meier Publishers, 1982).

Brisku, Adrian, *Political Reform in the Ottoman and Russian Empires: A Comparative Approach* (London: Bloomsbury, 2017).

Brookes, Douglas, 'Of Swords and Tombs: Symbolism in the Ottoman Accession Ritual', *Turkish Studies Association Bulletin*, 1993, 17(2), 1–22.

Brophy, James, *Popular Culture and the Public Sphere in the Rhineland, 1800–1850* (Cambridge: Cambridge University Press, 2009).

Brubaker, Rogers, *Nationalism Reframed: Nationhood and the National Question in the New Europe* (Cambridge: Cambridge University Press, 1996).

Bucur, Maria and Nancy Wingfield, *Staging the Past: The Politics of Commemoration in Habsburg Central Europe, 1848 to the Present* (West Lafayette, IN: Purdue University Press, 2001).

Burbank, Jane and Frederick Cooper, *Empires in World History: Power and the Politics of Difference* (Princeton, NJ: Princeton University Press, 2010).

Campos, Michelle, *Ottoman Brothers: Muslims, Christians, and Jews in Early Twentieth-Century Palestine* (Stanford, CA: Stanford University Press, 2011).

Cannadine, David, 'Splendor Out of Court: Royal Spectacle and Pageantry in Modern Britain, c. 1820–1977', in Sean Wilentz (ed.), *Rites of Power. Symbolism, Ritual, and Politics Since the Middle Ages* (Philadelphia, PA: University of Pennsylvania Press, 1985), pp. 206–43.

Çelik, Zeynep, *Empire, Architecture, and the City: French-Ottoman Encounters, 1830–1914* (Seattle, WA: University of Washington Press, 2008).

Cohen, Julia, *Becoming Ottomans: Sephardi Jews and Imperial Jews Citizenship in the Modern Era* (Oxford: Oxford University Press, 2014).

David-Fox, Michael, Peter Holquist and Alexander Martin (eds), 'The Imperial Turn', *Kritika: Explorations in Russian and Eurasian History*, 2006, 7(4), 705–12.

Davison, Roderic, *Reform in the Ottoman Empire, 1856–1876* (Princeton, NJ: Princeton University Press, 1963).

Davison, Roderic, *Essays in Ottoman and Turkish History, 1774–1923. The Impact of the West* (Austin, TX: University of Texas Press, 1990).

Deleon, Jak, *Anıtsal İstanbul (Gezgin Rehberi)* (Istanbul: Remzi Kitabevi, 2001).

Demirel, Fatmagül, 'A Modern Performance in Late Ottoman Times: Birthday Celebrations as Imperial Image-Making', in Suraiya Faroqhi and Arzu Öztürkmen (eds), *Celebration, Entertainment and Theatre in the Ottoman World* (London: Seagull Books, 2014), pp. 261–71.

Deringil, Selim, *The Well-Protected Domains. Ideology and the Legitimation of Power in the Ottoman Empire, 1876–1909* (London: I. B. Tauris, 1998).

Dimmig, Ashley, 'Fabricating a New Image: Imperial Tents in the Late Ottoman Period', *International Journal of Islamic Architecture*, 2014, 3(2), 341–72.

Doumanis, Nicholas, *Before the Nation: Muslim-Christian Coexistence and Its Destruction in Late Ottoman Anatolia* (Oxford: Oxford University Press, 2013).

Drinov, Marin, *Istoricheski Pregled na Bulgarskata Tsurkva ot Samoto i Nachalo i do Dnes* (Vienna: Sommer, 1869).

Duindam, Jeroen, *Dynasties: A Global History of Power, 1300–1800* (Cambridge: Cambridge University Press, 2016).

Ehala, Martin, *Signs of Identity: The Anatomy of Belonging* (London: Routledge, 2017).

Eissenstat, Howard, 'Modernisation, Imperial Nationalism, and the Ethnicisation of Confessional Identity in the Late Ottoman Empire', in Alexei Miller and Stefan Berger (eds), *Nationalizing Empires* (Budapest: Central European Press, 2015).

Eldem, Edhem, *Pride and Privilege. A History of Ottoman Orders, Medals and Decorations* (Istanbul: Ottoman Bank Archives and Research Centre, 2004).

Eldem, Edhem, 'Pouvoir, modernité et visibilité : l'évolution de l'iconographie sultanienne à l'epoque moderne', in Omar Carlier et Raphaëlle Nollez-Goldbach (eds), *Le Corps du leader. Construction et représentation dans les pays du Sud* (Paris: L'Harmattan, 2008), pp. 171–202.

Eldem, Edhem, 'Powerful Images – The Dissemination and Impact of Photography in the Ottoman Empire, 1870–1914', in Zeynep Çelik, Edhem Eldem and Hande Eagle (eds), *Camera Ottomana: Photography and Modernity in the Ottoman Empire, 1840–1914* (Istanbul: Koç University Press, 2015).

Eldem, Edhem, 'The Search for an Ottoman Vernacular Photography', in Markus Ritter and Staci G. Scheiwiller (eds), *The Indigenous Lens? Early Photography in the Near and Middle East* (Berlin: De Gruyter, 2018).

Ellis, Matthew, 'King Me: The Political Culture of Monarchy in Interwar Egypt and Iraq' (MPhil thesis, Exeter College, University of Oxford, 2005).

Erol, Merih, 'Surveillance, Urban Governance and Legitimacy in Late Ottoman Istanbul: Spying on Music and Entertainment during the Hamidian Regime (1876–1909)', *Urban History*, 1 November 2013, 40(4), 706–25.

Ersoy, Ahmet, *Architecture and the Late Ottoman Imaginary: Reconfiguring the Architectural Past in a Modernizing Empire* (Farnham: Ashgate Publishing, 2015).

Ersoy, Ahmet, 'Ottomans and the Kodak Galaxy: Archiving Everyday Life and Historical Space in Ottoman Illustrated Journals', *History of Photography*, August 2016, 40(3), 330–57.

Esenbel, Selçuk, 'Istanbul'da Bir Japon', *Istanbul Dergisi*, 9 (1994), 36–42.

Evered, Emine, *Empire and Education under the Ottomans: Politics, Reform and Resistance from the Tanzimat to the Young Turks* (London: I. B. Tauris, 2012).

Bibliography

Fahmy, Khaled, *All the Pasha's Men: Mehmed Ali, His Army, and the Making of Modern Egypt* (Cambridge: Cambridge University Press, 1997).

Findley, Carter, *Turkey, Islam, Nationalism and Modernity* (New Haven, CT: Yale University Press, 2010).

Finkel, Caroline, *Osman's Dream. The Story of the Ottoman Empire, 1300-1923* (London: John Murray, 2005).

Flemming, Katherine, *The Muslim Bonaparte: Diplomacy and Orientalism in Ali Pasha's Greece* (Princeton, NJ: Princeton University Press, 1999).

Fortna, Benjamin, *Learning to Read in the Late Ottoman Empire and the Early Turkish Republic* (Basingstoke: Palgrave Macmillan, 2012).

Fortna, Benjamin, *Imperial Classroom: Islam, the State, and Education in the Late Ottoman Empire* (Oxford: Oxford University Press, 2003).

Fujitani, Takashi, *Splendid Monarchy. Power and Pageantry in Modern Japan* (Berkeley, CA: University of California Press, 1996).

Gaonkar, Dilip, *Alternative Modernities* (Durham, NC: Duke University Press, 2001).

Gavin, Carney and Harvard Semitic Museum, 'Imperial Self-Portrait: the Ottoman Empire as Revealed in the Sultan Abdul-Hamid II's Photographic Albums, Presented as Gifts to the Library of Congress (1893) and the British Museum (1894)', *Journal of Turkish Studies*, 1989, 12.

Geisler, Michael, *National Symbols, Fractured Identities: Contesting the National Narrative* (Middlebury, VT: Middlebury College Press, 2005).

Georgeon, François, *Abdülhamid II: Le Sultan Calife (1876–1909)* (Paris: Fayard, 2003).

Georgeon, François, 'Le sultan caché : réclusion du souverain et mise en scène du pouvoir à l'époque de Abdülhamid II (1876–1909)', *Turcica*, 1997, 29, 93–124.

Georgov, Ivan, 'Materiali po nasheto vuzrazhdane', in *Sbornik za Narodni Umotvoreniya, Nauka i Knizhnina*, kniga XXIV, chart I (Sofia, 1908).

Gellner, Ernest, *Nations and Nationalism* (Ithaca, NY: Cornell University Press, 1983).

Gerov, Nayden, *Rechnik na Bulgarskiy Yazyik*, part I (Plovdiv, 1895).

Giloi, Eva, *Monarchy, Myth, and Material Culture in Germany, 1750–1950* (Cambridge: Cambridge University Press, 2011).

Giloi, Eva, 'Royally Entertained: Visual Culture and the Experience of Monarchy in Wilhelmine Prussia', *Intellectual History Review*, 2007, 17(2), 203–24.

Ginzburg, Carlo, *The Cheese and the Worms. The Cosmos of a Sixteenth-Century Miller* (London: Routledge & Kegan Paul, 1976).

Ginzburg, Carlo, *Clues, Myths, and the Historical Method* (Baltimore, MD: Johns Hopkins University Press, 1990).

Gluck, Carol, *Japan's Modern Myths: Ideology in the Late Meiji Period* (Princeton, NJ: Princeton University Press, 1985).

Gradeva, Rossitsa, 'Ottoman Policy towards Christian Church Building', *Etudes balkaniques*, 1994, 4, 14–36.

Gradeva, Rossitsa, 'Secession and Revolution in the Ottoman Empire at the End of the Eighteenth Century: Osman Pazvantoğlu and Rhigas Velestinlis', in Antonis Anastasopoulos and Elias Kolovos (eds), *Ottoman Rule and the Balkans, 1760–1850: Conflict, Transformation, Adaptation: Proceedings of an International Conference Held in Rethymno, Greece, 13–14 December 2003* (Rethymno: University of Crete, Department of History and Archaeology, 2007).

Gündüz, Irfan, *Osmanlılarda Devlet-Tekke Munasebetleri* (Ankara: Seha Neşriyat, 1984).

Habermas, Jürgen, *The Structural Transformation of the Public Sphere: An Enquiry into a Category of Bourgeois Society* (Cambridge, MA: Massachusetts Institute of Technology Press, 1989).

Halevi, Sa'adi ben Besalel, Isaac Jerusalmi, Aron Rodrigue and Sarah Stein, *A Jewish Voice from Ottoman Salonica. The Ladino Memoir of Sa'adi Besalel a-Levi* (Stanford, CA: Stanford University Press, 2012).

Hamadeh, Shirine, 'Splash and Spectacle: The Obsession with Fountains in Eighteenth-Century Istanbul', *Muqarnas*, 2002, 19, 123–48.

Hamadeh, Shirine, *The City's Pleasures: Istanbul in the Eighteenth Century* (Seattle, WA: University of Washington Press, 2008).

Hamann, Brigitte, 'Der Wiener Hof und die Hofgesellschaft in der zweiten Hälfte des 19. Jahrhunderts', in Karl Möckl (ed.), *Hof und Hofgesellschaft in den deutschen Staaten im 19 und beginnenden 20. Jahrhundert* (Boppard am Rhein: H. Boldt, 1990).

Hanioğlu, Şükrü, *A Brief History of the Late Ottoman Empire* (Princeton, NJ: Princeton University Press, 2008).

Hanscom, Christopher and Dennis Washburn (eds), *The Affect of Difference: Representations of Race in East Asian Empire* (Honolulu, HI: University of Hawaii Press, 2016).

Hanssen, Jens, *Fin de Siècle Beirut: the Making of an Ottoman Provincial Capital* (Oxford: Oxford University Press, 2006).

Hathaway, Jane, 'The Military Household in Ottoman Egypt', *International Journal of Middle East Studies*, 23 February 1995, 27(1), 39–52.

Haynes, D. E., *Rhetoric and Ritual in Colonial India. The Shaping of a Public Culture in Surat City, 1852–1928* (Berkeley, CA: University of California Press, 1991).

Herb, Guntram and David Kaplan, *Nested Identities: Nationalism, Territory, and Scale* (Lanham, MD: Rowman & Littlefield, 1999).

Heyd, Uriel, 'The Ottoman Ulema and Westernization in the Time of Selim III and Mahmud II', *Scripta Hierosolymitana: Studies in Islamic History and Civilisation*, vol. 9 (Jerusalem: Magnes Press Hebrew University, 1961).

Hobsbawm, Eric, *Nations and Nationalism Since 1780: Programme, Myth, Reality* (Cambridge: Cambridge University Press, 1990).

Hobsbawm, Eric and Terrence Ranger (eds), *The Invention of Tradition* (Cambridge: Cambridge University Press, 1983).

Bibliography

Hurewitz, J. C., 'The Europeanization of Ottoman Diplomacy: The Conversion from Unilateralism to Reciprocity in the Nineteenth Century', *Belleten*, 1961, 25(99), 455–66.

Inalcık, Halil, *Tanzimat ve Bulgar Meselesi* (Ankara: Türk Tarih Kurumu Basimevi, 1943).

Jelavich, Barbara and Charles Jelavich, *The Establishment of the Balkan National States, 1804–1920* (Seattle, WA: University of Washington Press, 1977).

Kabacalı, Alpay, *Tanzimat'tan II. Meşrutiyet'e imparatorluk ve nesnel tarihin prizmasından: Abdülhamid* (Istanbul: Creative Publishing, 2005).

Kafadar, Cemal, 'Eyüp'te Kılıç Kuşanma Törenleri', in Tülay Artan (ed.), *Eyüp: Dün/Bugün. Sempozyum, 11–12 Aralık 1993* (Istanbul: Tarih Vakfı Yurt Yayinlari, 1994).

Kafadar, Cemal, *Between Two Worlds. The Construction of the Ottoman State* (Berkeley, CA: University of California Press, 1995).

Kafadar, Cemal, 'On the Purity and Corruption of the Janissaries', *Turkish Studies Association Bulletin*, September 1991, 15(2), 273–80.

Kafadar, Cemal, 'Janissaries and Other Riffraff of Ottoman Istanbul: Rebels without a Cause?', in Baki Tezcan and Karl Barbir (eds), *Identity and Identity Formation in the Ottoman World. A Volume of Essays in Honor of Norman Itzkowitz* (Madison, WI: University of Wisconsin Press, 2007).

Karal, Enver Ziya, 'Gülhane Hatt-ı Hümayununda Batının Etkisi', *Belleten*, 1964, 28(112), 581–601.

Karaer, Nihat, *Paris, Londra, Viyana: Abdülaziz'in Avrupa Seyahatı* (Ankara: Phoenix Yayınevi, 2012).

Karateke, Hakan, *Padişahım Çok Yaşa! Osmanlı Devletinin Son Yüz Yılında Merasimler* (Istanbul: Kitab Yayinevi, 2004).

Karateke, Hakan, 'From Divine Ruler to Modern Monarch. The Ideal of the Ottoman Sultan in the Nineteenth Century', in Jörn Leonhard and Ulrike von Hirschhausen (eds), *Comparing Empires. Encounters and Transfers in the Long Nineteenth Century* (Göttingen: Vandenhoeck & Ruprecht, 2011).

Karateke, Hakan and Maurus Reinkowski (eds), *Legitimizing the Order: The Ottoman Rhetoric of State Power* (Leiden: Brill, 2005).

Karpat, Kemal, *The Politicisation of Islam: Reconstructing Identity, State, Faith, and Community in the Late Ottoman State* (Oxford: Oxford University Press, 2002).

Kasaba, Reşat, *A Moveable Empire: Ottoman Nomads, Migrants & Refugees* (Seattle, WA: University of Washington Press, 2009).

Kaynar, Mustafa, *Mustafa Reşit Paşa ve Tanzimat* (Ankara: Türk Tarih Kurumu Basımevi, 1954).

Kechriotis, Vangelis, 'Requiem for the Empire: "Elective Affinities" between the Balkan States and the Ottoman Empire in the Long 19th Century', in Sabine Rutar (ed.), *Beyond the Balkans: Towards an Inclusive History of Southeastern Europe* (Zurich: LIT Verlag, 2014), pp. 97–121.

Kedourie, Elie, *Nationalism in Asia and Africa* (New York: Meridian Books, 1970).

Keene, Donald, *Emperor of Japan: Meiji and His World, 1852–1912* (New York: Columbia University Press, 2002).

Keleş, Erdoğan, *Sultan Abdülmecid'in Rumeli Seyahatı, 1846* (Ankara: Birleşik Yayınevi, 2011).

Kennedy, Hugh, *The Prophet and the Age of the Caliphates* (London: Longman, 1986).

Kırlı, Cengiz, *The Struggle over Space: Coffeehouses of Ottoman Istanbul, 1780-1845* (PhD Dissertation, State University of New York-Binghamton, 2001).

Kırlı, Cengiz, 'Surveillance and Constituting the Public in the Ottoman Empire', in Seteney Shami (ed.), *Publics, Politics, and Participation: Locating the Public Sphere in the Middle East and North Africa* (New York: Social Science Research Council, 2010).

Kohlrausch, Martin, 'Loss of Control: Kaiser Wilhelm II, Mass Media, and the National Identity of the Second German Reich', in Milinda Banerjee, Charlotte Backerra and Cathleen Sarti (eds), *Transnational Histories of the 'Royal Nation'* (London: Palgrave, 2017).

Koloğlu, Doğan, 'Osmanlı Basını: İçeriği ve Rejimi', *Türkiye Ansiklopedisi: Tanzimat'tan Cumhuriyet'e*, vol. 1 (Istanbul: İletişim yayınları, 1983).

Konuk, Neval and Hanife Uslu, *Sultan II. Mahmud'un Rumeli Seyahatı ve Nişan Taşları* (Ankara: Merkez Repro, 2016).

Konyalı, Ibrahim Hakkı, *Söğütte Ertuğrul Gazi Türbesi ve Ihtifalı* (Istanbul: Sinan Matbaası, 1959).

Kraay, Hendrik, *Days of National Festivity in Rio de Janeiro, Brazil, 1823–1889* (Stanford, CA: Stanford University Press, 2013).

Kreiser, Klaus, 'Public Monuments in Turkey and Egypt, 1840–1916', *Muqarnas*, 1997, 14, 103–17.

Kuehn, Thomas, 'Ordering Urban Space in Ottoman Yemen, 1872–1914', in Jens Hansen, Stefan Weber and Thomas Philipp (eds), *The Empire in the City: Arab Provincial Capitals in the Late Ottoman Empire* (Beirut: Ergon Verlag, 2002).

Kuehn, Thomas, *Empire, Islam, and Politics of Difference: Ottoman Rule in Yemen, 1849–1919* (Leiden: Brill, 2011).

Kulstein, David, *Napoleon III and the Working Class: A Study of Government Propaganda under the Second Empire* (Los Angeles, CA: Ward Ritchie Press, 1969).

Kuneralp, Sinan, *Son Dönem Osmanlı Erkân ve Ricali, 1839–1922: Prosopografik Rehber* (Istanbul: Isis Press, 1999).

Kuneralp, Sinan, *Ottoman Diplomatic Documents on 'The Eastern Question'* (Istanbul: Isis Press, 2009).

Kunt, Metin, 'Ethnic-Regional (Cins) Solidarity in the Seventeenth-Century Ottoman Establishment', *International Journal of Middle East Studies*, June 1974, 5(3), 233–9.

Kushner, David, *The Rise of Turkish Nationalism, 1876–1908* (London: Frank Cass, 1977).

Bibliography

Kutluoğlu, Muhammed, *The Egyptian Question, 1831–1841: The Expansionist Policy of Mehmed Ali Paşa in Syria and Asia Minor and the Reaction of the Sublime Porte* (Istanbul: Eren, 1998).

Lacey, Robert, 'Royal Ritual in the Media Age', *Court Historian*, 2003, 8(1).

Lane-Poole, Stanley, *The Life of the Right Honourable Stratford Canning, Viscount Stratford de Redcliffe* (London: Longmans Green, 1888).

Lapidus, Ira, *A History of Islamic Societies* (Cambridge: Cambridge University Press, 1988).

Lessersohn, Nora, '"Provincial Cosmopolitanism" in Late Ottoman Anatolia: An Armenian Shoemaker's Memoir', *Comparative Studies in Society and History*, 2015, 57(2), 528–56.

Levy, Noemy and François Georgeon, *The Young Turk Revolution and the Ottoman Empire: The Aftermath of 1908* (London: I. B. Tauris, 2017).

Lewis, Bernard, *The Emergence of Modern Turkey* (London: Oxford University Press, 1961).

Lincoln, Bruce, *Nicholas I: Emperor and Autocrat of All the Russias* (Bloomington, IN: Indiana University Press, 1978).

Lockman, Zachary, *Contending Visions of the Middle East: The History and Politics of Orientalism* (Cambridge: Cambridge University Press, 2004).

Lory, Bernard, 'The Vizier's Dream: "Seeing St. Dimitar" in Ottoman Bitola', *History and Anthropology*, 2009, 20(3), 309–16.

Low, Morris, *Japan on Display: Photography and the Emperor* (London: Routledge, 2006).

Lyberatos, Andreas, 'The Application of the Tanzimat and Its Political Effects: Glances from Plovdiv and Its Rum Millet', in Maria Baramova et al. (eds), *Power and Influence in South-Eastern Europe, 16th–19th C.* (Berlin: LIT, 2013).

Lyberatos, Andreas, 'Through Nation and State. Reform and Nationalism "from Below" in the Late Ottoman Balkans. Introduction', *Turkish Historical Review*, 2016, 7(2), 121–33.

Makdisi, Ussama, *The Culture of Sectarianism: Community, History, and Violence in Nineteenth-Century Ottoman Lebanon* (Berkeley, CA: University of California Press, 2000).

Makdisi, Ussama, 'Ottoman Orientalism', *The American Historical Review*, June 2002, 107(3), 768–96.

Maksudyan, Nazan, *Orphans and Destitute Children in the Late Ottoman Empire* (New York: Syracuse University Press, 2014).

Mansel, Philip, *Constantinople: City of the World's Desire 1453–1924* (New York: St. Martin's Griffin, 1998).

Mansel, Philip, *Dressed to Rule. Royal and Court Costume from Louis XIV to Elizabeth II* (New Haven, CT: Yale University Press, 2005).

Marashi, Afshin, *Nationalizing Iran: Culture, Power, and the State, 1870-1940* (Seattle, WA: University of Washington Press, 2011).

Mardin, Şerif, *The Genesis of Young Ottoman Thought* [1962] (Syracuse, NY: Syracuse University Press, 2000).

Matossian, Bedross, *Shattered Dreams of Revolution: From Liberty to Violence in the Late Ottoman Empire* (Stanford, CA: Stanford University Press, 2014).

McClelland, Bruce, 'Sacrifice, Scapegoat, Vampire. The Social and Religious Origins of the Bulgarian Folkloric Vampire' (PhD dissertation, University of Virginia, 1999).

Mestyan, Adam, *Arab Patriotism: The Ideology and Culture of Power in Late Ottoman Egypt* (Princeton, NJ: Princeton University Press, 2017).

Meyer, James, *Turks across Empires: Marketing Muslim Identity in the Russian-Ottoman Borderlands, 1856–1914* (Oxford: Oxford University Press, 2015).

Mikhail, Alan and Christine Philliou, 'The Ottoman Empire and the Imperial Turn', *Comparative Studies in Society and History*, October 2012, 54(4), 721–45.

Miller, Alexei and Alfred Rieber (eds), *Imperial Rule* (Budapest: Central European Press, 2004).

Miller, Alexei and Stefan Berger (eds), *Nationalizing Empires* (Budapest: Central European Press, 2015).

Mitchell, Timothy, *Colonising Egypt* (Cambridge: Cambridge University Press, 1988).

de Montalbo, Jules Martin and Raymond Richebé, *Armoiries et décorations* (Paris: P. Ollendorff, 1897).

Mueller, Frank, *Royal Heirs in Imperial Germany. The Future of Monarchy in Nineteenth-Century Bavaria, Saxony and Württemberg* (London: Palgrave, 2017).

Murphey, Rhoads, *Exploring Ottoman Sovereignty: Tradition, Image and Practice in the Ottoman Imperial Household, 1400–1800* (London: Continuum International Publishing Group, 2011).

Murray-Miller, Gavin, 'A Conflicted Sense of Nationality: Napoleon III's Arab Kingdom and the Paradoxes of French Multiculturalism', *French Colonial History*, spring 2014, 15, 1–38.

Naltchayan, Nazaret, 'Kaiser Wilhelm II's Visits to the Ottoman Empire: Rationale, Reactions and the Meaning of Images', *Armenian Review*, summer 1989, 42(2), 47–91.

Necipoğlu, Gülru, 'Suleyman the Magnificent and the Representation of Power in the Context of Ottoman-Habsburg-Papal Rivalry', *The Art Bulletin*, September 1989, 71(3), 401–27.

Necipoğlu, Gülru, *Architecture, Ceremonial, and Power: The Topkapi Palace in the Fifteenth and Sixteenth Centuries* (Cambridge, MA: Massachusetts Institute of Technology Press, 1991).

Necipoğlu, Gülru, 'Framing the Gaze in Ottoman, Safavid, and Mughal Palaces', *Ars Orientalis*, 1993, 23, 303–18.

Necipoğlu, Gülru, 'Dynastic Imprints on the Cityscape: the Collective Message of Imperial Funerary Mosque Complexes in Istanbul', in Jean-Louis Bacque-Grammont and Aksel Tibet (eds), *Cimetières et traditions funéraires dans le monde islamique*, vol. II (Ankara: Turk Tarih Kurumu Basimevi, 1996).

Bibliography

Nicoletti, Manfredi , 'D'Aronco e la Turchia', in Marco Pozzetto and Elettra Quargnal (eds), *D'Aronco Architetto* (Milan: Electa, 1982).

Özbek, Nadir, 'The Politics of Welfare: Philanthropy, Voluntarism and Legitimacy in the Ottoman Empire, 1876–1914' (PhD dissertaion, State University of New York-Binghamton, 2001).

Özbek, Nadir, 'Imperial Gifts and Sultanic Legitimation during the Late Ottoman Empire, 1876–1909', in Michael Bonner, Mine Ener and Amy Singer (eds), *Poverty and Charity in Middle Eastern Contexts* (Albany, NY: State University of New York Press, 2003).

Özcan, Abdulkadir, 'II. Mahmud'un Memleket Gezileri', in Bekir Kütükoğlu (ed.), *Prof. Dr. Bekir Kütükoğlu'na Armağan* (Istanbul: Edebiyat Fakültesi Basımevi, 1991).

Özendes, Engin, *Photography in the Ottoman Empire, 1839–1919* (Istanbul: Haşet Kitabevi A. Ş., 1987).

Özendes, Engin and Erol Makzume, *Ottoman Court Painter Fausto Zonaro* (Istanbul: Yapı Kredi Kültür Sanat Yayıncılık, 2003).

Özlu, Nilay, 'From Palace to Museum: The Topkapi Palace during the Long Nineteenth Century' (PhD dissertation, Bogazici University, 2018).

Öztuncay, Bahattin, *The Photographers of Constantinople: Pioneers, Studios and Artists from Nıneteenth-Century Istanbul* (Istanbul: Aygaz, 2006).

Paulmann, Johannes, *Pomp und Politik: Monarchenbegegnungen in Europa zwischen Ancien Régime und Ersten Weltkrieg* (Paderborn: F. Schöningh, 2000).

Peirce, Leslie, *The Imperial Harem. Women and Sovereignty in the Ottoman Empire* (Oxford: Oxford University Press, 1993).

Peleggi, Maurizio, *Lords of Things: The Fashioning of the Siamese Monarchy's Modern Image* (Honolulu, HI: University of Hawaii Press, 2002).

Peng, Ying-chen, 'A Palace of Her Own: Empress Dowager Cixi (1835–1908) and the Reconstruction of the Wanchun Yuan', *Nan Nu*, 2012, 14(1), 47–74.

Philliou, Christine, *Biography of an Empire: Governing Ottomans in an Age of Revolution* (Berkeley, CA: University of California Press, 2011).

Pilehvarian, Nuran, Nur Urfalıoğlu and Lütfi Yazıcıoğlu (eds), *Fountains in Ottoman Istanbul* (Istanbul: Yapı-Endüstri Merkezi Yayınları, 2000).

Piterberg, Gabriel, *An Ottoman Tragedy. History and Historiography at Play* (Berkeley, CA: University of California Press, 2003).

Plunkett, John, *Queen Victoria: First Media Monarch* (Oxford: Oxford University Press, 2009).

Podeh, Elie, *The Politics of National Celebrations in the Arab Middle East* (New York: Cambridge University Press, 2014).

Quataert, Donald, 'Clothing Laws, State and Society in the Ottoman Empire, 1720–1829', *International Journal of Middle East Studies*, August 1997, 29(3), 403–25.

Quataert, Donald, *The Ottoman Empire, 1700–1922* (Cambridge: Cambridge University Press, 2000).

Radev, Ivan, *History of the Bulgarian Literature during the Revival* (Veliko Turnovo, 2007).
Redhouse, James, *Turkish Ottoman-English Dictionary* (Istanbul: Sev Matbaacilik ve Yayıncilik, 1997).
Redhouse, James, *A Turkish and English Lexicon* (Istanbul: İstanbul Cagrı Yayınları, 2006).
Reinkowski, Maurus, 'The Imperial Idea and Realpolitik – Reform Policy and Nationalism in the Ottoman Empire', in Jörn Leonhard and Ulrike von Hirschhausen (eds), *Comparing Empires. Encounters and Transfers in the Long Nineteenth Century* (Göttingen: Vandenhoeck & Ruprecht, 2011).
Reynolds, Michael, *Shattering Empires: The Clash and Collapse of the Ottoman and Russian Empires, 1908–1918* (Cambridge: Cambridge University Press, 2012).
Riasanovsky, Nicholas, *Nicholas I and Official Nationality in Russia, 1825–1855* (Berkeley, CA and Los Angeles, CA: University of California Press, 1959).
Rodrigue, Aron and Nancy Reynolds, '"Difference" and Tolerance in the Ottoman Empire', *Stanford Humanities Review*, 1996, 5(1), 81–92.
Rohdewald, Stefan, 'Nationale Identitäten durch Kyrill und Method: Diskurse, Praktiken und Akteure ihrer Verehrung unter den Südslawen', in Sabine Rutar (ed.), *Beyond the Balkans: Towards an Inclusive History of Southeastern Europe* (Zurich: LIT Verlag, 2014), pp. 357–76.
Ruoff, Kenneth, *Imperial Japan at Its Zenith: The Wartime Celebration of the Empire's 2600th Anniversary* (Ithaca, NY: Cornell University Press, 2010).
Safrastjian, Ruben, 'Ottomanism in Turkey in the Epoch of Reforms in XIX C.: Ideology and Policy I', *Etudes Balkaniques*, 1998, 24(4), 72–86.
Sami, Şemseddin, *Kamus-i Türki* (Istanbul: Kapı Yayınları, 2011).
Schama, Simon, 'The Domestication of Majesty: Royal Family Portraiture, 1500–1850', *The Journal of Interdisciplinary History*, 1986, 17(1), 155–83.
Scheffler, Thomas, 'The Kaiser in Baalbek: Tourism, Archeology, and the Politics of Imagination', in Helene Sader, Thomas Scheffler and Angelika Neuwirth (eds), *Baalbek: Image and Monument, 1898–1998* (Stuttgart: Franz Steiner Verlag, 1998).
Schoolfield, George, *Helsinki of the Czars* (Columbia, SC: Camden House, 1996).
Schull, Kent, *Prisons in the Late Ottoman Empire: Microcosms of Modernity* (Edinburgh: Edinburgh University Press, 2014).
Schull, Kent, 'Comparative Criminal Justice in the Era of Modernity: A Template for Inquiry and the Ottoman Empire as Case Study', *Turkish Studies*, December 2014, 15(4), 621–37.
Shaw, Stanford, *Between Old and New. The Ottoman Empire under Sultan Selim III, 1789–1807* (Cambridge, MA: Harvard University Press, 1971).
Shaw, Stanford, *History of the Ottoman Empire and Modern Turkey* (Cambridge: Cambridge University Press, 1977).
Shaw, Stanford, and Ezel Shaw, *History of the Ottoman Empire and Modern Turkey*, 2 vols. (Cambridge: Cambridge University Press, 1976–7).

Bibliography

Shaw, Wendy, *Possessors and Possessed: Museums, Archeology, and the Visualisation of History in the Late Ottoman Empire* (Berkeley, CA: University of California Press, 2003).
Smith, Anthony, *The Ethnic Origins of Nations* (New York: Basil Blackwell, 1986).
Spivak, Gayatri, *A Critique of Postcolonial Reason: Towards a History of the Vanishing Present* (Cambridge, MA: Harvard University Press, 1999).
St. Laurent, Beatrice and Andras Riedlmayer, 'Restorations of Jerusalem and the Dome of the Rock and Their Political Significance, 1537–1928', *Muqarnas*, 1993, 10, 76–84.
Stein, Sarah, 'The Permeable Boundaries of Ottoman Jewry', in Joel Migdal (ed.), *Boundaries and Belonging: States and Societies in the Struggle to Shape Identities and Local Practices* (Cambridge: Cambridge University Press, 2004).
Stephanov, Darin, 'The Ruler and the Ruled Through the Prism of Royal Birthday Celebrations. A Close Look at Two Documents', in Maria Baramova et al. (eds), *Power and Influence in South-Eastern Europe, 16th–19th Century* (Berlin: LIT Verlag, 2013), pp. 263–70.
Stephanov, Darin, 'Solemn Songs for the Sultan. Cultural Integration through Music in the Late Ottoman Empire, 1840s–1860s', in Aspasia Theodosiou, Panagiotis Poulos and Risto Pennanen (eds), *Ottoman Intimacies, Balkan Musical Realities* (Helsinki: Suomen Ateenan-instituutin säätiö, 2013), pp. 13–30.
Stephanov, Darin, 'Patriotism in Transition: The Thought of Butrus al-Bustani, Mehmed Said Pasha and Ziya Gokalp', in Adel Bishara (ed.), *Butrus al-Bustani. Spirit of the Age* (Melbourne: IPhoenix Publishing, 2014).
Stephanov, Darin, 'Sultan Abdülmecid's 1846 Tour of Rumelia and the Trope of Love', in Virginia Aksan and Veysel Şimşek (eds), *Living Empire: Ottoman Identities in Transition, 1700-1850* (Istanbul: ISAM, 2014), pp. 475–501 [Special Issue: *The Journal of Ottoman Studies*, 2014, 44].
Stephanov, Darin, 'Sultan Mahmud II (1808–1839) and the First Shift in Modern Ruler Visibility in the Ottoman Empire', *Journal of the Ottoman and Turkish Studies Association*, 2014, 1(1–2), 129–48.
Stephanov, Darin, 'Public Celebrations of Emperor Nicholas I (1825–1855) in the Grand Duchy of Finland: Typology, Dynamics, Impact', in Vladimir Lapin and Yulia Safronova (eds), *400th Anniversary of the Romanov Dynasty, 1613-2013. The Politics of Memory and the Monarchic Idea* (Saint Petersburg: European University Press, 2016), pp. 89–103.
Stephanov, Darin, 'Ruler Visibility, Modernity and Ethnonationalism in the Late Ottoman Empire', in Kent Schull and Christine Isom-Verhaaren (eds), *Living in the Ottoman Realm: Sultans, Subjects, and Elites* (Bloomington, IN: Indiana University Press, 2016), pp. 259–71.
Stephanov, Darin, 'Bulgar Milleti Nedir? [What is a Bulgar Community of Co-Religionists?]: Syncretic Forms of Belonging in Mid-Nineteenth-Century Istanbul', in Richard Wittmann and Christoph Herzog (eds),

'Istanbul' – 'Kushta' – 'Constantinople': Diversity of Identities and Personal Narratives in the Ottoman Capital (1830–1900) (London: Routledge, 2018).

Stephanov, Darin, 'Cannon Salvos for the Monarch. Notes on the Ceremonial Usage of Artillery at Nineteenth-Century Ottoman and Russian Accession, Coronation and Other Public Dynastic Festivities', unpublished paper.

Stone, Norman, Sergei Podbolotov, and Murat Yaşar, 'The Russians and the Turks: Imperialism and Nationalism in the Era of Empires', in Alexei Miller and Alfred Rieber (eds), *Imperial Rule* (Budapest: Central European Press, 2004), pp. 27–45.

Stoyanov, Manyo, *Bulgarska Vuzrozhdenska Knizhnina*, vols 1 & 2 (Sofia: Nauka i Izkustvo, 1957–9).

Sungu, Ihsan, 'II. Mahmud'un Izzet Molla ve Asakir-i Mansure haqqinda Bir Hattı', in *Tarih Vesikaları*, vol. 1 (Istanbul: Maarif vekilliği, 1941–2).

Taki, Viktor, *Tsar and Sultan: Russian Encounters with the Ottoman Empire* (London: I. B. Tauris, 2016).

Talbot, Michael, 'The Exalted Column, the Hejaz Railway and Imperial Legitimation in Late Ottoman Haifa', *Urban History*, 28 May 2015, 42(2), 246–72.

Talbot, Michael, 'Accessing the Shadow of God: Spatial and Performative Ceremonial at the Ottoman Court', in Dries Raeymaekers and Sebastiaan Derks (eds), *The Key to Power? The Culture of Access in Princely Courts, 1400–1750* (Leiden: Brill, 2016).

Tezcan, Baki, *The Second Ottoman Empire: Political and Social Transformation in the Early Modern World* (Cambridge: Cambridge University Press, 2012).

Todorova, Maria, *Anglia, Rossia i Tanzimat. Vtoraya Chetvert XIX Veka* (Moscow: Nauka, 1983).

Todorova, Maria, *Imagining the Balkans* (Oxford: Oxford University Press, 1997).

Todorova, Maria, *Bones of Contention: The Living Archive of Vasil Levski and the Making of Bulgaria's National Hero* (Budapest: Central European Press, 2009).

Truesdell, Matthew, *Spectacular Politics: Louis-Napoleon Bonaparte and the Fete Imperiale, 1849–1870* (New York: Oxford University Press, 1997).

Tziovas, Dimitris (ed.), *Greece and the Balkans: Identities, Perceptions and Cultural Encounters since the Enlightenment* (London: Ashgate, 2003).

Tuğlacı, Pars, *The Role of the Balian Family in Ottoman Architecture* (Istanbul: Yeni Çığır, 1990).

Unowsky, Daniel, *The Pomp and Politics of Patriotism: Imperial Celebrations in Habsburg Austria, 1848–1916* (West Lafayette, IN: Purdue University Press, 2005).

Unowsky, Daniel and Laurence Cole (eds), *The Limits of Loyalty: Imperial Symbolism, Popular Allegiances, and State Patriotism in the Late Habsburg Monarchy* (New York: Berghahn Books, 2007).

Bibliography

Unruh, Holly, 'Imaging an Empire: The Photographic Collection of Sultan Abdülhamid II' (MA thesis, University of California at Santa Barbara, 1996).

Ünver, Rüstem, 'Architecture for a New Age: Imperial Ottoman Mosques in Eighteenth-Century Istanbul' (PhD dissertation, Harvard University, 2013).

Wang, Cheng-hua, '"Going Public": Portraits of the Empress Dowager Cixi, Circa 1904', *Nan Nu*, 2012, 14(1), 119–76.

Weber, Eugene, *Peasants into Frenchmen: The Modernisation of Rural France 1870–1914* (London: Chatto & Windus, 1977).

Wharton, Alyson, *The Architects of Ottoman Constantinople. The Balyan Family and the History of Ottoman Architecture* (London: I. B. Tauris, 2015).

Wilentz, Sean (ed.), *Rites of Power: Symbolism, Ritual, and Politics Since the Middle Ages* (Philadelphia, PA: University of Pennsylvania Press, 1985).

Will, Pierre-Etienne, 'Views of the Realm in Crisis: Testimonies on Imperial Audiences in the Nineteenth Century', *Late Imperial China*, June 2008, 29(1), 125–59.

Wishnitzer, Avner, *Reading Clocks, Alla Turca: Time and Society in the Late Ottoman Empire* (Chicago, IL: University of Chicago Press, 2015).

Wodak, Ruth, 'Fragmented Identities: Redefining and Recontextualizing National Identity', in Paul Chilton and Christina Schaefner (eds), *Politics as Text and Talk: Analytic Approaches to Political Discourse* (Philadelphia: John Benjamins Publication Company, 2002), pp. 143–69.

Worringer, Renee, '"Sick Man of Europe" or "Japan of the Near East"?: Constructing Ottoman Modernity in the Hamidian and Young Turk Eras', *International Journal of Middle East Studies*, May 2004, 36(2), 207–30.

Wortman, Richard, *Scenarios of Power: Myth and Ceremony in Russian Monarchy*, vols 1 and 2 (Princeton, NJ: Princeton University Press, 1995–2000).

Yaycıoğlu, Ali, *Partners of the Empire: The Crisis of the Ottoman Order in the Age of Revolutions* (Stanford, CA: Stanford University Press, 2016).

Yosmaoğlu-Turner, Ipek, *Blood Ties: Religion, Violence and the Politics of Nationhood in Ottoman Macedonia, 1878–1908* (Ithaca, NY: Cornell University Press, 2013).

Yılmaz, Gülay, 'Becoming a Devshirme: The Training of Conscripted Children in the Ottoman Empire', in Gwyn Campbell, Suzanne Miers and Joseph C. Miller (eds), *Children in Slavery through the Ages* (Athens, OH: Ohio University Press, 2009), pp. 119–34.

Yosmaoğlu, Ipek K., 'Chasing the Printed Word: Press Censorship in the Ottoman Empire, 1876–1913', *The Turkish Studies Association Journal*, 2003, 27(1–2), 15–49.

Yuhang, Li, 'Oneself as a Female Deity: Representations of Empress Dowager Cixi as Guanyin', *Nan Nu*, 2012, 14(1), 75–118.

Zandi-Sayek, Sibel, 'Ambiguities of Sovereignty: Property Rights and Spectacles of Statehood in Tanzimat Izmir', in Sahar Bazzaz, Yota Batsaki and Dimiter Angelov (eds), *Imperial Geographies in Byzantine and Ottoman Space* (Cambridge, MA: Harvard University Press, 2013).

Zarinebaf, Fariba, 'Models: A View from the Ottoman Margin', *Kritika: Explorations in Russian and Eurasian History*, spring 2011, 12(2), 489–99.

Ze'evi, Dror, 'Kul and Getting Cooler: The Dissolution of Elite Collective Identity and the Formation of Official Nationalism in the Ottoman Empire', *Mediterranean Historical Review*, 1996, 11, 2, 177–95.

Zürcher, Erik, *Turkey: A Modern History* (London: I. B. Tauris, 2004).

Index

References to notes are indicated by n; references to images are indicated by *italics*

11 May *see* St Cyril and St Methodius day

Abdülaziz, Sultan, 4, 20, 37–8, *96*, 129, 202–3
 and accession, 95–103, 104–5
 and Bulgars, 104–12, 114–21
 and deposition, 131
 and Rumelia, 112, 114
Abdülhamid II, Sultan, 4, 127–31, 183–6, 205
 and early reign, 132–41
 and late reign, 151–76
 and mid-reign, 141–51
 and negative symbolic encounters, 176–83
Abdülmecid, Sultan, 4, 37–8, *39*, *48*, 84–5, 129
 and Bulgars, 64–78, 80–4
 and celebrations, 47, 49
 and Gülhane Rescript, 16–17
 and medals, 45, 47
 and public image, 57–62
 and Rumelia, 62–3
 and tomb, 138
 and trope of love, 50–7
Abu-Manneh, Butrus, 137
act/process of naming, 37, 69, 81, 83, 204
Ahmed III, Sultan, 13, 14, 158
Ahmed Kemaleddin Efendi, 140
Ahmed Pasha, 180
Albania, 27, 29n1, 42, 124n61, 149, 191n98
Alexander I of Russia, Tsar, 209
Alexander II of Russia, Tsar, 103, 115, 142, 169, 190n70, 209–10
Alexander III of Russia, Tsar, 164, 169
Ali Tepedelenli, 16
Ali Bey, 118, 119

Ali Pasha, 112, 129
Ankara, Battle of, 9
April Revolt, 120
architectural monuments, 7, 129–30; *see also* fountains
Arifi Pasha, Ahmed, 118
Armenians, 28, 38, 63, 112, 114, 153, 196n190
 and the Russian Empire, 209
Asim Pasha, Mehmed, 119
asylums, 152, 153
Ataullah Pasha, 181, 182
audiences *see* target audiences
Auldjo, John, 19
Auspicious Event (*Vaka-yı Hayriye*), 16, 18
auto-Orientalism, 148–9, 183
Aya Sofya (Hagia Sophia), 129, 131, 133

Balabanov, Marko, 120, 126n92
Bayezid I, Sultan, 9
Bayezid II, Sultan, 12
Bayraktar Mustafa Pasha, 15, 21
Beirut, 165, 167
Belchev, Nikola Gerov, 81, 82–3, 94n146
Berlin, 28–9
beys (chieftains), 9
Birovski, Toma M., 107
Bogoridi, Stefan, 187n8
blood connection, 66, 80, 84, 99, 102, 203, 204
blood, last drop of, 107–9
Bonneval, Comte de, 14
Boris I of Bulgaria, Tsar, 110, 124n50
Bosnia, 179
Bulgaria, 79–80, 81–2, 83, 86n3, 111, 119–21, 202–4
 and monument, 163, *164*

233

Ruler Visibility and Popular Belonging

Bulgaria (*cont.*)
  and Muslim school, 155–6
  and personification of, 80–5, 108, 204
  and victimisation of, 80–5, 204
  and sanctification of, 80, 121, 203
Bulgarian Revolutionary Central
    Committee, 120
Bulgars, 2, 5, 38, 61, 119–20
  and Abdülaziz, 98–102, 104–12,
    114–17, 202–3
  and Abdülhamid II, 176–7
  and Abdülmecid, 58, 63, 64–78
  and Russia, 117–18
Burmov, Todor, 62–3, 80, 90n83, 111
Büyükdere, 6
Byron, Lord, 6

Cage (*Kafes*), 129, 139
calendars, 25, 47, 103–4, 203
Canning, Sir Stratford, 17
Catherine II of Russia, Tsarina, 21
celebrations, 2, 4, 13, 15, 17, 85n1
  and Abdülaziz, 95–107, 120–1, 203–4
  and Abdülmecid, 47, 49, 51, 200–1
  and Mahmud II, 24–9, 199
  and Nicholas I, 207, 209, 211
  see also ceremonies; St Cyril and St
    Methodius day
censorship, 117, 119, 141, 185, 212
ceremonies, 2–3, 4, 9
  and Abdülaziz, 116–17, 178–9
  and Abdülhamid II, 128, 140–1,
    178–80, 205
  and Abdülmecid, 42
  and Mehmed Murad Efendi, 51–2
  and Mehmed Reşad Efendi, 51, 52
  and Murad V, 131, 134
  and school examinations, 72–3
  and sword girding, 10–11
  see also celebrations; target audiences
centralisation, 42–3, 85, 178, 200, 202,
    212
  and Mahmud II rule, 9, 12, 17, 24, 26–7,
    30n9
centre, Ottoman, 4, 201, 203–5, 209, 212
  and Abdülaziz rule, 96, 105–6, 110, 112
  and Abdülhamid II rule, 145, 160, 173,
    177, 179–83, 196n192
  and Abdülmecid rule, 37, 42–3, 55–6,
    62, 71, 74, 85, 91
  and Mahmud II rule, 15, 16, 21, 23,
    24–9
Cevdet Pasha, Ahmet, 103

Charles V, Holy Roman Emperor, 12
Choragic monument, 160, 164–5, *166*, 167
clothing, 2, 19, 22, 63, 72, 101, 110, 114,
    155, 199
  and Abdülhamid II, 133–4, 183
  and Abdülmecid, 41, 63
  and Mahmud II, 17–18, 22–3, 199
compatriots (*sootechestvennitsyi*), 61, 116
consciousness, group/(macro-)communal/
    mass, 2, 5, 3n6, 203
  and Abdülaziz rule, 110–11, 117, 121
  and Abdülmecid rule, 38, 74, 81
Constantinople, 9, 12, 31n18
cosmic/grand spatial metaphor, 51–4, 78,
    83–4, 97, 107, 108, 115
Crimea, 16, 21
Crimean War, 34n79, 122n26, 141
cross-dating, 122n31
  and Abdülaziz rule, 104
  and Abdülhamid II rule, 151, 171, 183,
    185, 192n116, 196n192
  and Abdülmecid rule, 201
  and Nicholas I rule, 211, 213n9
cult of personality *see* personality cult

Dardanelles, 16, 22
D'Aronco, Raimondo, 163
Davidov, Penyo, 65, 68, 69, 72, 75, 81
Daynelov, Yosif, 101–2, 122n15
decorations *see* medals and orders
Deed of Agreement (*sened-i ittifaq*), 15
Deringil, Selim, 30n5, 127, 136, 156
Drinov, Marin, 119, 125n86
duty/obligation (*zimmet/vacibe/feriza*), 56,
    59, 60–1, 71, 108–9, 116, 182
  of devotion to the ruler (*ubudiyet*), 27,
    55, 57, 89n59, 197n214
duty/obligation to the ruler, 4, 26–7, 98,
    108, 204
  and Abdülmecid rule, 44, 55, 56, 59–61,
    71
  and Abdülhamid II rule, 154–5, 182
duty to the 'us'-group, 109, 116, 119, 204
dynastic pantheon, 141–2, 148, 183, 184
dynasticism, 54, 128–31, 138–40, 141–3,
    209

Eastern Question, 16, 34n79
Ebu'suud, 21
Edirne, 22, 60–1
education, 58, 72–3, 74, 76–7, 210–11; *see
    also* students
Egypt, 11, 16, 18, 179–80

Index

enemies of the ruler, 81–4, 94n150, 107, 136, 204
enemies of the 'us'-group, 82, 117, 204
Ertuğrul, 130, 149
Erzurum, 28
Eski Zağra (Stara Zagora), 62, 116–17, 125n73
Ethem Pasha, 107–8
ethnicity, 1, 4, 86n3, 128, 213n13
  and Abdülhamid II rule, 149, 186n5, 205
ethnonational, 1–2, 5, 8, 30n6, 37–8, 86n3, 204, 205–6
  and Abdülaziz rule, 102, 109, 123n39
  and Finland, 210
ethnoreligious, 23
Eugenie, Empress, 141, 146
Eyüp tomb, 10, 31n18, 102–3, 132–3

faith, 4, 201–2, 204, 209
  and Abdülaziz rule, 97–8, 110
  and Abdülhamid II rule, 131, 142–3, 152, 155, 176, 182, 184, 204–5
  and Abdülmecid rule, 43, 51, 52–3, 58, 59, 61, 64, 67, 68–9, 90n92, 92n107
  and Mahmud II rule, 23–4, 26, 30n8
faith, inclusive/integrative/universalist, 17, 21, 24, 26, 57, 70, 200, 204
faithful subjects, 56, 58, 100, 108–9, 210
familial (father–children) metaphor, 200, 202, 204, 210–11
  and Abdülmecid rule, 37, 59, 60, 61, 69
  and Mahmud II rule, 4, 23
  and Nicholas I rule, 210–11
fatherland, 2, 202, 204
  and Abdülaziz rule, 118, 120
  and Abdülhamid II rule, 138, 141, 155
  and Abdülmecid rule, 60, 61, 79, 85, 94n14, 202
  and Nicholas I rule, 211
felicity, 153–4
Filibe (Plovdiv), 43, 79, 89n69, 111–12, 117–18, 119, 125n76, 125n84, 196n197
Fındıklı Mosque, 133
Finland, 207, 209–12
Fonton, Joseph, 13
Fotinov, Konstantin, 72, 92n109, 92n111
fountains, 7, 13
  and Abdülhamid II, 157–76, *157–75*
France, 14, 28, 178–9
Franz Joseph I, Emperor, 118, 130, 141, 146

Friday prayers, 19, 131–3, 147–8, 180–2
Friendship of the ruler, 40–1, 43–4
Fuad Pasha, 103, 129

Gabrova (Gabrovo), 62, 77, 90n78, 90n81, 93n132
Generosity of the ruler, 54, 58–60, 66, 76, 151, 185
Germany, 143–6
Gerov, Nayden, 63, 79, 90n85
  and Russia, 117, 118, 122n23, 125n84
ghazi title, 9, 11, 18, 30n8
Ghika, Alexander, 26–7
Ginzburg, Carlo, 3
grace of the ruler (*inayet*), 28, 36n122, 44–7, 53, 55, 89n57, 176
Great Britain, 15–16
Greece, 16, 21, 22, 150
Gruev, Yoakim, 79, 93n140
guilds (*esnaf, taife*), 11, 31n31
Gülhane Rescript, 4, 16–17, 137, 199–201
  and Abdülmecid rule, 37, 43, 64, 69, 87n20, 91n94
Gümüşgerdan, Mihail, 117

halberdiers (*baltacı*), 148
Hamidian establishments, 152–5, 185
healthcare, 58, 62, 152, 185
heart/love (*ihlas*), 44, 87n24, 97
heart as bond between ruler and ruled, 201
  and Abdülaziz rule, 97, 98–9, 101, 107–8
  and Abdülmecid rule, 49–51, 54–61, 70, 82, 85
  and Nicholas I rule, 210, 212
heart, kin-loving, 109–10
helmet crown, 12–13
Herzegovina, 179
Hobhouse, John, 6, 15
holy image/personage of the ruler, 29, 51, 53, 144, 176, 179, 181–2
holy to the 'us'-group, 109–11, 119
hospitals, 58, 134, 152–3, 168, 185
Hurshid Pasha, 116–17, 118
hymns *see* songs of praise

Iași Treaty (1792), 14
Ibrahim Hakkı, 181–2
Ibrahim Paşa, 13, 177
identity, 1, 82, 116, 206
identification, group/macro-communal, 38, 78–84, 86n3
Ignatiev, Count Nikolay, 118

Ruler Visibility and Popular Belonging

Ikonomov, Todor, 116, 125n71, 125n72
Iliev, Atanas, 116–17, 125n73, 125n74
illuminations, 25–6, 29, 49–52, 62, 98, 104, 112, 134, 150, 179, 182
Imperial Portrait (*tasvir-i hümayun*), 19–20, 28–9, 36n122, 36n124, 150
Iran, 28
Istanbul, 16, 21; *see also* Constantinople
Izmit, 23
Izvorski, Stefan, 72–3, 81, 92n110, 94n150

Janissaries, 6, 11–12, 13, 14, 15, 31n24, 31n25, 31n26, 31n32
   and abolition, 16, 17, 18, 40, 128, 129, 135, 149, 199, 207
Jerusalem, 137, 143–5, 160, 167–8, 194n148, 194n161
Jews, 2
   and Abdülaziz rule, 98, 105, 114
   and Abdülhamid II rule, 133, 153, 167, 192n104
   and Abdülmecid rule, 38, 61, 63, 69, 77, 87n19, 93n135
   and Mahmud II rule, 23, 34n89
   and the Russian Empire, 209
Justice of the ruler, 23, 52–3, 64, 116, 133, 137, 138

Kafadar, Cemal, 9, 12
Kamil Pasha, Mehmed, 118
Keçecizade Izzet Molla, 21–2
kin, of the same (*ednorodets/edinorodets*), 58, 101–2
Kırlı, Cengiz, 22–3
Kızanlık (Kazanluk), 62, 64, 90n81
Kotel (Kazan), 73, 110

Lancers (*Mızraklı*), 19, 148–9
Levski, Vasil, 120, 126n94
Linsen, Johan G., 210–11
Lom (Lom Palanga), 79, 107, 123n40
London, 25, 28, 29, 49, 161, 171, 176, 187n6, 190n71, 195n170
love for the ruler *see* trope of love
loyalty to the ruler, 199, 203, 204
   and Abdülaziz rule, 110, 117, 120, 125n65
   and Abdülhamid II rule, 136, 150, 152, 154, 177, 180, 182, 184, 185
   and Abdülmecid rule, 37, 38, 42, 73
   and Mahmud II rule, 16, 20, 26
   and Nicholas I rule, 210–11
loyalty to the 'us'-group, 37, 204

Lyberatos, Andreas, 43, 87n23, 89n69
Lyuboslovie (magazine), 72, 73, 92n111

Macedonia, 176–7, 196n186
macro-mapping, 84, 93n142, 204
macro-territorial attachment, 2, 38, 79–84, 201
Mahmud Celaleddin, Prince, 139–40
Mahmud II, Sultan
   and Abdülhamid II, 138–9
   and annual ruler celebrations, 2–3, 24–9
   and Christians, 23–4
   and early reign, 14–16
   and medals, 44–5
   and reform, 16–17, 128–9, 199–200
   and Russia, 207–9
Maronites, 182–3, 197n219
Mecca, 18, 21, 145
medals, 12, 19, 38, 44–5, *45–6*, 47, 84, 143, 201
media, 12, 20, 73–4
Mehmed Ali, 16, 18, 20, 209
Mehmed II, Sultan, 9, 12, 138
Mehmed Murad Efendi, 51–2, 139–40
Mehmed Reşad Efendi, 51, 52–3, 140
Mehmed Rüşdi Pasha, 112
Mehmed V, Sultan, 30n5, 186
Mehmed VI, Sultan, 186
mercy/charity of the ruler
   and Abdülaziz rule, 99, 107
   and Abdülmecid rule, 50, 53, 59–61, 70
   and Abdülhamid II rule, 151–4
   and Mahmud II rule, 22, 35n91
mercy/charity of the ruled, 155
messengers, ceremonial
   and Abdülhamid II rule, 135, 147
   and Abdülmecid rule, 40, 42–3
microregional, 2, 78–9, 202
Midhat Pasha, 112, 136, 188n39
Mihail Sturdza, 51–7, 88n46
Mikhail Romanov, 130, 142
militarisation of the image of the ruler, 204
   and Abdülaziz rule, 98, 108, 200
   and Abdülhamid II rule, 133–6, 148–9, 151, 183
   and Abdülmecid rule, 40, 63, 84
   and Mahmud II rule, 6, 10, 17–20, 199, 209
militarisation of the image of the 'us'-group, 84, 204
millet, 1, 2, 3, 30n6
   and Abdülaziz rule, 95, 98, 114, 121n2, 124n63

Index

and Abdülhamid II rule, 133
and Abdülmecid rule, 38, 43, 50, 86n2, 201–2
and Mahmud II rule, 24
and Murad V rule, 187n19
millet-ism, 202
mobilisation for the ruler, 59, 61, 70–1, 83–4, 108, 204
mobilisation for the 'us'-group, 37, 80, 82, 83–4, 204
modernisation, 127, 207
modernising effects, 37, 128, 185
modernity, 3, 5, 16–17, 134, 201, 212
modern state, 3, 97, 148, 168, 184, 185, 212
Moldavia, 16, 21, 25, 33n56, 35n104, 51–7, 88n46
Moltke, Helmuth von, 23
monogram (*tuğra*), 7, 13, 29, 114, 130, 141, 145, 150, 155, 189n40
monogram of Nicholas I, 211
mother metaphor, 80
motherland, 85, 204
Murad I, Sultan, 11, 32n33
Murad IV, Sultan, 10–11, 137
Murad V, Sultan, 129–32, *132*, 133–5, 137–8, 181, 188n39, 189n43
Mustafa I, Sultan, 11
Mustafa IV, Sultan, 14
Mustafa Reşid Paşa, 17, 24, 129
and Abdülmecid, 42, 60, 75–6
myth of naming, 151, 185
mythic/mythological, 66, 79, 119, 126n94, 130, 141
mythology of power, 95, 129, 137, 157, 184, 185

Napoleon I, Emperor, 14, 44
Naser al-Din Shah Qajar, 142, 145
Navarino, Battle of, 18
Necipoğlu-Kafadar, Gülru, 9
Nelson, Admiral Horatio, 44
Nicholas I of Russia, Tsar, 19, 138, 197n220, 207–8, *208*, 209–12, 213n7, 213n9
Nicholas II of Russia, Tsar, 130, 198n224

oath-taking ceremony (*biat*), 140–1
obelisks, 160–1, *162*, 163–4, 194n150
Obshti, Dimiter, 120, 126n94
Orders (decorations), 32n47, 38, 44–5, *45*, *46*, 47, 84, 134, 182, 201

organic metaphor, 204
and Abdülaziz rule 101, 107, 108
and Abdülmecid rule, 37, 52, 59, 78, 87n23
Osman I, Sultan, 9, 11, 102–3, 130, 137–8
Osman II, Sultan, 11, 15, 31n21
Ottoman Foreign Ministry (*Hariciye Nezareti*), 25, 118, 122n25, 125n83, 179
Ottoman Renaissance, 129–30

Patrick, Mary, 146
patriotic, 102, 154–5
patriotism, 1
Paul I of Russia, Emperor, 13
Pazvantoğlu, Osman, 16, 33n58
people (*narod*), 72, 75, 77, 81, 98–9, 110, 114–16
people (*narodnost*), 112, 117, 124n60
personality cult, 4, 67, 70, 85, 91n103, 104, 129, 151, 176, 183, 185, 205, 212
Peter I of Russia, Emperor, 19, 142
Phanariots, 16, 33n56, 36n109, 82, 94n152, 100
piety, 4, 25, 52, 53, 58, 89n55, 133, 152, 153, 158, 175, 185, 205
populace, 4, 10, 27, 57, 62, 65, 69, 121, 133
popular (*naroden*), 58, 92n111, 101, 108–10, 116
Porfiriy, Archbishop, 72, 73
'Prayer-Song for Many Years (*Mnogoletstvie*)', 77, 82, 83
propaganda, 128, 178
Prophet's birthday (*mevlid*), 25
public gaze, 7, 10, 17, 139, 199
public image of the ruler, 3, 38, 42, 53, 57–62, 186, 207
public/group memory, 111, 119, 121, 173, 203, 205
public mind/consciousness, 107, 123n31
and Abdülaziz rule, 107
and Abdülhamid II rule, 139, 151, 192n116, 193n145
and Abdülmecid rule, 41, 59, 74
public space, 14, 86n1, 212
public space/sphere, 3, 29, 37, 85, 85n1
and Abdülaziz rule, 118
and Abdülhamid II rule, 176, 178, 185–6
and Abdülmecid rule, 81, 85
and Nicholas I rule, 212

Razgrad, 74, 105
reciprocity, 15–16, 41, 44–5, 47, 73, 82, 103, 135, 141, 145, 173, 177, 199
refugees, 152–3, 188n32, 192n123
regalia, 12, 75, 92n126, 94n155, 142
religio-cultural, 2, 78, 109, 123n39
requisite(s)/necessities (*levazım/muktaza/iktiza*), 26, 40–1
  of devotion (*ubudiyet*), 26, 35n106, 43, 87n12
  of gratitude (*teşekkür*), 41, 43
  of illumination (*şehrayin*), 35n106, 52
  of inner exhilaration (*inşirah-ı derun*), 51, 88n45
  of mutual friendship (*muhadenet*), 41
  of mutual, sincere friendship (*muhalasat*), 40
  of praise (*mahmedet*), 41
  of pure affection (*safvet*), 41
  of rejoicing (*meserret*), 35n106
  of respect (*riayetkari*), 40
  of submission (*rıkkiyet*), 26, 35n106
  of veneration (*ihtiramiye*), 25
requital (*vuzdayanie*), 107–8
Reşid Bey, 182–3
Rococo architecture, 13, 157–8
royal accession day (*cülus-i hümayun*), 4, 24, 103–4, 120, 122n31, 128–9, 138, 187n9, 190n76
  and Abdülaziz, 4, 103–5, 111–12, 119, 120, 178, 203
  and Abdülhamid II, 150, 151, 152–4, 156–8, 176–7, 178–80, 193n134, 196n189
  and Abdülmecid, 47, 49, 200–1
  and Mahmud II, 24–5, 28, 49, 103, 199
royal accession day, Alexander II, 209–10
royal accession day, Nicholas I, 207
royal birthday (*veladet-i hümayun*), 4, 105, 128–9, 187n9, 190n76
  and Abdülaziz, 103–4, 107, 123n40, 203
  and Abdülhamid II, 152, 154, 156, 179
  and Abdülmecid, 45, 47, 49, 50, 74, 88n34, 105
  and Mahmud II, 24–9, 103, 199
royal birthday, Nicholas I, 207
royal portraits, 4, 12, 14, 63, 187n13, 189n42, 205
  and Abdülaziz, *96*, 110
  and Abdülhamid II, 130, 135–7, 150, 184, 192n107
  and Abdülmecid, 20, *39*, *48*
  and Mahmud II, 19–20, 28–9, 199

  and Murad V, *132*, 135–6
  and Nicholas I, 19, *208*
ruler visibility, 3–5, 6–8, 9–14, 37–8, 127–31
  and Abdülaziz, 95–7, 109–10
  and Abdülhamid II, 132–41, 205
  and Abdülmecid, 38, 40–4, 67, 84, 200–1
  and Mahmud II, 17–20, 199
  and Nicholas I, 207, 212
Rum (Hellene-minded or Helenised), 2
  and Abdülaziz rule, 100, 105, 109, 111, 112, 124n56
  and Abdülmecid rule, 38, 73, 78, 86n3, 89n69, 94n151, 94n152
  and Mahmud II rule, 22
Rumelia, 5, 15, 21, 32n52, 86n4, 92n108, 177, 203
  and Abdülaziz, 98, 112, 116, 202
  and Abdülmecid, 38, 51, 57, 60, 62, 64–5, 72–3, 85, 86n4, 201
  and Mahmud II, 23, 26, 27, 34n89, 59, 209
  see also Bulgars
Rusçuk (Ruse), 62, 63, 79, 90n81, 107–8, 112, 116, 117, 119, 123n43, 124n61, 125n70
Russia, 5, 11, 13, 14, 16, 19, 23, 103, 115, 117–18, 120, 122n26, 125n66, 125n84, 134, 154, 179, 182–3, 213n13
  and architecture, 157, 168–9
  and Christians, 20–2, 34n79
  and dynastic pantheon, 141–3
  and Finland, 209–12
  and ruler visibility, 138, 198n224, 207–12
Russo-Ottoman Wars, 18, 20, 21, 23, 34n79, 86n3, 117, 120, 178, 186n1, 196n199, 204, 209

Sacred, 100, 144–5
  and Abdülaziz rule, 103, 119
  and Abdülhamid II rule, 138, 141–2, 144–5, 151, 177, 182, 185, 186
  and Abdülmecid rule, 37, 57, 61, 75–6
sacrifice (*kurban*), 66, 68, 91n99
sacrifice for the people/subjects, 84
sacrifice for the ruler, 71, 78, 107–8, 181, 204
sacrifice for the 'us'-group, 204
Sadık Rifat Pasha, 42

Index

Safavids, 12
St Cyril and St Methodius day, 77, 79, 109–12, 120–1, 201, 203, 210
Şakir Pasha, 179–80, 197n203
salvos, 15, 25, 33n55, 49, 51–2, 53, 62, 101, 104, 178
Samakov (Samokov), 98, 99
scenario of power, 54, 58, 73, 75–6, 79, 84, 130, 131, 138, 201
secular, 16–17, 37, 127, 199–200
secular celebration, 79, 120, 154, 201
secular power, 53, 75
Selim I, Sultan, 10, 11, 138, 189n49
Selim II, Sultan, 10, 31n19
Selim III, Sultan, 14, 15, 16, 18, 19, 21, 30n5, 32n48, 44, 128, 139, 150, 187n6
Serbia, 16, 21, 64, 120, 191n103
Shaw, Stanford, 21, 32n48
Shivarov, Ilia, 99–100
Silistre (Silistra), 23, 26, 62
simplicity of the image of the ruler, 6, 18, 41, 133–4, 183
Slade, Adolphus, 6
social pact between ruler and ruled, 37, 44, 51–4, 59, 60, 68, 84, 107, 204
Sofya (Sofia), 98–9, 100, 196n197
Söğüt, 129, 149
songs of praise and prayer
  and Abdülaziz, 99–101, 104–5, 107, 109–12, 115–17, 120, 201
  and Abdülmecid, 38, 62, 64–78, 81–5, 91n97, 91n104, 93n130, 93n131, 93n135, 94n149, 94n150, 201
  and Finland, 210–11
  and Nicholas I of Russia, 210–11
Stambolski, Hristo, 62, 63, 90n79, 123n43, 124n64, 146, 191n103
Stara Zagora Uprising, 120
Stoyanov, Ilarion (Makariopolski), 59, 60, 61, 72, 80–1, 90n73, 91n97
Süleyman I (the Magnificent), Sultan, 10, 12, 21, 139
Şumnu (Shumen), 22, 23, 72–3, 79, 94n150, 116
supra-regional, 2, 74
surveillance, 185
sword girding, 10–11, 32n53, 102, 137–8, 183
  and Abdülaziz, 101, 102–3, 138, 203
  and Abdülhamid II, 31n20, 132–3, 135, 136–9, 147, 188n27, 189n43
  and Abdülmecid, 40, 43, 137–8

  and Mahmud II, 15, 31n20, 137
  and Murad V, 137, 89n43
symbolic power/acts/markers of the ruler, 4, 7–8, 10–12, 21, 44, 75–6, 78, 80–1, 84–5, 85n1, 109–10, 121, 129–31, 133, 137, 144, 148, 160, 167, 178, 184, 189n40, 189n49, 194n146, 201, 207
symbolic interaction between ruler and ruled, 37–8, 44, 50, 58, 65, 67–8, 70, 75, 86n1, 100, 103, 106–8, 115, 118, 143, 160, 167, 185, 186n5, 200, 202, 204–5, 207, 212
symbolic markers of the ruled, 93n139, 109–10, 167
symbolic encounters, negative, 176–83, 185, 205
symbolic over-extension, 205, 206n3
syncretic, 67, 70, 76–7, 80, 91n101, 103, 111, 119, 144, 149, 178, 203, 212
syncretic regalia, 75, 83, 102, 107, 108, 202
syncretic sacred, 100, 102
Syria, 11, 143–4, 145

Takvim-i Vekayi (newspaper), 20, 40, 49–50, 59
Tanzimat ('Reordering') reforms, 8, 17, 199–200
  and Abdülmecid, 37, 42–3, 64–5, 69, 72, 75, 85, 137, 201
  and Mahmud II, 8, 17, 199–200
target audiences/listeners, 3, 8, 19, 25, 38, 61, 121, 127, 136, 183
Tatarcık Abdullah Efendi, 21
Tatar-Pazarcık (Pazardzhik), 109–10, 114
tax collectors (*muhassıl*), 42–3, 47, 87n30
tax farming (*iltizam*), 11
Tekfurdağ, 22
temporal continuum/axis, 30n6, 56, 66, 76, 82, 99, 106, 110, 119, 139, 204
throne, 9–11, 14–15, 37, 40, 52–4, 75, 77, 95, 100–2, 107–8, 120, 132, 134–5, 138–40, 156, 173, 186, 207
Tırnova (Turnovo), 51, 62, 64–70, 75, 79, 90n81, 98–9, 104–7, 112
totality/totalisation for the ruler, 27, 44, 56, 60–1, 97–8, 106, 108, 115, 178, 185, 204
totality/totalisation for the 'us'-group, 82, 94n153, 204
Tott, Baron François de, 14
trade, 11, 90n92

239

Treaty of Iași, 14
Treaty of Küçük Kaynarca, 20–1, 189n49
Treaty of Paris, 122n26
trope of love by the ruler, 23, 38, 41, 65, 71, 73, 82, 106, 108, 200, 210
trope of love for the ruler, 4, 27, 38, 49–59, 61, 70–1, 82, 84–5, 100, 101, 200–1, 210
Tsankov, Dragan, 81, 82, 94n145
Tsarigradski Vestnik (newspaper), 73–4, 75, 77, 92n116, 189n52, 201
Tulip Period (*Lale Devri*), 13
Tupchileshtov, Nikola, 59–60, 90n74

Umar, Caliph, 103, 137, 144, 189n47, 189n49
unity for the ruler, 23, 27, 37, 56, 60–1, 85, 88n38, 97, 100, 108, 204
unity for the 'us'-group, 37, 82–3, 94n153, 204
universal kingship, 12, 17, 200
universalised faith, 17, 57, 200, 204n8

Varna, 23, 62, 116
Vassaf Efendi, 23

Vazov, Ivan, 77
Vecih Efendi, 21–2
Vehbi Efendi, 118
Vidin, 16, 107, 123n40, 124n62, 155–6
Vienna, 25, 28–9, 118, 129, 179, 187n6
village, 2, 22, 24, 86, 152

Wahhabis, 18
Wallachia, 16, 21, 25–7, 33n56, 35n104, 65, 117
Wilhelm II, Kaiser, 143–7, 149, 150–1, 184, 191n93
and fountain, 171, *171*, 173–4

Yanya (Ioannina), 16, 105, 152
Yazıncızade Abdülvehab Efendi, 20
Yemen, 152, 168, 179–80, 197n203
Yoannovich, Hadzhi Nayden, 64, 65, 68, 69, 72, 79, 90n90, 108
Youssouf Izzedin, Prince, 139–40, 192n109

Zafirov, Spas, 76, 93n130, 94n149
Zhelev, Tsani, 76, 93n130, 94n149
Zouave (*Zühaf*), 148–9

EU representative:
Easy Access System Europe
Mustamäe tee 50, 10621 Tallinn, Estonia
Gpsr.requests@easproject.com

www.ingramcontent.com/pod-product-compliance
Lightning Source LLC
Chambersburg PA
CBHW051054230426
43667CB00013B/2295